The Ultimate Medicine Personal Statement Guide

UniAdmissions

Published by *RAR Medical Services Limited, trading as* **Infinity Books**
www.uniadmissions.co.uk
info@uniadmissions.co.uk
Tel: 0208 068 0438

The Ultimate Medicine Personal Statement Guide

Dr David Salt

Dr Rohan Agarwal

UniAdmissions

About the Authors

David is **Director of Services** at *UniAdmissions*, taking the lead in product development and customer service. David read medical sciences at Gonville and Caius College Cambridge, graduating in 2012, completed his clinical studies in the Cambridge Clinical School and now works as a medical doctor.

David is an experienced tutor, having helped students with all aspects of the university applications process. He has authored five books to help with university applications and has edited four more. Away from work, David enjoys cycling, outdoor pursuits and good food.

Rohan is the **Director of Operations** at *UniAdmissions* and is responsible for its technical and commercial arms. He graduated from Gonville and Caius College, Cambridge and is a fully qualified doctor. Over the last five years, he has tutored hundreds of successful Oxbridge and Medical applicants. He has also authored ten books on admissions tests and interviews.

Rohan has taught physiology to undergraduates and interviewed medical school applicants for Cambridge. He has published research on bone physiology and writes education articles for the Independent and Huffington Post. In his spare time, Rohan enjoys playing the piano and table tennis.

INTRODUCTION

Medical school is, and always has been, extremely competitive. It consistently attracts the top students from every school. Therefore medical schools have the most difficult decisions to make. They have to decide who are the very best amongst a sea of excellent applicants. And their duty goes beyond simply allocating the space to the highest achievers: those who may deserve it most. Medical schools are selecting the doctors of the future – those who will look after the health of many generations across the course of their career, and who will rise through the ranks to, in turn, train new doctors and shape the health service of the future.

This decision, therefore, has vast and wide-ranging consequences. Medical schools have both a moral and indeed a legal duty to properly assess applicants and choose the ones who will make the best doctors. But how do they decide, and how can you convince them that you are the one who deserves that all important place?

Although the personal statement is just one component of the applications process, it is the only component that, before interview selection takes place, provides the admissions tutor with information about the real you. It is your opportunity to show your reasons for choosing medicine, your motivation and your personal skills which will make you succeed as an excellent doctor of the future.

This book first guides you through the process of writing your personal statement, giving top tips and advice to help you show yourself in the best possible light whilst avoiding common pitfalls. Next, there are 101 successful medical personal statements from recent applicants. Each is labelled with the student's applications and the outcome, and comes with a commentary showing you the stronger and weaker points of the statement to help you hone the structure and content of your own.

So, what are you waiting for?!

THE BASICS

Your <u>Personal</u> Statement

Applying to university is both an exciting and confusing time. You will make a decision that will decide the next 3-6 years and potentially your entire life. Your personal statement is your chance to show the universities you apply to who you really are. The rest of the application is faceless statistics – the personal statement gives the admissions tutor the opportunity to look beyond those statistics at you as an individual: the person they may spend four to six years training and who may eventually become a doctor.

Some people may tell you there is a right and wrong way to write a personal statement, but this is a myth. One of the reasons we produced this book is to show you the vastly different styles that successful personal statements have. Yes, there are rules of thumb that can help you along the way, but never lose sight of the fact that this is your opportunity to tell <u>your</u> story.

How does the Process Work?

University applications are made through the online UCAS system. You can apply to 4 universities (and a 5th non-medical option). After receiving the outcomes of all applications, you make a confirmed (i.e. first) and reserve choice. Your place at university is only confirmed once you've achieved the conditions set out in the conditional offer.

It's important to remember that the **same application will be sent to all of your choices**. There is therefore, little point in applying to completely unrelated subjects e.g. English for your fifth choice. Many applicants don't even apply to a fifth university. Of the ones that do, most opt for a scientific course e.g. Biomedical Science.

Other than exam marks, GCSE grades and teacher references, the only part of the application which you have direct control over is your personal statement. This is your chance to convince the reader (i.e. admissions tutor) to give you a place at their university. Although not a job interview, it is important to treat the personal statement with the respect it deserves.

The Timescale

For medicine, be aware of an earlier deadline, **15 October** – if you don't get your application in on time it won't be considered. Remember that **schools often have an earlier internal deadline** so they can ensure punctuality and sort out their references in time. Different schools have different procedures, so it is very important that you know what the timescale is at your school before the end of your AS year. Internal deadlines for medicine can be as early as the beginning of September, which is only a couple of weeks after the summer break. Submitting earlier can be good- as it frees up your time to concentrate on admission test preparation, interview preparation and your A2 studies.

What are the requirements?

➢ Maximum 4000 characters
➢ Maximum 47 lines
➢ Submitted by the early deadline – 15 October

What do Admissions Tutors look for?

Academic ability

This is the most obvious. Every university will have different entrance requirements for the same course titles, so make sure that you are aware of these. Some universities may have extra requirements, e.g. Medical applicants to UCL must have three full A levels and one AS. It is your responsibility to ensure that you meet the entry criteria for the course that you're applying to.

Extra-curricular activities

Unlike in the US, the main factor in the UK for deciding between candidates for university places is their academic suitability for the course to which they have applied, and little else. Whilst extra-curricular activities can be a positive thing, it is a common mistake for students to dedicate too much of their Personal Statement to these. There is however an important place for subject-related extra-curricular activities in a personal statement i.e. work experience.

Passion for your subject

This is the most important part of a personal statement. This is what makes your statement personal to you, and is where you can truly be yourself, so do not hold back! Whether you've dreamt of being a doctor since birth or a historian since learning to read, if you are truly passionate about your chosen subject this will be shine through in the personal statement.

It is not necessary for you to have wanted to do a particular subject for your entire life. In fact, it is entirely possible to choose a subject because you found a course that really appealed to you on a university open day. Whatever the case, you should find reasons to justify your decision to pursue a course that will cost a lot of time and money. If the personal statement does not convince the reader that you're committed to medicine, then you'll likely be rejected.

I have the grades, will I be accepted?

In short – not necessarily. Achieving the entrance grades required is considered to be the basic requirement for all successful applicants, and will certainly be the case for all applicants who gain interviews. If an applicant's personal statement is terrible but they meet the minimum grade criteria, they may still be rejected. Likewise, if an applicant's personal statement is amazing but they fall slightly under the minimum grade requirements, the applicant may still be accepted.

Application Timeline

Component	Deadline
Research Courses	June + July
Start Brainstorming	Start of August
Complete 1st Draft	Mid-August
Complete Final Draft	End of August
Expert Checks	Mid-September
Submit to School	Late September
Submit to UCAS	Before 15th October

1) Researching Courses

This includes both online research and attending university open days. Whilst some of you reading this guide will already know that you want to apply for medicine, some may not have decided. Course research is still very important even if you're certain you want to study medicine. This is because the 'same' courses can **vary significantly** between universities. Some courses have a very separated pre-clinical science and clinical transition, whereas others are fully integrated where clinical experience starts from day one. Some are taught traditionally with lectures and practicals, whereas others have a much more self-directed problem-based learning (PBL) style. Do your course research and decide which style of course is best for you. As only one personal statement is sent to all universities that you apply to, it is important that you write in a way that addresses the different needs of each university you apply to.

If you cannot make it to university open days (e.g. if you are an international applicant), you can usually email a department and request a tour. If you allow plenty of time for this, quite often universities are happy to do this. Be proactive – do not sit around and expect universities to come to you and ask for your application! The worst possible thing you can do is appear to be applying to a course which you don't understand or haven't have researched.

You're highly recommended to research the course content of courses that you interested in. Every university will produce a prospectus, which is available printed and online. This will help to not only choose the 4 universities that you should apply for, but also be aware of exactly what it is that you are applying for.

2) Start Brainstorming

At this stage, you will have narrowed down your subject interests and should be certain that you're applying for medicine (if you're not then check out our "*Ultimate Personal Statement Guide*" for other non-medical subjects).

A good way to start a thought process which will eventually lead to a personal statement is by simply listing all of your ideas, why you are interested in your course and the pros and cons between different universities. If there are particular modules which capture your interest that are common across several of your university choices, do not be afraid to include this in your personal statement. This will not only show that you have a real interest in your chosen subject, but also that you have taken the time to do some research.

3) Complete First Draft

This will not be the final personal statement that you submit. In all likelihood, your personal statement will go through multiple revisions and re-drafts before it is ready for submission. In most cases, the final statement is wildly different from the first draft.

The purpose of completing a rough draft early is so that you can spot major errors early. It is easy to go off on a tangent when writing a personal statement, with such things not being made obvious until somebody else reads it. The first draft will show the applicant which areas need more attention, what is missing and what needs to be removed altogether.

4) Re-Draft

This will probably be the first time at which you receive any real feedback on your Personal Statement. Obvious errors will be spotted, and any outrageous claims that sound good in your head, but are unclear or dubious will be obvious to the reader at this stage.

It is important to take advice from family and friends, however with a pinch of salt. Remember that the admissions tutor will be a stranger and not familiar with the applicant's personality.

5) Complete Final Draft

This will not be the final product, and until now, you probably won't have had much real criticism. However, a complete draft with an introduction, main body and conclusion is important as you can then build on this towards the final personal statement.

6) Expert Check

This should be completed by the time you return for your final year at school/college. Once the final year has started, it is wise to get as many experts (teachers and external tutors) to read through the draft personal statement as possible

Again, you should take all advice with a pinch of salt. At the end of the day, this is your UCAS application and although your teachers' opinions are valuable, they are not the same as that of the admissions tutors. In schools that see many Oxbridge and Medical applications, many teachers believe there is a correct 'format' to personal statements, and may look at your statement like 'number' in the sea of applications that are processed by the school. There is no 'format' to successful personal statements, as each statement should be **personal** to you.

At schools that do not see many Oxbridge/Medical applications, the opposite may be true. Many applicants are coerced into applying to universities and for courses which their teachers judge them likely to be accepted for. It is your responsibility to ensure that the decisions you make are your own, and you have the conviction to follow through with your decisions.

7) Final Checks

Armed with a rough draft, and advice from friends, family and teachers you should be ready to complete your final personal statement.

8) Submit to School

Ideally, you will have some time off before submitting your statement for the internal UCAS deadline. This is important because it'll allow you to look at your final personal statement with a fresh perspective before submitting it. You'll also be able to spot any errors that you initially missed. You should submit your personal statement and UCAS application to your school on time for the internal deadline. This ensures that your school has enough time to complete your references.

9) Submit to UCAS

That's it! Take some time off from university applications for a few days, have some rest and remember that you still have A levels/IB exams to get through (and potentially admissions tests and interviews).

GETTING STARTED

The personal statement is an amalgamation of all your hard work throughout both secondary school and your other extracurricular activities. It is right to be apprehensive about starting your application and so here are a few tips to get you started…

General Rules

If you meet the minimum academic requirements then it is with the personal statement that your application to university will be made or broken. With many applicants applying with identical GCSE and A-level results (if you're a gap year student) the personal statement is your chance to really stand out and let your personality shine through. As such there is no concrete formula to follow when writing the personal statement and indeed every statement is different in its own right. Therefore throughout this chapter you will find many principles for you to adopt and interpret as you see fit whilst considering a few of these introductory general rules.

Firstly: **space is extremely limited**; as previously mentioned a maximum of 4000 characters in 47 lines. Before even beginning the personal statement utilise all available space on the UCAS form. For example do not waste characters listing exam results when they can be entered in the corresponding fields in the qualifications section of the UCAS form.

Secondly: always remember **it easier to reduce the word count** than increase it with meaningful content when editing. Be aware that is not practical to perfect your personal statement in just one sitting. Instead write multiple drafts starting with one substantially exceeding the word limit but containing all your ideas. As such starting early is key to avoid later time pressure as you approach the deadline. Remember this is your opportunity to put onto paper what makes you the best and a cut above the rest – you should enjoy writing the personal statement!

Lastly and most importantly: **your statement is just one of hundreds that a tutor will read**. Tutors are only human after all and their interpretation of your personal statement can be influenced by many things. So get on their good side and always be sympathetic to the reader, make things plain and easy to read, avoid contentious subjects and never target your personal statement at one particular university (unless you're only applying there!).

When Should I Start?

TODAY!

Although it might sound like a cliché, but the earlier you start, the easier you make it. Starting early helps you in four key ways:

1) The most important reason to start early is that it is the **best way to analyse your application**. Many students start writing their personal statement then realise, for example, that they haven't done enough work experience, or that their extra reading isn't focused enough. *By starting early, you give yourself the chance to change this.* Over the summer, catch up on your weak areas to give yourself plenty to say in the final version.

2) **You give yourself more time for revisions.** You can improve your personal statement by showing it to as many people as possible to get their feedback. With an earlier start, you have more time to modify, thus improving the final result.

3) **Steadier pace.** Starting early gives you the flexibility of working at a steadier pace – perhaps just an hour or so per week. If you start later, you will have to spend much longer on it, probably some full days, reducing the time you have for the rest of your work and importantly for unwinding, too.

4) **You can finish it earlier.** If you start early, you can finish early too. This gives you time to change focus and start preparing for the UKCAT, BMAT (if needed), and for your interviews, which can sometimes start by mid-November.

What people *think* is best:

What is *actually* best:

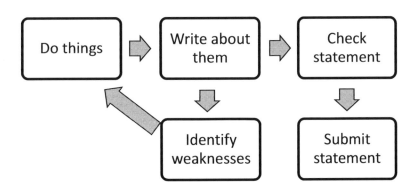

Doing your Research

The two most important things you need to establish are: ***What course? + What University?***

If you're unsure where to begin, like most things in life, success with the personal statement begins with preparation and research.

Your choice of university is entirely personal and similar to your course choice; it needs to be somewhere that you are going to enjoy studying. Remember that where you end up will form a substantial part of your life. This could mean going to a university with a rich, active nightlife or one with strict academic prowess or perhaps one that dominates in the sporting world. In reality each university offers its own unique experience and hence the best approach is to attend as many open days as feasibly possible. At which you will have the opportunity to meet some of your potential tutors, talk to current students (who offer the most honest information) and of course tour the facilities.

The best way to prevent future stress is to start researching courses and universities early i.e. 12 months before your apply through UCAS. There is a plethora of information that is freely available online, and if you want something physical to read, you can request free prospectuses from most UK universities. It is important to remember that until you actually submit your UCAS application, **you** are in control. Universities are actively competing against one another for **your** application! When initially browsing, a good place to start is by simply listing courses and universities which interest you, and 2 pros and cons for each. You can then use this to shortlist to a handful of universities that you should then attend open days for.

There are no right choices when it comes to university choices, however there are plenty of wrong choices. You must make sure that the reasons behind your eventual choice are the right ones, and that you do not act on impulse. Whilst your personal statement should not be directed at any particular one of your universities, it should certainly be tailored to the course you are applying for.

With a course in mind and universities short listed your preparation can begin in earnest. Start by ordering **university prospectuses** or logging onto the university's subject specific websites. You should be trying to find the application requirements. Once located there will be a range of information from academic demands including work experience to personal attributes. Firstly at this point **be realistic with the GCSE results you have already achieved and your predicted A-level grades**. Also note that some universities will require a minimum number of hours of work experience – this should have been conducted through the summer after GCSE examinations and into your AS year. Work experience is not something to lie about as the university will certainly seek references to confirm your attendance. If these do not meet the minimum academic requirements a tutor will most likely not even bother reading your personal statement so don't waste a choice.

If you meet all the minimum academic requirements then focus on the other extracurricular aspects. Many prospectuses contain descriptions of ideal candidates with lists of desired personal attributes. Make a list of these for all the universities you are considering applying to. Compile a further list of your own personal attributes along with evidence that supports this claim. Then proceed to pair the points on your personal list with the corresponding requirements from your potential universities. It is important to consider extracurricular requirements from all your potential universities in the interest of forming a **rounded personal statement applicable to all institutions**.

This is a useful technique because one university may not require the same personal attributes as another. Therefore by discussing these attributes in your statement, you can demonstrate a level of ingenuity and personal reflection on the requirements of the course beyond what is listed in the prospectus.

Always remember that the role of the personal statement is to **show that you meet course requirements by using your own personal experiences as evidence**.

Taking your First Steps

A journey of one thousand miles starts with a single step...

As you may have already experienced, the hardest step of a big project is the first step. It's easy to *plan* to start something, but when it *actually* comes to writing the first words, what do you do? As you stare at the 47-line blank page in front of you, how can you fill it? You wonder if you've even done that many things in life. You think of something, but realise it probably isn't good enough, delete it and start over again. Sound familiar?

There is another way. The reason it is hard is because you judge your thoughts against the imagined finished product. So don't begin by writing full, perfectly polished sentences. Don't be a perfectionist. Begin with lists, spider diagrams, ideas, rambling. Just put some ideas onto paper and **write as much as possible** – it's easy to trim down afterwards if it's too long, and generally doing it this way gives the best content. Aim to improve gradually from start to finish in little steps each time.

Your Personal Statement...

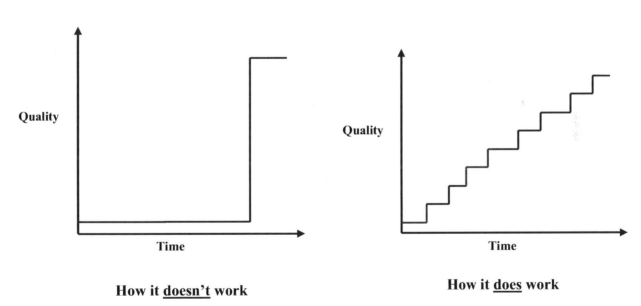

How it **doesn't** work   How it **does** work

Brainstorming

If writing prose is too daunting, start by using our brainstorm template. Write down just three bullet-points for each of the 12 questions below and in only twenty minutes you'll be well on your way!

Why medicine?

What areas of medicine interest you the most?

What are your 3 main hobbies and what skills have they developed?

What have you chosen to read outside the A-level syllabus?

Do you have any long-term career ideas/aspirations?

What did you learn from your work experience?

Have you won any prizes or awards?

What is your favourite A-level subject and why?

What are your personal strengths?

Have you attended any courses?

Have you ever held a position of responsibility?

Have you been a part of any projects?

The Writing Process

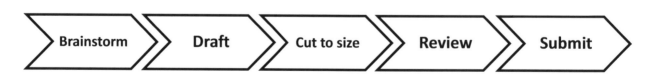

Brainstorm → Draft → Cut to size → Review → Submit

Why Medicine?

What areas of medicine interest you the most?

What are your 3 main hobbies? What skills have they developed?

1)

2)

3)

What have you chosen to read outside the A-Level syllabus?

Do you have any long term career ideas or aspirations?

What did you learn from your work experience?

Have you won any prizes or awards?

What is your favourite A-level subject and why?

What are your personal strengths?

What courses have you attended?

What positions of responsibility have you held?

What projects have you been involved in?

What is the Purpose of your Statement?

An important question to ask yourself before you begin drafting your personal statement is: how will the universities I have applied to use my personal statement? This can dramatically change how you write your personal statement. For the majority of courses that don't interview, the personal statement is directly bidding for a place on the course.

However, given that you're applying for medicine, you will almost certainly have to go through an interview process. Therefore, your personal statement will require substantially more thought and tactics. The first thing to establish is the role of the personal statement in the context of the interview. At this point it is well worth going through the application procedures in prospectuses and on university websites.

The first option is that the personal statement is solely used for interview selection and discounted thereafter. In this case the interviewer is going to want to discuss material that isn't including in your personal statement. As such, make sure you leave yourself room to talk more at interview. Make sure you have extra material to expand on the key points in your personal statement to avoid being left in a difficult position.

Alternatively the personal statement can represent a central component of the interview. Many universities adopt an interview protocol whereby the interviewers run through the personal statement from start to finish questioning the candidate on specific points. This technique has many benefits for the interviewer as it allows them to assess the presence of any fraudulent claims (it is very hard to lie to a tutor face to face when they starting asking for specifics), it gives the interview clear structure but also allows the interviewer to bring pre planned questions on specific personal statement points.

However from the candidate's point of view this can lead to an oppressive, accusative and intense interview. There are techniques to take control back into your own hands like, for example, "planting" questions within your personal statement. This can be achieved in many ways. The phrase "for example" can be helpful here. If you describe an experience and give some examples, it gives the impression of an incomplete list, allowing you to provide extra detail at interview.

Finding the Right Balance

The balance of a personal statement can have a significant effect on the overall message it delivers. Whilst there are no strict rules, there are a few rules of thumb that can help you strike the right balance between all the important sections.

As a medical applicant, the **most important point** is to dedicate enough space to talking about your work experience. This is absolutely essential – a good discussion of your work experience answers *almost all* the questions the admissions tutor will want to find out about you. **Discussing work experience can show why you've chosen medicine, your motivation, knowledge and professional awareness.** It can also be used to highlight any specific areas of interest, hints at future career plans and to guide questions at interview. In short, it is one of the best ways to make you stand out.

Extra-curricular activities are a great way of supporting your skills. However, you need to be careful that this is the supporting act and not the headliner. It is generally recommended to spend no more than a quarter of the personal statement discussing extra-curricular activities, leaving the other three-quarters for discussing your motivation for medicine, reading and work experience.

The following template gives a suggestion how to balance the different sections:

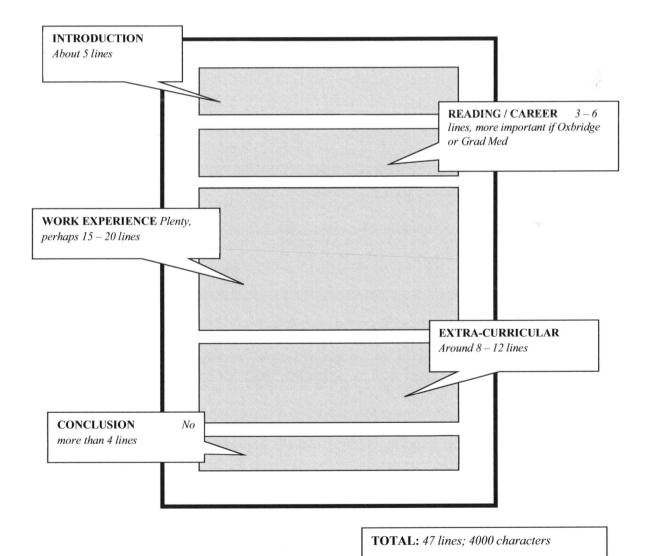

INTRODUCTION
About 5 lines

READING / CAREER   *3 – 6 lines, more important if Oxbridge or Grad Med*

WORK EXPERIENCE *Plenty, perhaps 15 – 20 lines*

EXTRA-CURRICULAR
Around 8 – 12 lines

CONCLUSION   *No more than 4 lines*

TOTAL: *47 lines; 4000 characters*

Structuring Your Statement

This may sound obvious, but many applicants fail to write personal statements which have a proper structure. Personal statements are not monologues of your life, or a giant list of your achievements. They are instead a formal piece of prose written with the aim of helping you secure a place at medical school.

The Introduction

The Opening Sentence

Rightly or wrongly, it is likely that your personal statement will be remembered by its opening sentence. It must be something short, sharp, insightful and catch the reader's attention. Remember that admissions tutors will read several hundred personal statements and often their first impression is made by your opening sentence which is why it needs to be eye catching enough to make the tutor sit and pay particular attention to what you have written. It does indeed set the standard for the rest of the personal statement.

If this seems a daunting prospect (as it should!) then here are a few pointers to get you started:

➢ Avoid using overused words like "passionate", "deeply fascinating" and "devotion".
➢ Avoid using clichéd quotes like the infamous "I have always been fascinated with the intracies of the human body".
➢ If you are going to use a quote then put some effort into researching an obscure yet particular powerful – don't forget to include a reference.
➢ Draw on your own personal experiences to produce something both original and eye-catching.

In many ways it is best that you save writing your opening statement till last; that way you can assess the tone of the rest of your work but also write something that will not be repeated elsewhere.

If you are really stuck with where to begin try writing down a memory and then explain how it has affected your relationship with your subject.

Whilst the opening statement is important, it is not something to stress about. Although a strong opening statement can make the personal statement; a bad one rarely breaks it.

Why Medicine?

The introduction should answer the most important question of all – **why medicine?**

*Why do **YOU** want to study medicine?*

It is essential to show your genuine reasons and motivation. The first thing to consider is whether you genuinely want to be a doctor. You need to be certain that your motivation comes from yourself and not from external sources such as teachers or family.

Once you are certain medicine is the right choice for you, there are a few key styles you can use- as shown below. By reading the example personal statements, you will see different ways successful applicants have used these building blocks to customise their own feelings towards a medical career.

Personal illness: If you have had a personal experience of healthcare and this has motivated you to study medicine.

Family illness: If the illness of a friend or family member has ignited your interest.

Making a difference: If you have seen people facing difficulties or suffering and you would like to help in the capacity of a doctor.

Academic interest plus experience: If your interest has spiralled out of a love of the biological sciences – but must be supported by practical experience, as work as a doctor is very different from academic science.

Suggestion plus experience: If someone has suggested the idea of medicine to you, made you think and investigate, and then you realised it would be a great choice for you.

Whichever reason style you choose to go with, or if you have a completely different reason altogether, a good answer always has a few key features. A good answer to the "why medicine" question will always tell a story with three key points:

> ➢ When you first thought about medicine as a career
> ➢ How you went about learning what the job is actually like
> ➢ Why you have decided it is the right choice for you

Try to avoid clichés when describing your route into medicine. Some people will say they've wanted to be a doctor ever since they were born – but of course, this simply isn't true and therefore it isn't helpful. The admissions tutor wants to see a simple and honest story about your journey, helping them assess how carefully you have considered your choice and how suitable a choice it is.

The *exact* phrase: *"from a young age I have always been interested in"* was used more than 300 times in personal statements in 2013 (data published by UCAS), and substituting "young" for "early" gave an additional 292 statements – these phrases can quickly become boring for admissions tutors to read!

There are certain things that raise red flags, phrases that will count against you if you write them. These include: saying that medicine is a respected career, saying that doctors are well paid, saying that you want to be a doctor because of other people telling you to, saying you want to be a doctor because other professions are worse in some way and making direct comparisons to law or engineering.

These phrases are all bad because they don't show your interest in the actual work that doctors do. Doctors may be well respected, but this fact alone won't motivate you to succeed at medical school and in a medical career – you need to be interested in what doctors *do*. The same applies to choosing medicine because it's a stable professional occupation. Likewise, if you're choosing medicine because someone else told you it would be a good choice (or suggested medicine or law but you don't like law), you may lack this personal motivation that medical schools know is essential for success.

The Main Body

In the rest of your text your aim should be to demonstrate your suitability for the course by exemplifying your knowledge of the course structure and its requirements through personal experience. Again there are no rigorous guidelines on how to do this and it is very much down to your own writing style. Whereas some prefer a strict structure, others go for a more synoptic approach, but always remember to be consistent in order to achieve a flowing, easy to read personal statement.

This point ties in closely with writing style. You want one that the tutor will find pleasing to read; and as everyone prefers different styles the only way to assess yours accurately is to show your drafts to as many people as possible. That includes, teachers, parents, friends, siblings, grandparents – the more the better, don't be afraid to show it round!

Despite the lack of a standardised writing method, there is of course a list of standard content to include. In general you are trying to convey your academic, professional and personal suitability for the course to the tutor. This needs to be reiterated whilst demonstrating clear, exemplified knowledge of the course structure and its demands. The biggest problem then in achieving these goals, with all the other candidates also trying to convey the same information, is in producing an original personal statement and remaining unique.

The easiest way to overcome this is to integrate your own personal experiences, reflections and emotions – both demonstrating passion and insight.

More practically, it is a good idea to split the main body into two or three paragraphs, in order to avoid writing one big giant boring monologue.

Part One: This should cover why you are suited for medicine. This will include your main academic interests, future ambitions and what makes medicine right for you. It is a good idea for you to read up the course syllabuses, and find something that catches your interest above others. If you have read anything outside of the A-level/IB syllabus related to your chosen course which has inspired you then this is the place to mention it.

Part Two: This section should still be about why you're suited to your chosen course with a particular focus on work experience. If you've had to overcome any significant challenges in life and wish to include these in your personal statement, then this is normally the best place to do so. Similarly, any relevant prizes & competitions should be included here. However, it is important to remember not to simply list things. Ensure that you follow through by describing in detail what you have learned from any experiences mentioned.

Part Three: This is the smallest part of the main body and is all about extra-curricular activities. It is easy to get carried away in this section and make outrageous claims e.g. claim to be a mountain climber if all you have ever climbed is a hill at the end your street etc. Lying is not worth the risk given that your interviewer may share the same hobby that you claim to be an expert in!

Avoid making empty statements by backing things up with facts. For example: *'I enjoy reading, playing sports and watching TV',* is a poor sentence and tells the reader nothing. The applicant enjoys reading, so what? Which sports? Doesn't everyone like watching TV? If the applicant is in a sports team, or plays a particular sport recreationally with friends then they should name the sport and describe what their role is. Likewise, the applicant should actually describe how their hobbies relate to them as a person and ideally their subject.

What to Include

Still a little stumped? Here is a summary of a few useful pointers to get you started:

➤ **Sports and other hobbies** – these are particularly important for the vocational courses like medicine and dentistry as they offer a form of stress relief amidst a course of intense studying whilst also demonstrating a degree of life experience and well roundedness. By all means discuss international honours, notable publications or even recent stage productions. Remember to reflect on these experiences offering explanations of how they have changed your attitude towards life or how they required particular dedication and commitment.

➤ **Musical instruments** – Again an excellent form of stress relief but also a great example of manual dexterity if your course requires this. Do not be afraid to mention your favourite musical works for that personal touch but also any grades you have obtained thus demonstrating commitment and a mature attitude that can be transferred to any field of study.

➤ **Work experience(s)** – Don't bother wasting characters by citing references or contacts from your work experience but rather discuss situations that you were presented with. Describe any situations where you showed particular maturity/professionalism and explain what you learnt from that experience. It is always advisable to discuss how your work experience affected your view of the subject field, either reinforcing or deterring you from your choice.

➤ **Personal interests within the field of study** – This is a really good opportunity to show off your own genuine interest within the subject field. Try to mention a recent article or paper, one that isn't too contentious but is still not that well known to show depth of reading. Reflect on what you have read offering your own opinions, but be warned, you will almost certainly be called up on this at interview if you have one.

➤ **Personal attributes** – exemplify these through your own personal experiences and opinions. As mentioned previously many courses will list "desired" personal attributes in their prospectus - you must include these as a minimum in your personal statement. Try to add others of your own choice that you think are relevant to the subject in order to achieve originality – here are a few to inspire you:

  o Honesty
  o Communication skills
  o Teamwork
  o Decision making
  o Awareness of limitations
  o Respect
  o Morality
  o Ability to learn
  o Leadership
  o Integrity

➤ **Awards** – be they national or just departmental school awards, it always worth trying to mention any awards you have received since about the age of 15/16. A brief description of what they entailed and what you learnt from the experience can add a valuable few lines to your personal statement. Providing proof of long term dedication and prowess.

Together, discussion of all these points can demonstrate reasoned consideration for the course you have applied for. This is particularly appealing for a tutor to read as it shows a higher level of thinking by giving your own reflection on the course requirements.

The Conclusion

The conclusion of your personal statement should be more about leaving a good final impression than conferring any actual information. If you have something useful to say about your interest and desire to study medicine, you shouldn't be waiting until the very end to say it!

Admissions tutors will read hundreds of personal statements every year, and after about the fifth one all start looking very much the same. You should try to make your statement different so it stands out amongst the rest. As the conclusion is the last thing the admissions tutor will read, it can leave a lasting influence (good or bad!) The purpose of a conclusion is to tie up the entire statement in two or three sentences.

A good conclusion should not include any new information, as this should be in the main body. However, you also need to avoid repeating what you have said earlier in your personal statement. This would be both a waste of characters and frustrating for the tutor. Instead it is better to put into context what you have already written and therefore make an effort to keep your conclusion relatively short – no more than 4 lines.

The conclusion is a good opportunity to draw on all the themes you have introduced throughout your personal statement to form a final overall character image to leave the tutor with. Unless there is anything especially extraordinary or outrageous in the main body of your personal statement; the tutor is likely to remember you by your introduction and conclusion. The conclusion therefore is a good place to leave an inspiring final sentence for the tutor.

Some students will make a mention in here about their career plans, picking up on something they have observed in work experience or have encountered during reading. This can be a good strategy as it shows you're using your current knowledge to guide your future aspirations. If you do this, try to do so with an open mind, suggesting areas of interest but being careful not to imply you are less interested in others.

You have to spend a long time at medical school and as a junior doctor doing everything before you have the option to specialise in any one field, so admissions tutors need to be certain your interest extends into all areas. Secondly, don't sound too fixed about your plans. There is a lot more to see before you can make an informed career choice, so by all means show your particular interests but avoid sounding as though you are closing any options off.

It is important to avoid sounding too arrogant here and over selling yourself. Instead adopt a phrase looking forward in time – perhaps expressing your excitement and enthusiasm in meeting the demands of your course requirements, or looking even further ahead, the demands of your career. For example, consider a phrase like: *'driven by my love of medicine, I am sure that I will be a successful doctor and take full advantage of all opportunities should this application be successful'* rather than *'I think I should be accepted because I am very enthusiastic and will work hard'*. The sentiment behind both of these statements is positive, however the second sounds juvenile whereas the first is aspirational, confident and yet humble.

Work Experience

Work experience is a great way to demonstrate your commitment to medicine. It cannot be over-stressed just how vital it is. It is so essential that I have *never* heard a case of someone getting an offer for medicine without work experience.

During the work experience itself it is wise to keep a notebook or a diary with a brief description of each day, particularly noting down what events happened and importantly what you learnt from them. Whilst there is a designated section of the UCAS form for work experience details, the personal statement itself must be used to not only describe your experiences but also reflect on them. Making sure to discuss the following points:

➤ How did certain situations affect you personally?
➤ How did the experience alter your perspective on the subject field?
➤ Were there particular occasions where you fulfilled any of the extracurricular requirements listed within prospectuses?
➤ Most importantly how did your experience(s) confirm your desire to pursue the field of study into higher education?

Why Work Experience?

Medical schools value work experience so highly because it shows you have a number of essential traits.

Work experience shows you're informed. You're making a potentially lifelong commitment to a profession – so how do you know you'll be suited to it? Rather than basing your ideas of a medical career on the media or stories you hear from others, the best way to convince the admissions tutor you know what the job actually entails is to go and experience it for yourself. Getting as much varied work experience as possible opens your eyes to the work that doctors and other caring professionals actually do, demonstrating you have a realistic understanding of the profession better than any words can. If you have good work experience, admissions tutors are confident you're choosing medicine for the right reasons.

Work experience shows you're committed. Arranging work experience can be hard – you may need to approach multiple people and organisations before you get a 'yes'. Therefore, if you have a good portfolio of work experience, it shows you have been proactive. It shows you have gone to the effort for the sole purpose of spending your free time in a caring environment. This shows drive and commitment – impressive qualities that will help you gain that valuable place!

Arranging Work Experience

Arranging work experience can be hard. If you're finding it difficult to get exactly what you want, please don't be disheartened. You are facing the same difficulty that tens of thousands of students before you have also faced.

With work experience, it's a very good idea to start early. The earlier you approach people, the more likely you are to be accepted. It is not really practical to start seeking work experience until after you turn 16 due to age restrictions within the work place – especially where confidential information is concerned! So conduct your work experience during the summer after your GCSE examinations and throughout your AS year. This can be achieved through private arrangements you yourself make but it always worth consulting your schools careers officer as well. Remember that any part-time/summer paid jobs also count as work experience and definitely worth mentioning as they show an additional degree of maturity and professionalism.

If you are able to keep up a small regular commitment over a period of months it really helps to show dedication. It's a good idea to always carry a notebook when you're on work experience. Use it to note down anything interesting you see or hear about to make certain you don't forget!

Types of Work Experience

Medical Shadowing

This is where you spend time watching doctors or other healthcare professionals going about their work. It is a great opportunity to learn about the day-to-day activities of people working in healthcare. You will see both the interesting and stressful sides of the job. But it can be hard to organise. Aim to get some direct work experience with doctors, but if you aren't able to get much then you can supplement with any of the other good types of work experience as below.

Medical Volunteering

This includes voluntary work in any medical or care-related setting such as a hospital, GP surgery, hospice or care home. Care homes can present good opportunities to volunteer with helping with entertainment activities for the residents, so this is something to consider getting involved in. Alternatively, consider volunteering at the hospital as a "show and tell" guide to help patients find where they are looking for. It doesn't matter that you are not actually providing the care – what matters is that you are in an environment where you are interacting with people who need help and are learning about how they are cared for. Although most seek a voluntary placement, this is not essential; you could take a job in a caring setting. For example, you could work as a hospital porter or a healthcare assistant, either of which would provide a great insight into the workings of the hospital from two very different perspectives. This can be a particularly good option if you're planning on a gap year: you can work for a few months to gain valuable experience and save up some money, then use the money if you intend on any travelling.

Non-Medical Volunteering

This might include working in a charity shop, library or similar. This is a good way of showing commitment and public service, however, you won't learn about healthcare this way. It can make up the majority of the work experience, but in addition, you need to do something which gives you the opportunity to actually learn about healthcare.

Becoming a Member

It's good to get as involved as possible with your local health community. By becoming a member of any local health-related organisations, you can demonstrate a willingness to do something to help people. You could become an associate at the hospital, allowing you to vote in Governors' elections. Another possibility is to train as a first aider and join St John's Ambulance (but if you're considering this make sure to plan ahead as sometimes it can take a while to get started). Keep on the lookout for any local health-related projects – perhaps you could help by delivering leaflets to raise awareness of a new service for example.

Attending Courses

Whilst this is not strictly work experience, this section is the best place to discuss courses. It is not necessary to attend medicine preparation courses, but there are some good options available. Make sure you check what the course offers before enrolling, and only attend if there is something you will directly benefit from.

Professional Awareness

Awareness of the medical profession takes a number of forms. It includes knowledge of the day-to-day duties of a doctor, the multi-disciplinary teams doctors work in, the legal and ethical frameworks doctors operate in, the different medical specialties, training routes, the organisation of the NHS, the latest news regarding healthcare, and the outlook for the profession as a whole.

It is important to have a good awareness of these areas as without understanding the profession, you can't make an informed decision to join it. It's essential that you use your personal statement to show you have developed a good understanding of the profession through your research, reading and work experience. This will then be assessed further at interview.

Discuss any issues that have arisen through your work experience. If, for example, you saw a doctor explaining a procedure to obtain consent from a patient, you can discuss how this has made you think. You can tie it into your reading around the principle of giving valid consent (i.e. it must be voluntary, informed and given freely without pressure). The patient must be competent to make the decision (that they can understand the information, retain it, weigh up the options and communicate their decision). By relating what you see to your learning, you demonstrate interest and an enquiring mind.

Think critically about what you see and what you read. Be certain to include a few instances where in one way or another, you demonstrate an awareness of some professional issues. This once again shows you are well informed about the work of doctors, the provision of healthcare, and the difficulties facing doctors and the NHS.

Remember the most important professional attributes of a doctor. One is a commitment to learning – doctors never stop learning as they progress through their career towards specialties and keep up to date with new developments. Show that you are driven by new knowledge and are able to learn independently with self-discipline. Another is diligence – no one wants a doctor who heroically tries to solve every problem themselves. Doctors work in teams and the success of the medical team requires doctors to ask for advice if there's a difficult problem; it also requires doctors to work to systems and to raise concerns if there is any form of problem. Make sure you come across as a diligent person who would be a good humble team worker. Another is honesty – doctors have to be extremely honest and trustworthy. Studies repeatedly show doctors are the most trusted professionals; one job of the next generation of doctors is to maintain this outstanding reputation.

Extra-Curricular

It is important to show you are a balanced person, not someone whose only focus is work. Extra-curricular activities can really strengthen your personal statement by showcasing your skills. Remember that there is no *intrinsic* value in playing county level rugby or having a diploma in acting – you will not win a place on excellence in these fields. The value comes from the skills your activities teach you. Regardless of whether you're outstanding at what you do or you just do it casually, remember to reflect on what you've gained from doing it. There will always be something positive to say and it may be more valuable than you think.

There are three very important ways that extra-curricular activities can strengthen your application, so make sure to use them to their full capability.

You should use your extra-curricular activities to highlight skills that will help you in medicine. You play football – talk about how this has helped your teamwork; you play chess – surely this has improved your problem-solving? By linking what you do to the skills you've developed, you take a great opportunity to show the admissions tutor just how well-rounded you are. By showing how you have developed these critical skills you demonstrate, you are a strong applicant.

Interests outside work give you a way to relax. Medical studies and work as a doctor can be stressful, and admissions tutors have a duty of care towards students. By accepting someone who knows how to relax, they are ensuring you'll strike the right balance between studies and relaxation, keeping yourself fresh and healthy through difficult times.

Showing you have enough time for extra-curricular activities can support your academic capabilities. If you are the member of an orchestra, a sports team and you keep a rock collection, you were clearly not pushed to the absolute limit to get the top grades you achieved. For a student without other interests, it might suggest to the admissions tutor they are struggling to keep up with the current workload and may not be able to cope with the additional demands of a medical course.

Skills

Throughout this book we talk about skills – abilities that you have developed through your work and experiences that will equip you to be a good medical student and doctor. Here follows a discussion of some of the major skills it is useful to demonstrate in your personal statement. Remember that this isn't a tick-box exercise – you don't need to provide evidence for every single skill we discuss. This is merely to give you some guidance towards the key skills you may want to focus on as you write your personal statement.

Teamwork

Doctors work as part of a large team comprising lots of other doctors and different healthcare professionals such as nurses and physiotherapists. In order to achieve good outcomes for the patients, effective teamwork is essential. You can demonstrate your teamwork through team sports, musical ensembles and collaborative projects.

Time-management

Doctors are very busy. As you may have seen in your work experience, they constantly have a long and varied task list including prescribing, patient reviews, referrals, letters, phone calls, meetings and more. As such, they need to be able to manage their time well to prioritise the most important tasks, and to work quickly and efficiently to make sure they complete everything that needs doing. Show your time-management skill by balancing a number of different activities at the same time.

Working under pressure

Doctors can work under a lot of pressure, whether this is because they have so much to do or because some particular task is critical to get right. It's important that doctors can remain calm under pressure so they work well and avoid becoming too stressed. Show that you can work under pressure by working as a first aider, competing in high-level sport, becoming a sports official, taking responsibility for something important in a group activity or helping run an event with a committee or society.

Communication

Good communication is one of the most important skills that a good doctor has. This is essential both in talking to patients and the rest of the healthcare team. Talking to patients, it is important to be able to explain clearly what is going on and to be able to answer their questions. Doctors also need to be able to put patients at ease, and sometimes break bad news in a caring and sensitive manner. Talking to the rest of the healthcare team, it is important to be able to communicate plans clearly and suggest your ideas in a logical way. You can show your communication proficiency in a vast number of ways – absolutely anything where you need to talk to communicate ideas to another person. If it is under any particular pressure then bonus points!

Self-directed learning

Some medical schools have a very structured teaching programme. Others, such as the PBL (problem-based learning) courses rely much more on individual research and learning. But at any medical school and then afterwards as a doctor, you will be required to use your own initiative to both work out what you need to learn and then to learn it. Therefore, you need to show you have this ability to seek out and learn information for yourself. Demonstrate this ability by reading outside the normal curriculum, by reading books and articles about medicine or by taking on an extra self-taught course or module.

Organisation

Similar to time management, but doctors have to be organised to ensure they never forget about something important to do. Show your organisational skill by being a member of a society or committee, planning some form of event, organising a group activity or a teaching scheme.

Leadership

Doctors have to be leaders of the medical team, making medical decisions and discussing plans with others involved in the care. Therefore to make a good doctor, it helps to have some natural leadership ability. Show your leadership skills by taking a prefect role in school (describe what you're responsible for, don't just name-drop the title), by leading a project, by sitting on a committee, by conducting a music group or by captaining a sports team. DoE (Duke of Edinburgh) awards can be a good way of showing leadership as well as a number of other positive personal qualities.

Teaching

Training as a doctor is a long process, and even once qualified, doctors embark on a process of lifelong learning to advance their knowledge and keep up to date with new developments. All through the training process, more senior doctors help by teaching medical students and more junior doctors. Even going back to the ancient Hippocratic Oath, the duty for doctors to train the next generation is a central theme. Therefore, teaching is an important skill of any doctor. Show your teaching skill by presenting a project in school, helping to teach younger students, teaching a musical instrument or helping with sports coaching, for example.

Achievements and awards

Not a specific skill of course, but medical schools are looking for the very best applicants. If you have won any particular prizes or awards either through school or though a society, or you have done particularly well in the UKMC (Maths Challenge) or a science Olympiad, then it would be great to mention it on your personal statement. It's just one extra thing to help your abilities stand out from the rest.

Oxbridge

There's nothing fundamentally different about Oxford and Cambridge to other medical schools, but there are certain things you need to be aware of when applying. There is a spectrum of how scientific the education is at different medical schools, ranging from just learning the essential scientific basics through to extensive scientific detail.

Oxford and Cambridge both lie at the extreme scientific end of this spectrum. The first three years of study is almost entirely science with minimal patient contact. In the third year, you have the opportunity to do your own original research or written project. To enjoy this course, you really need to be excited by science.

Because you submit the same personal statement to all your choices, you must make sure your statement is applicable to all universities. So you can't talk about Oxbridge in it, but you can lay a few simple foundations. It is a good idea to make some mention of scientific reading, or some scientific project like a lab project in your personal statement. This certainly won't put another university off, but it gives Oxford or Cambridge a hint that you have a natural curiosity for science. You really don't need to be too strong with this: a little hint is all you need. The interviews are very scientific in focus and give all the opportunity the admissions tutors need to see how you respond to scientific problems. At Oxbridge, the main criteria for admissions selection are: academic performance, admissions test performance and interview performance. The personal statement is a significantly smaller consideration and so you need not worry about focussing too much to Oxford or Cambridge. Make sure that the personal statement covers all the general medical things that are important for every university you are applying for.

In addition, Cambridge sends out an extra questionnaire called the SAQ (Supplementary Application Questionnaire) once they receive your UCAS form. Included in this is space for a specific 1,200 character personal statement, which goes only to Cambridge and is your opportunity to tell the admissions tutor any extra things you would like Cambridge to know. Consider using this to highlight why you feel the scientific focus of the Cambridge course would be good for you. There isn't an equivalent for Oxford.

Deferred Entry and Gap Years

It is always advisable to apply to university during your A2 year – at the very least it is a useful experience and you can always apply again next year if you are unsuccessful. In attending university a year later, you are a year older, bringing more maturity and life experience to the course – the benefits of this are clear to see in course like medicine!

If you are planning to take a gap year, always apply whilst in A-level year unless there is a reason you would not be able to gain a place (e.g. grades/predictions too low, you need to sit more exams). Applying for deferred entry allows you to go on your gap year, safe in the knowledge that you have secured a place upon your return. If things then don't go to plan, you have time to improve your application and a second chance in which to apply to different medical schools.

You'll need to tweak your statement slightly if you're applying for deferred entry. You will need to demonstrate to the tutor that you are filling your gap year with meaningful experiences in order to help you grow as a person. Therefore discuss your gap year plans in a brief paragraph, describing what you hope to achieve, what life skills you hope to learn, and how these are both transferable and applicable to your course. In addition, a year of deferred entry gives you opportunity to work and save in order to fund your progress through what is a very expensive time at university.

This is a good opportunity once again to show your commitment. If your gap year plans include any volunteering work, use this to support your vocation of public service. If you have already made plans, it shows that you're organised.

To make a strong application, you should be spending a significant proportion of your gap year doing things that support your application: work experience, voluntary work and activities that build your skills. Discuss in your personal statement why you chose to do these things, what you are learning from them and how it has affected your desire to study medicine. Make sure you account for all time and give reasons for everything you do, tying it back to your path towards (hopefully) becoming a doctor. A good application should draw upon your gap year to reinforce your skills and commitment; it should give positive reasons why you have chosen to take a gap year. Taking a gap year gives you good opportunities to expand your experiences, but you have to remember that it also brings expectations – therefore if you don't take these opportunities you stand to weaken your application.

Going on a gap year is a choice for you to make; overall, you are equally likely to get an offer with or without taking a gap year.

Re-applying

If instead you are reading this during a gap year because of an unsuccessful first application do not be disheartened. Applying a second time puts you in a much stronger position as you have your A-level grades in hand. Do mention your failure first time round in your personal statement, but also reflect on it and discuss why you think this happened. More importantly, discuss what you have done to address these issues to improve yourself as a candidate. Re-applying shows strength of character, resilience and determination- qualities desired by any course tutor at any institution.

Extra Reading

Reading above and beyond what you would need to for your school studies is a great way to show genuine enthusiasm. Therefore, a good personal statement will include at least some discussion of this extra reading.

If you are applying to Oxford or Cambridge, where the medical course is pure academic science for the first three years, discussing scientific reading is a good way to show your love of science to the admissions tutor. It also has the added benefit of suggesting your areas of particular interest which can help guide the interview discussion to your strongest topics.

Make sure you don't fall into the trap of thinking a long list of books will impress – this isn't the point. [**The idea is you show what you have learned**]from each of the books and how it has influenced your decision to study medicine. This shows that you haven't just looked at the pages of the book as you've turned them over, but rather that you have understood and thought about them. When discussing your learning, try to make specific points rather than generic ones. For example, a weaker statement might say:

"I read Thinking Fast and Slow by Daniel Kahneman, which helped me understand the way decisions are made".

Whereas a stronger statement may say:

"I particularly enjoyed Thinking Fast and Slow by Daniel Kahneman, which made me realise the importance of shortcuts in making quick and accurate decisions."

Mature and Graduate Applicants n/a··· paras.

If you're applying as a mature student or to graduate entry medicine, talking about your previous work and career is important.

If you have been working for a number of years, then a large chunk of your relevant life story will be due to your employment. Your journey to medicine will describe your previous career path, the moment you thought about a change, how you investigated medicine as a career and why you now believe it is the right path for you.

Coming from a professional background, the skills you have learned in the workplace will be significant and begin to overtake extra-curricular activities as a way of demonstrating core attributes such as time-management, communication and team working. In addition, you may have undertaken professional learning in your job such as reading books or attending courses – be sure to draw upon this to support your ability to undertake the lifelong learning required of a doctor.

Admissions tutors are not looking to see how similar your current job is to medicine. You will learn what you need to know at medical school. They are looking for the general skills you have learned that will help make you a good doctor, and research/experience outside of work to confirm your interest. There is, however, an exception to this – if you work within science and are applying to 4-year accelerated grad-med courses, be sure to talk about your scientific education. Describe the scientific skills you have learned such as data interpretation, because this shows your aptitude for science and your suitability for picking up new technical knowledge quickly.

Standing out from the crowd

You may have heard people saying that a good personal statement helps you stand out from the crowd – and this is certainly true. Admissions tutors read <u>hundreds</u> of personal statements, so to be in with the best chance yours should offer something a bit different to leave a lasting good impression.

Whilst standing out from the crowd is easy, the line between standing out for the <u>right</u> and the <u>wrong reasons</u> is a <u>fine one and you have to tread carefully</u>.

The easiest ways to add some originality are in your reading and activities. There will be countless people who play football but less who play ice hockey; everyone reads New Scientist and Student BMJ (both excellent resources you should look at) but fewer people read Nature. It is not more valuable to do something less popular, but it can make it easier for the reader to see your personal statement as original. This is not about going out and enrolling with an extreme ironing club – it is about taking time to identify the things you already do and skills you have that are a bit more interesting than the generic activities and just giving them a mention to show a wide variety of interests.

Many medical schools will score the personal statement based on a <u>marking grid.</u> You'll gain marks for evidence of performance in different areas depending on your assessed level of achievement. These areas may include <u>interest in medicine</u>, <u>variety of work experience,</u> <u>evidence of altruism/volunteering</u>, <u>communication skills</u> and <u>general skills</u>. Ensure you cover all the areas described in the section guide to make sure you hit all the <u>key scoring points</u>.

Proof-reading the personal statement is extremely important – not just you, but also by showing it to friends, family and teachers to get their opinions. Firstly, it's so easy to ignore your own mistakes, because as you become familiar with your own work you begin skimming through rather than reading in-depth. But also, this allows people to assess the writing style – by gathering lots of opinions you can build up a good idea of the strongest areas (which you should expand) and the weakest areas (which you should modify).

Don't try to force anything into the personal statement. Allow it to grow and showcase your wide variety of skills. Make sure there is a smooth flow from one idea to the next. Allow it to tell your story. Make sure all the spelling and grammar are accurate. Then, your personal statement will shine out from the average ones to give you the best possible chance.

Interviews

As a medical applicant, you are almost certain to be interviewed before any offer is made – and this fact adds extra complexity to the writing of your personal statement.

In any interview, you can expect to be asked questions on the content of your personal statement – about your work experience, your reading, your extra-curricular activities and so on. This makes it especially important to be completely honest. And I don't mean just avoiding *explicit* lies (you shouldn't be doing that anyway; doctors and medical students are legally bound by a moral code) – this includes all the little traps that are so easy to fall into – the book you intend to read, the operation you 'watched' but didn't fully see and so on. That book you were genuinely *planning* to read might turn out to be terrible, but you're then committed to reading it front to back in case your interviewer probes your interest in it. Likewise, if you couldn't see an operation in your work experience because there were 5 broad-shouldered surgeons blocking your view, it might be sensible to avoid bringing it up. Your interviewer might be a specialist shoulder surgeon and ask all about posterior dislocation and the rotator cuff muscles, leaving you feeling silly if you cannot answer about an operation you claim to have watched.

But this isn't all bad news – **it can actually be a very positive thing**. By writing about all the subjects that interest you most in your personal statement, you have the opportunity to guide the interview discussion towards those areas you love, know most about and would enjoy discussing. By doing so, you give yourself an opportunity to show your knowledge and enthusiasm to the interviewer – traits which will go a long way in convincing them you are the right person to fill that elusive place at medical school.

Therefore, it is important that you use your personal statement as part of your interview preparation. Read and re-read your statement before the interview to make certain you are ready to talk about anything you may be asked questions on. Not only does this give you a great chance of answering these questions well, it can give you an overall feeling of assurance that you are well prepared, lending confidence to make your overall performance more polished. What's more, if you have all your personal statement information at the front of your mind, answering general questions about your experiences is much easier as you have a great bank of information to quickly draw upon.

Omissions

It can be difficult to work out exactly where the line stands when it comes to omitting certain information.

Of course, you should only include things that emphasise your best points. But sometimes leaving certain things out can cause problems.

For example, let's imagine you worked for half an hour a month at a care home over a 6 month period. If you said in your personal statement you had worked at a care home for 6 months, you could reasonably expect interview questions on it. If it emerged that you had only spent three hours there in total, the interviewer would not be impressed, and would be left doubting the truthfulness of the whole personal statement. Far better to just say you arranged a few sessions helping in a care home, then discuss what you learned from it and avoid the risk of being left looking silly.

Another circumstance when not to omit details is when there is something that needs explaining. Perhaps you've taken a year out of the normal education pathway to do something different or because you were experiencing some difficulty. Whilst the personal statement is not the place to discuss extenuating circumstances, it should tell the story of your recent path through life. If there are any big gaps, it is likely to concern the person reading it that you have something to hide. Make sure you explain your route and the reasons for it, putting it in the context of your journey towards a medical career.

Things to Avoid

Whilst there are no rights and wrongs to writing a personal statement, there are a few common traps students can easily fall into. Here follows a discussion of things that are best avoided to ensure your personal statement is strong.

Stating the obvious – this includes phrases like "I am studying A-level biology which has helped me learn about human biology in the human biology module". Admissions tutors can see from the UCAS form what A-level subjects you are studying and the learning you claim is obvious.

University names – the same personal statement goes to all universities, so don't include any university names. Only include specifics of the course if they are common to all the courses you are applying to.

Harsh criticism – it's great to show two sides of anything and it's perfectly acceptable to disagree with things. However, it is wise to avoid excessively strong criticism of anything for two reasons. Firstly, you are still early in your academic journey. Questioning established knowledge makes a good scientist, but dismissing the work of eminent scientists will make you seem ignorant and should be avoided. Secondly, you never know who is going to interview you – it could be the person you are criticising, or a close friend or work colleague of theirs. I am aware of one Cambridge interview where a student had strongly criticised a book in their personal statement. Guess who the interviewer turned out to be....

Controversy – avoid controversy in any form, be it strong opinions or any other reason. You don't want to make an impression for the wrong reasons, and if you irritate the reader you're making life needlessly difficult.

Lists – everything needs to be included for a reason. Very few things have an intrinsic value, rather the value comes from the knowledge you gain and the skills you develop by doing the activities. Therefore, reeling off a long list of sports you play won't impress anyone. Instead, focus on specifics and indicate what you have learned from doing each thing you mention.

Flattery – this includes flattery of either people or universities. Saying how much you dream of being a doctor or how much you admire someone's work will not win you a place.

Detail about your A-level subjects – all students study broadly similar A-levels and they are included on your UCAS form. Admissions tutors are looking for ways you are unique and have differentiated yourself from others. They know that most applicants study broadly similar A-levels, so this won't help you stand out. As it won't do anything to convince someone you are suited for medicine, it is a waste of words and unnecessary.

Things that happened before GCSE – if something *started* when you were nine and you have continued it up until today then you should absolutely include it as it shows great commitment and the opportunity to develop many skills. However, if you are considering mentioning the archery you stopped four years ago, please resist the temptation. Putting something that finished a long time ago signals to the reader that you don't have much going on now – not the impression you want to be making.

Include books you haven't read – this is risky. Even if you *genuinely* intend to read the book, you can't make any intelligent observations about it if you haven't done so yet. In addition, you are then committed to finishing it even if you find it very dull, or you risk being caught out in an interview.

Stick to things you have already read. If you don't have much to say, pick some short books and journal articles and make a start today!

Starting too late – the later you begin writing, the harder you make the task. By starting early you can do little and often, making it a much more enjoyable experience. You get more time to review, proof-read and show it to others. And by considering your personal statement early, you have a chance to do extra things to fill in any gaps or weak areas that you spot.

Extenuating circumstances – the personal statement is to tell your story. It is not the place for extenuating circumstances. If any are applicable, this is for teachers to write in the reference. Make sure you know who is writing it and meet with them to help explain the full story.

Plagiarism – it goes without saying that you must not plagiarise, but I feel no "things to avoid" list would be complete without the most important point. Plagiarism of another personal statement is the easiest way to get yourself into big trouble. UCAS use sophisticated detection software and if any significant match shows up (not necessarily the whole statement, just a few identical sentences is enough), then universities you apply to will be notified and are likely to blacklist your application.

Power Words

Certain words can be useful as they help you show how motivated, dynamic and enthusiastic you are. These words are often termed 'power words'. For example, just substituting the word 'made' for 'created' or 'established' can give a much more dynamic and proactive feel to the writing. The following list of power words is provided for you to dip into – you will find that including just a few of these words in the correct context will help to strengthen the writing.

Absorbed	Established	Minimised	Reorganised
Accomplished	Exceeded	Modernised	Secured
Achieved	Expanded	Monitored	Spearheaded
Analysed	Explored	Moved	Streamlined
Assembled	Formulated	Obtained	Strengthened
Attended	Gained	Organised	Targeted
Authored	Improved	Overhauled	Taught
Awarded	Influenced	Participated	Trained
Broadened	Initiated	Prevented	Transformed
Collaborated	Instigated	Promoted	Underlined
Committed	Integrated	Protected	Understood
Communicated	Learned	Purchased	Undertook
Created	Led	Pursued	Updated
Customised	Listened	Qualified	Upgraded
Determined	Maximised	Ranked	Valued
Enabled	Manoeuvred	Recognised	Volunteered
Enthused	Mentored	Realised	Won

The Reference

The UCAS reference is often neglected by many applicants; it's an untapped resource that can give you an edge over other applicants. In order to plan your use of the reference you first need to establish how it will be used – again consult prospectuses or subject websites. Does it actually count towards your application score or rather is it only consulted in border line candidates? Furthermore the reference could certainly affect the way in which the tutor perceives what you have written and indeed what they infer from it.

Either way, in order to get the most out of your reference you need to actively participate in its creation. The best way to achieve this is to ask a teacher who you are particularly friendly with to write it. Even if this is not possible, ask for a copy of your reference before it is submitted to UCAS. This way you can ensure that the personal statement and reference complement one another for maximum impact.

The reference is best used for explanations of negative aspects within your application – e.g. deflated exam results, family bereavements – or even addition of new information if you run out of space in your personal statement. In this respect the reference is a backdoor through which you can feed more information to the tutor in order to strengthen your application.

If there is a teacher who is willing to go through your reference with you, complete your personal statement first before starting on the reference itself. This way you will have a clear idea of the content and tone of the majority of your application as well as anything that may be missing which you would like to add.

The reference is the one place for your teachers to be completely unreserved- superlatives and complements mean a lot more coming from someone other than yourself. One such example of this is the opportunity for your teachers to discuss how they have actively noticed your initiative and passion, going above and beyond in pursuing the subject in question.

Using the Personal Statements

This book contains 100+ medical personal statements. Each one is an actual personal statement that was successful in getting the applicant into medical school.

There is a table at the back of the book showing which statements were successful at different universities – we include this for interest only and don't suggest you over-analyse. It might be useful to take a *slightly* closer look at any that were successful for your top choices, but always bear in mind that the similarities between different medical schools are much greater than the differences, and in any case, you have to write a personal statement equally applicable to all of your choices.

All personal statements come with comments, drawing your attention to the stronger and weaker points of that personal statement. Don't look immediately at this. First, read the personal statement yourself and get a feeling for the general style of writing. Then, test yourself: decide which you think the strongest and weakest parts are. After that, look at the comments on the statement. By using the book this way, you develop your own critical reading skills – skills which you can then apply to your own personal statement, allowing you to build in improvements.

We include these personal statements for several reasons including:

➢ To show you different approaches to "why medicine" questions
➢ To help you gauge what a good balance is between different sections
➢ To prove there are many different routes to success
➢ To suggest ideas of high-impact phrases to use
➢ To give insight into the many work experience options that exist
➢ To show how you can link experiences to skills and learning
➢ To show you that writing a successful statement is within your reach
➢ To help you assess when your personal statement may be nearly ready

---

IT CANNOT BE OVERSTRESSED HOW IMPORTANT IT IS THAT YOU **DO NOT COPY** FROM THESE PERSONAL STATEMENTS

UCAS uses anti-plagiarism software called *Copycatch*. This software checks your submission against all previous personal statements and any in your year of entry too. If any significant similarity is detected, then all universities you apply to are notified. You can use the examples for inspiration and comparison, but everything you write in your own statement must be your own original work, and must be completely truthful to you.

I'd like to give a final word of warning. We are aware there are companies and individuals who will write personal statements for you. We strongly recommend against getting anyone else to write your personal statement. In doing so, you run the risk that they are plagiarising material without you knowing, thus jeopardising your entire application. In addition, this will breach the declaration that the statement is your own original work. Follow our top tips, take inspiration from the examples and put in some hard work – you'll be sure to produce an excellent personal statement.

UNDERGRADUATE
PERSONAL STATEMENTS

Statement 1

Helping to care for children during work experience this summer at an HIV clinic in Botswana has strengthened my determination to pursue a career in medicine. It was emotionally challenging to witness children suffering, but I was inspired by the tremendous efforts of the team to help improve the lives of their patients.

My interest in medicine stems from my fascination with science and has been consolidated through work experience placements in general practice, radiology, pathology and pharmacy. One experience that has left a lasting impression was a rare opportunity of observing a newborn on ECMO whilst shadowing a Radiologist at University Hospital, Southampton. It was eye-opening to see how the pediatric intensive care team worked hard to keep the baby alive. I have gained an insight into the breadth of careers within medicine and the incredible teamwork that occurs behind the scenes during work experience with a Pathologist at Whittington Hospital. At Barnes Surgery, sitting in on GP consultations gave me an opportunity to see how building rapport and utilizing good communication skills can help in building a professional and supportive relationship, giving the patient ownership over their treatment. Attending a Medlink course enabled me to learn from the experiences of different specialists.

Learning about the complexities of the human body in Biology sparked my curiosity to learn more in Chemistry and understand the relationship between drugs and the medical conditions they are targeted to treat. To further my interest in science I took part in the 'Siemens - The Next Big Thing' national competition, which my team won with an idea of a desalination plant providing purified water and cheap electricity for poor countries. Another inspirational experience was being awarded a scholarship for the Honeywell Leadership Academy at the US Space Centre where I developed leadership and teamwork skills through STEM based challenges.

Motivated by my experience in Botswana, I undertook an EPQ on the prevention of HIV transmission in Africa, focusing on the latest advances in treatments and the necessity of education and social support. To research for this project, and to generally learn about advances in medicine, I have attended lectures focusing on new treatments for HIV, cancer relapses and Parkinson's disease and have read related articles in the Biological Sciences Review. All this has helped to develop my analytical and independent research skills.

Outside school, volunteering at a care home for the elderly, where I organise activities and assist with feeding, has given me a deeper understanding of the palliative care of the elderly. I have developed my ability to interact with young children from working at Kumon Math's over the past two years. I have a passion for music and have taught myself to play the piano and drums and have been a long-term member of the school choir.

At school, I have been awarded prizes in English, Math's and Science. I am also a keen sportsperson and have been awarded Borough sports prizes in netball, tennis and athletics. I have set up a school basketball team and organized professional coaching. I volunteered for a year-long National Social Enterprise competition to raise funds for the Wings of Hope children's charity and out of five hundred competing teams, my team won one of the five top prizes. Being Head of House and a member of the Head Girl Team has enhanced my time management, interpersonal and communication skills. Through a month-long expedition to Mongolia and the Gold DofE award, I have improved my problem solving, organization and teamwork skills and have learnt to work well under pressure.

My experiences have shown me that medicine is a challenging and demanding profession, however, I believe that I have the determination, intellectual curiosity and commitment to undertake the vast level of lifelong learning that medicine is going to entail.

Universities Applied to:

➤ University College: Offer
➤ Imperial College: Rejected
➤ Birmingham: Rejected
➤ Bristol: Interview + Rejected

Good Points:

Well-written and well-structured statement. It provides a good overview of a very diverse education career, covering a variety of medically relevant topics. The student clearly has spent a lot of time and effort gearing her education towards studying medicine. Having diverse experiences is definitely helpful as it shows determination and dedication to the subject matter.

Bad Points:

The entire statement presents essentially a list of different achievements. There is very little information on the student's original motivation for studying medicine. Whilst it starts well with the emotional side of experiences gathered during work experience in Botswana, the student fails to provide any reason for studying medicine other than her interest in science. This is a let-down as most students applying for medicine will have a scientific interest. In addition, simply listing achievements can easily come across as bragging. There is a very fine line between providing an insight into previous accomplishments and showing off, which is not a quality sought in doctors.

Overall:

The statement is strong but would have been a lot stronger if the student had managed to tie her experiences closer to the motivation for studying medicine. Whilst it is good to provide a list of achievements in a competitive course such as medicine, listing them without purpose has little effect. Most medical applicants will have a history of academic excellence and diverse medical work experience, what is going to make a difference for the application is the connection between previous achievement and the relevance for medicine.

NOTES

Statement 2

"I haven't eaten all day and I don't know if I will last the night". This is one of forty similar messages left within an hour on my house answering machine and was one of the first signs of my Grandma's dementia. I began to read books on dementia as she deteriorated further which helped us cope with the challenges ahead. She has been diagnosed with Vascular Dementia and our family has been in close contact with Primary Care and the community mental health team. I was moved by their compassion and unique work ethic, which motivated me to pursue a career in Medicine.

Keen to learn more about medicine, I attended a Medical Taster Weekend at King's College London. I learned about the process of becoming a doctor and the importance of listening and history taking. Soon afterwards, I arranged work experience on the Gastroenterology Ward at Epsom General Hospital. My most memorable patient was a 70-year-old man who came in with jaundice; I accompanied doctors throughout the diagnostic process. It was detective-like; running blood tests and CT scans with the results unfortunately showing he had liver cancer. This amplified the low-points in medicine, that as a Doctor you will be dealing with people at their most vulnerable moments, however seeing the doctors providing the patient individual and holistic care was uplifting. I appreciated the multidisciplinary team working together to aid his physical and emotional recovery. I have now completed 10 weeks of work experience. Having spent a week in an Endocrine Clinic I have become fascinated by Diabetes and its current and future treatments. I recently read an article about commercially available continuous glucose monitors, which soon will be used alongside artificial pancreases.

Volunteering in a government hospital in Gambia for a month affirmed my career choice in medicine. I realized the importance of empathy in Medicine as I assisted with a prolonged labor where the mother tragically died, speaking to the family afterwards was the most difficult task I have ever undertaken, but I was proud to say "Everyone tried their very best." The whole experience was emotionally challenging as all around me patients were suffering from illnesses that could be prevented by improvements in infrastructure and education. Nevertheless, it was inspiring seeing the medical team-work assiduously to achieve the best results possible.

For the past year, I have been volunteering at a care home for adults with learning disabilities. Maintaining composure was difficult, particularly when they would throw tantrums or refuse to eat, but I have enjoyed the patient interaction and it has developed my interpersonal skills. This experience has given me the confidence to spend nine weeks in a Summer Camp in America with children who have learning disabilities.

I have been competing nationally in swimming for 5 years, and now have completed my National Pool Lifeguard Qualification, which required me to learn first aid. My first aid skills became useful on my Duke of Edinburgh Gold expedition when a team member scalded their hand with hot water. D of E has also given me the opportunity to develop team-working skills and learn British Sign Language.

In Year 13, I was awarded school prizes in Math and Chemistry, and the Pickle prize for outstanding charitable endeavors. I was also awarded the prestigious Silver UKMT Award for scoring in the top 12% of a national math's competition.

Last year, I volunteered in a national social-enterprise scheme, to raise money and awareness for the Wings of Hope Charity. Out of 500 teams, my team was invited to the House of Lords and presented with one of five prizes for raising over £3000.

Through my experiences I understand the challenges that come with a career in Medicine but my scientific curiosity, empathetic nature and sheer determination are all attributes that will help me become a great doctor.

Universities Applied to:
➤ Sheffield: Offer
➤ Liverpool: Offer
➤ Glasgow: Rejected
➤ Leeds: Offer

Good points:
Well-written and good style. Excellent personal entry into the statement. Giving insight into what motivates the student to pursue a career in medicine is centrally important. Having a concrete case to tie this motivation to is helpful as it gives the statement a human and individual touch and also provides material to discuss during the interview. The student also displays extensive work experience, which is a strength.

Bad points:
Whilst the statement gives insight into various medical experiences in the past, it only superficially ties them to new skills learned. This is important because work experiences only really have a purpose if they help to further the student's abilities. The achievements section at the end of the statement is somewhat at the wrong place. Whilst the achievements are impressive, listing them must serve a purpose that shows personal development.

Overall:
Overall this is a good statement. The strengths definitely lie in the personal touch with the motivation to study medicine. Unfortunately, it loses strength as the student fails to tie previous experiences to lessons learned that are relevant to studying medicine. This is a pity as the student has quite extensive past experiences that certainly provided very relevant learning points.

NOTES

Statement 3

Sitting in front of Mrs D, beside the Royal Marsden consultant I was shadowing, I realised that as a doctor, treating a patient's emotional concerns is just as important as treating the actual disease. A simple smile can work wonders. I also learnt how successful and worthwhile the mammography screening programme was, causing a 15% reduction in mortality rates. However, an article in the student BMJ made me think about the possible emotional, financial and physical stresses that overdiagnosis can cause. At Medlink I was excited to start developing my own practical skills by using an ophthalmoscope. I was then amazed whilst witnessing a bronchoscopy, at both the doctor's anatomical knowledge and dexterity.On my work experience on a respiratory ward at East Surrey Hospital I was struck by the seamless coordination of doctors, nurses, lab scientists and specialist teams. Doctors must be able to act as a leader within a team, so that the patients feel comfortable and secure.

At the Royal Marsden, seeing medicine as an academic pursuit as well as a practical one, cemented my passion for the field. I became inspired to read The Molecular Biology of Cancer by Lauren Pecorino and Cancer by Paul Scotting which, whilst fascinating, left me eager for more answers than they (or current research) could provide. As stem cells' infinite ability to divide is drawn from the up-regulation of telomerase - as for cancer cells - does this feature cause them to acquire so many mutations that they end up inextricably linked to tumorigenesis? Furthermore, is cancer an inevitable price we pay for life? It was then, through studying depolarisation and the cardiac cycle in biology, that I started to wonder why malignant cardiac tumours are so rare. I find the extent of current research awe inspiring but was also excited to discover that in every avenue of medicine I looked, I had so many questions that are still, as yet, unanswerable.

Medicine also requires strong interpersonal skills. Helping out at The School for Profound Education was daunting and had a steep learning curve for me, especially the challenge of communicating wholly non-verbally. However, I found that devoting my time to the care and support of these children through a range of activities from changing feed bags to wheelchair barn dancing was immensely satisfying. Helping the 'learners' to enjoy life's full potential made me realise, that despite the huge commitment, being a doctor and dedicating yourself to ensuring people get the most out of their lives would always be rewarding and worthwhile. I was also interested to learn and research further the conditions some of the children had - a common example among the girls being Retts syndrome.

I have been elected as a Senior Prefect and also House Captain at my school. Finding time to relax is vital in medicine and I find playing guitar (grade VI) and piano perfect for me to do so. I have enjoyed engaging with German both in and outside of school, as an exciting opportunity to learn not just a language but also more about a foreign culture; participating in various international exchanges has enabled me to appreciate this first-hand. I developed teamwork skills on my Gold Duke of Edinburgh expedition, and have been Club Captain of my swimming club for the last two years. Through perseverance and determination I have pushed myself to succeed in competitions and I strive to approach academic life with a similar drive. As a voluntary ASA qualified swimming teacher, and through teaching English skills at my school, I have had valuable experience of the challenges of helping, leading and interacting with young children - in particular when I had to clear the pool and improvise a session in an emergency.

I aspire to be the doctor aiding Mrs D through such tough times. When I retire I hope to be able to look back on my career and know that I have made a positive impact on society. Medicine would allow me to achieve this.

Universities applied to:
➢ Oxford: Offer
➢ Sheffield: Interview + Rejected
➢ Bristol: Interview + Rejected
➢ Edinburgh: Rejected

Good points:
The student demonstrates some good reflections on their work experience. This is very relevant as the experience only really becomes relevant for providing strength to the statement if it is put into the right context and met with adequate reflection from the student's side. The student correctly underlines the correlation of soft and academic skills in the practice of medicine. This is important as it is a commonly underestimated relationship. In addition to the clinical work experience, the student also provides a good range of non-clinical experiences that all contribute to their personal development. Particularly relevant in this context are lessons learned teaching as well as communication skills.

Bad points:
At instances, the statement lacks a clear structure and a clear message. The information provided is a little all over the place. This is a pity as the unorganised structure makes it very difficult to follow the content and learn about the student, which significantly weakens the overall expressive power of the statement. In addition, the statement remains vague and does not deliver the full extent of reflections on experiences possible. This leaves the statement superficial and falling short of the potential expressive strength.

Overall:
An average statement that is, unfortunately, let down by some stylistic and content weaknesses that make it difficult to draw the maximum amount of information about the student from the statement. With some more or less minor improvements to structure and depth of reflection, this statement could be very strong. In the form presented here, it does provide some insight into the student's character and into what they considers important, but the statement sells itself short due to lack of detail.

NOTES

Statement 4

For me medicine offers an academically and mentally challenging profession which amalgamates my fascination with the human body and my desire to work with a variety of individuals with their own individual problems on a day to day basis. It offers a chance to make a real difference to the lives of others.

My passion for the subject has been fuelled by additional reading, namely various books on the brain such as Greenfield's 'Guided Tour of the Brain' and Sacks' 'The Man Who Mistook his Wife for a Hat'. As well as giving me a good grounding in the current understanding of the brain it has revealed how much of it remains a tantalising mystery. I have also borrowed past A level textbooks from school that cover areas of the syllabus that have since been cut such as the anatomy and function of the human eye and I keep up to date with medical affairs using the <u>Science and Health sections of the BBC news website</u>.

I have explored my interest in the subject through work experience. My first placement was with a neurologist who specialised in MS. The one-on-one consultations showed me the all-important need for tact when dealing with difficult issues that needed to be addressed. It also highlighted the great potential for progress in medical research which is exciting for me.

During my second week-long placement in a general practice I observed a GP dealing with a broad spectrum of individuals who presented cases ranging from gynaecological issues and chest infections to severe depression and even minor operations. For me, it emphasised the range of skills required to *range* be a doctor: the knowledge of the physiological systems that underpin each illness and how specific treatments will affect these systems, knowledge that has a constant need to be replenished due to advances in medical research and technology; the vital interpersonal skills and clarity of communication required to convey what may be a complicated concept to someone with little scientific knowledge; and even the manual skills involved in thoroughly examining patients and carrying out minor operations.

I volunteer weekly in a residential care home for severely disabled adults, most of whom have acute *sub for the hospice* cerebral palsy. Feeding and brushing the teeth of the residents has taught me a lot about the value of patience and empathy in dealing with the seriously disabled. I thoroughly enjoy getting to know the habits of many of the residents and although none of them has any coherent method of communication each individual has a unique personality that I have come to appreciate over time. While challenging, finding unconventional methods of communication with the residents is very rewarding. Helping the elderly during church events has also highlighted for me the value of care and understanding for fragile individuals. Working with these people has really made me realise that I want to devote my life to using my intelligence, diligence and enthusiasm for the good of others; I think medicine is a natural career choice given this perspective.

I believe my <u>extracurricular</u> activities have taught me valuable skills that will prove useful as a medic. I am part of the Nottingham Youth Orchestra and the East Midlands Youth String Orchestra. Playing as a part of these ensembles requires individual prowess as well as an ability to coordinate finely with the many other members of the orchestra. In addition, during my weekly shift at a restaurant I have the role of training new employees which highlights my ability to explain with clarity and to be friendly and welcoming.

Attending Medlink and speaking with doctors and other members of the NHS has made me appreciate how challenging a career in medicine will prove yet I am certain that this is the right choice for me as it offers personal challenge, continual development and the opportunity to make a real difference in people's lives. I hope you will give me the chance to fulfil this aspiration.

Universities applied to:
- Oxford: Offer
- Newcastle: Offer
- Birmingham: Offer
- Bristol: Rejected

Good points:
This is an excellent statement. It is well-written and well-rounded providing a wide range of insight into the educational career of the student. It also gives a good impression of previous work experience and the student ties these experiences well into the whole picture of medicine. It makes it clear how these experiences have contributed to their choice of medicine as a subject which is very helpful for an examiner reading this statement. The student also ties his past work experience to lessons learned that they sees relevant for medicine. This is important, as work experience can only be useful if it teaches relevant lessons.

Bad points:
The paragraph addressing the interest in the scientific side of medicine is somewhat superficial. Whilst it is good to show interest in anatomy and a desire to stay up to date with current medical developments, this is also something that is expected from students aiming to study medicine. It therefore serves little purpose as a distinguishing feature from other applicants.

Overall:
A very good statement that ticks all relevant boxes and only has a few minor weaknesses. These weaknesses have little impact on the overall quality as the student manages to demonstrate a variety of lessons and experiences that support their choice of medicine as a career.

NOTES

Statement 5

The first time I announced I wanted to be a doctor; my parents were amused but indulgent. Their reactions are understandable, considering that I was eight at the time. From a young age I have always been intrigued with the human body and it has only grown from that time. My fascination with science is one of the reasons I want to study Medicine. The continuous learning throughout my career; constant new discoveries and technologies; as well as the variety in each day are part of the attraction of Medicine.

To form a realistic image of a profession in Medicine I have undergone various work experience which has allowed me patient contact and a chance to observe professionals. I arranged my first two-week placement at St James Hospital in 2008, where I learnt basic practice such as, data confidentiality and hand hygiene which is becoming more important with the emergence of the new superbug, NDM-1. In 2009 I had another two-week placement in Castlehill Hospital, where I gained knowledge of how the management and administration of a hospital operate. This is useful knowledge for understanding how much the government demands for savings from the NHS will truly affect quality of care. My work experience has strengthened my resolve to pursue a medical career. Volunteering regularly at Harrogate Hospital over the past year has given me recurring interaction with a hospital environment. *[handwritten note: mrsa patient.]* *[handwritten note: sub per my hospital volunteering]*

My A level choices confirm my enthusiasm for science and demonstrate that I am able to cope with a heavy workload and rise to a challenge, which have already resulted in an achievement of an A* grade in my A-level Mathematics. I enjoy reading and keeping up to date with the latest developments in science; I am a subscriber to "Biological Science Review" and regularly read the "New Scientist". I am currently writing an EPQ on the ethics of organ donation which is self-motivated and gives me a chance to be in charge of my learning. I participated in my school's Medical Package, which enabled me to attend a Hospice Day, hospital tours and lectures and much more. I am also the creator and president of the Medical Debate Society at my school. We meet weekly to discuss common medical controversial topics.

I try to balance my interest in science with a variety of other activities. As a Senior Prefect and a School Council Member, I have excellent organisation, time management and leadership skills, along with the ability to negotiate. My communication and listening skills have developed through Charity Committee, debating and Netball. As a member of the Boxing club I have learnt self-discipline and determination. I am a philanthropic individual and enjoy assisting others. I am a volunteer at my Sunday school and local library. Paired tutoring is a scheme I am also involved in, where I help a younger student who has difficulty reading. Taking part in the Duke of Edinburgh scheme has shown me the importance of perseverance and motivation to succeed.

I am a focused and determined person with a fierce commitment to studying Medicine. I believe I have the academic capability and drive to succeed in a Medicine course at university. My aspiration is to become a Paediatrician and one of the top experts in my field.

Universities applied to:
- Cambridge: Offer ✗
- Imperial College: Offer ✗
- Newcastle: Offer
- University College: Offer ✗

Good points:

A strong, well-written statement that demonstrates a varied history of academic excellence. The student provides good insight into how the early desire to be a doctor has shaped their development, both academically as well as individually. This demonstrates great dedication to the subject matter as well as the intellectual and motivational facilities necessary to perform well in a demanding course such a medicine. The student demonstrates good academic performance and discipline.

Bad points:

The statement is very focussed on academic performance and academic detail. Personal experiences and lessons learned during patient exposure are somewhat limited, which is a pity as the student shows considerable clinical experience. It would complete and strengthen the picture of academic excellence significantly if the student had been able to add clinical and inter-person lessons learned during their time in the hospital. This includes skills such as communicating information which are essential in medicine.

Overall:

A good statement providing good insight into the impressive academic performance of the student. Unfortunately the student sells themselves somewhat short by ignoring the non-academic side of medicine that is equally as important as academia. Having had the hospital exposure, it would have been easy to add this in order to achieve an even better statement.

NOTES

Statement 6

In the summer of 2008, my grandfather was diagnosed with Parkinson's disease. At the tender age of 11, I was oblivious to the neurological disorder's implications. On a Saturday afternoon that summer, my father suddenly collapsed and had a seizure in the cold foods section of a supermarket. I have never been as terrified as I was when I watched froth come out of his mouth. Following this episode, he was diagnosed with photosensitive epilepsy, leaving me jarred and increasingly concerned about my family's health.

I view doctors as leaders in both the medical field and in society. As Head Boy of my school, I strive to do the same among my peers and in my community. I am proud to have won "Student of the Year" twice and to have represented the school varsity football team for three years. I have developed responsibility and communication skills by attending six conferences in four continents for Model United Nations, the highlight of which was leading 800 delegates as President of the General Assembly at DIAMUN, the largest conference in the Gulf region. As President of the Water for Life Club, I raised AED 75,000 (~GBP12,300) for the Aqua Initiative, a UK-based charity that provides clean water to developing nations. Inspired to do more, I embarked on an unforgettable service trip to the Sasenyi Primary School in Kenya, where I immersed myself in the local community by helping with school construction and interacting with children. Back in Dubai, I helped found the Interact Club and served as its President. We initiated frequent visits to the Senses Center, the only residential facility for special needs children in the UAE. Knowing that I can make a difference in the lives of others is something that satisfies me greatly, which further motivates me to pursue medicine.

I was also fortunate enough to attend a three week Global Leaders Program at Cambridge University and take a fascinating online course by Brown University. From the latter, I developed a fundamental understanding of neuroscience, modern neurotechnology, neurological disorders and scientific writing. With my grandfather in my mind, I created a presentation on Parkinson's disease aimed at relatives of patients. I genuinely take pleasure in knowing that pursuing a medical career is an ongoing process of learning and reflection that will enable me to benefit individuals and society.

I have also gained direct experience in the medical field by shadowing Dr. William Murrell at the Dr. Humeira Badsha Medical Centre in Dubai. We had lengthy discussions about upcoming research papers on gold-induced cytokines, quality and compliance in biologics, platelet rich plasma and stem cell therapy. In addition, I observed the versatile soft skills he utilized that I could relate to. For example, when working with a conservative woman from Saudi Arabia, he spent more time building trust before treatment. I then spent one insightful week at the Saudi German Hospital, where I shadowed an array of doctors with varied skill sets and specialties, thoroughly observing both real-life surgeries and clinical treatment. Though I was able to satisfy my curiosity to an extent, I am now more interested than ever in pursuing a career in medicine.

This summer, I visited my grandfather only to find out that his condition had worsened. The man who worked from dawn to dusk and still had the energy to take me around Dubai while I was growing up could now barely move across the living room without support; it is a truly heartbreaking sight. I now appreciate the importance of medical care as I understand that patients are not the only ones who suffer, entire families do. It is my dream to pursue medicine as it combines what I strive for - leadership, empathy and initiative, which are characteristics that I believe are most essential for doctors. I feel a drive inside of me, pushing me to become a person who can make a crucial impact on the health and lives of my family, my community and the world.

Universities applied to:
- King's: Offer
- Cambridge: Rejected
- Queen Mary: Offer
- University College: Offer

Good points:

This is a powerful statement that demonstrates the student's personal relation to medicine. Gaining insight into the emotional motivation of this student to pursue a career in medicine is a definite strong point providing a good impression of the student's character. The student's varied experiences prior to their application all are demonstrated to serve a purpose to make them a better doctor down the line. The student manages to provide an overview over both- subject academic knowledge as well as non-academic knowledge, such as communication skills and the doctor-patient relationship. This is important as these lessons are a necessity when practicing medicine.

Bad points:

There are very few obvious bad points. It would be interesting to hear if the student has any particular scientific interest. Also, whilst it is true that leadership, empathy and initiative are central qualities of doctors, these qualities also include scientific excellence. It would also contribute to the quality of the statement to provide more detail relating to lessons learned during work experiences.

Overall:

A very strong statement that gives an excellent impression of the student providing good insight into their motivation to study medicine. It becomes obvious that the student is very driven and highly motivated to successfully complete a medical degree, which is an important point of interest in the personal statement.

NOTES

Statement 7

I realise that medicine may not always have positive outcomes, having witnessed two deaths at a young age. However, the inevitable fallibility of the human body has driven my desire to acquire a better understanding of the complicated processes and mechanisms of our body. I am captivated by the prospect of lifelong learning; the rapid and ceaseless pace of change in medicine means that there is a vast amount of knowledge in an astonishing number of fields.

Work experience and volunteering have intensified my desire to pursue the profession; it gave me the chance to observe doctors diagnosing problems and establishing possible routes of treatment; I found the use of monoclonal antibodies in kidney transplantation fascinating. A doctor needs to be skilled, dexterous and creative. Medicine is a scientific discipline that requires a profound understanding of the physiology of the body, but the application of medicine can be an art, especially when communications between the doctor and the patient can influence the outcome of the treatment. I admire the flexibility of doctors; an inpatient needs to be approached with sensitivity and reassurance, whereas an acute admission patient would benefit more from hands-on assessments. I have been volunteering at Derriford Hospital since 2010. The most valuable part is taking time to converse with the patients to alleviate their stress and appreciate their concerns, demonstrating my understanding of the importance of listening. I appreciate that the quality of life is more important than the quantity of years, as a recent death at the ward made me realise that despite all the technological advances and our increasing understanding of the human body, there is a limit to what we can achieve.

My Nuffield Bursary project was based on finding potential medical treatments for sepsis by working on the molecular genetics of bacteria infected cells. Using theory to interpret laboratory experiments allowed me to show how an enzyme was involved in the inflammatory response mechanism.

My skills of organisation and time management were recognised by the Individual Achievement Award for my role as Finance Director in the Young Enterprise team. I used my leadership skills to assign team members to tasks to which their talents were best suited and demonstrated effective communication and teamwork to meet the deadlines. I took part in the British Mathematical Olympiad after receiving the Gold and Best in School prize for the Senior Maths Challenge last year. Regular participation in the Individual and Team Maths Challenge enhanced my lateral thinking. The numerous awards I have won such as Best Results at GCSE and Bronze in the Physics Olympiad not only show my ability in a range of subjects but also my commitment to my academic career. As a subject mentor, I developed my ability to break down problems, explaining them in a logical, analytical yet simpler way. I cherished the opportunity to work with the younger pupils; enabling them to grasp new concepts, and I believe that discussing ideas, problems or case studies with colleagues will be even more rewarding.

A keen pianist, I have been playing for 14 years. At the age of 12, I became the pianist for the Children's Amateur Theatre Society. Perseverance was essential as I was learning numerous songs each week showing commitment, resilience and attention to detail, which are transferable skills applicable to medicine. Playing in front of 300 people regularly helped me to build my confidence and taught me to stay calm under pressure. Playing the piano is a hobby that I love and I will continue to pursue it to balance my academic life.

I believe I possess the ability, devotion, diligence and determination required for this course that demands a holistic understanding of both the sciences and the arts. I will relish the challenges on an academic and personal level and I look forward to following this vocation in the future.

Universities applied to:

- ➤ Cambridge: Offer
- ➤ Imperial College: Interview + Rejected
- ➤ Cardiff: Interview + Rejected
- ➤ Bristol: Rejected

Good points:

Well-written statement that guides the reader well from one point to the next providing good insight into personal development and the motivations to becoming a doctor. The student shows that they have a very diverse background, both academically as well as related to work experience. One of the strongest parts of the statements is that the student recognizes the limitations of medicine and acknowledges the challenges to the delivery of medical care that come with those limitations. The student is also able to demonstrate experiences made in non-medical fields and how they contributed to their personal development. This is important as some of the skills necessary to becoming a good doctor are transferable from other professions.

Bad points:

The student provides extensive detail on awards and prizes won. This part is somewhat unnecessary as it does not add anything to the quality of the statement itself. Most, if not all students applying for medicine will have a history of academic excellence, therefore listing awards and achievements is less relevant. This space could be better used to provide more insight into lessons learned on work experience.

Overall:

A strong statement with a lot of information on the student's development and academic achievements. The statement succeeds at raising interest in the student and providing an overview of the individual's development. There are a few minor weaknesses that could be optimized in order to improve the overall strength of the statement even further.

NOTES

Statement 8

The combination of scientific knowledge, getting actively involved in people's lives and the job satisfaction is what made me choose a career in medicine. I enjoy the reasoning behind science but the complexity of the human mind and illness intrigues me as it can defy logic.

My enthusiasm for science was sparked after learning about topics such as the DNA and nervous control. I was amazed how minute molecules control the whole system. Taking maths has built a desire to solve challenging problems which doctors face on a daily basis. I extensively read about the medical field and after 'Life at Extremes' by Frances Ashcroft I was intrigued how the body reacts to maintain homeostasis. Stirred by my placements, I researched further about Alzheimer's and to what extent it affects people. Through volunteering at a care home, I saw how dementia, a condition where medicine has limited answers, affected patients. Seeing the impact it had, I was motivated to write an extended project on "Should Physician assisted suicide be legalised in the UK?" After researching about how other countries have implemented it and the impact it has on them I have been able to reach a conclusion of my own.

Listening to talks made by consultants in various fields, I was surprised by the diversity of medicine. In the course I saw a live knee operation through a video link. I was inspired by the precision of the surgery, the impact on the patient's life and the personal satisfaction that this could generate. To understand about the profession I shadowed doctors and I learnt that versatility and resilience is vital when dealing with acute and chronic problems. These skills were enhanced during my voluntary work at Elhap. By working with children with learning difficulties, I adapted to their different needs and focused on their individual interests which are crucial when working in the NHS. To help children overcome their anxieties, I tailored activities which encouraged group play and interaction. However some had little verbal communication, which urged me to be patient and pick up non-verbal cues. Through my voluntary work I have become an attentive listener and developed as a compassionate person; qualities I believe will put me in good stead when I am a doctor.

I am the Deputy Head of School Council. This requires being reliable, liaising with senior management and work through problems with other members of school council to ensure an effective solution is reached. My team-work skills were enriched whilst working towards my Gold Duke of Edinburgh where it was important to be supportive towards other members who struggled trekking the mountains. I realised having the ability to work effectively in a team is key when I observed a multi-disciplinary team make a collaborative decision on the patient's next step regarding treatment.

I feel I maintain a good work life balance. As the leader of the orchestra, I have performed at the Barbican thus developing my teaching skills. I organise and participate in musical evenings for the residents at the care home and I encourage them to take part. Music has made me self-disciplined and effective in time management which will help me cope and prioritise work load in the future. One of the key skills I have developed from volunteering as a lifeguard is foreseeing potential problems which will be helpful as a doctor when promoting health and preventing diseases. My post certificate in LAMDA has made me more articulate and has improved my presentation skills whilst understanding the broader aspect of communication.

Contributing to a vast medical field and to its progress excites me. Although I am aware of some of the challenges that doctors face; breaking bad news, comforting patients in distress and working unsociable hours, I feel I will be privileged to be in a profession where every day is different, brings new challenges and to have the opportunity to impact positively people's lives.

Universities applied to:

➢ Oxford: Offer
➢ King's: Offer
➢ Imperial College: Offer
➢ Nottingham: Offer

Good points:

Well-written statement, proving insight into a diverse range of individual interests. The student lists a wide range of academic and work experience related skills and explains how they contributed to their desire to study medicine and strengthened their ability to be a good doctor down the line by teaching valuable lessons. Providing insight into other sources of learning such as the school council shows breadth in their experiences contributing to the impression of a well-rounded individual. There is also some relation to the scientific basis of medicine and the student's interest in particular areas of medical research. The student manages to draw satisfactory conclusions from their experiences which is important to achieve a complete picture.

Bad points:

There are some minor points that provide room for improvement. The most obvious one is the issue of euthanasia. Whilst it is very interesting that the student has been dealing with this issue and spent time forming an opinion, the personal statement might not be the right place to address this, as there is not enough room to sufficiently address the issue in-depth.

Overall:

Good statement, many strong points and some minor weak points that could easily be corrected making space for further elaboration on past experiences.

NOTES

Statement 9

I want to join the medical profession as it combines my fascination for human biology with a commitment to have a positive influence on people's lives.

I have done many forms of work experience which gave me some insight into the demands of the medical profession. I spent a week in the General Surgery department of the Royal Free Hospital where I observed daily ward rounds, talked to patients and learned how to take a patient history. The sensitive nature of the patient-doctor relationship demonstrated the importance of explaining procedures to patients, especially in cases where the patients were suffering from ascites and pancreatitis. It was hard to miss the satisfaction practising doctors received and how multidisciplinary teamwork was essential in the management of patients. During my week at a GP surgery I observed consultations and enjoyed watching doctors use symptoms, test results and problem solving skills to reach a diagnosis. It was interesting to see GPs tackle social as well as medical issues and it emphasized the significance of listening. Accompanying a doctor on a home visit, I met a 42 year old male with lung cancer. As well as valuing the use of palliative care to improve the quality of life of patients and their families facing the problems associated with chronic diseases, I was impressed by how the doctor coped with the responsibility of the family's hopes and expectations.

For the last year I have volunteered at Meadow Wood School for children with disabilities. Helping a child with cerebral palsy cut in a straight line for the first time and seeing him start to learn how to dress independently made me more aware of the challenges and rewards of supporting people with conditions such as autism and cerebral palsy. For six months I have been a nursing home visitor, gradually developing a deeper insight into the nature of degenerative diseases. By talking with residents I believe I have become more empathetic, a crucial quality that a doctor should possess. Skills I have gained through these experiences are patience and the ability to communicate with people of all ages verbally and non-verbally, highlighting the ingenuity needed to practise Medicine. After taking a St John's Ambulance First Aid course as a part of my Gold D of E, I gained the skills to help people who are injured or acutely unwell and used these skills volunteering in the junior school sick bay.

I have particularly enjoyed studying genetics and genetic disorders. After reading an article in the New Scientist about the Human Genome Project, I was interested by how research in human genetics has led to medical advances in molecularly targeted treatments of diseases such as chronic myeloid leukaemia. To develop this interest I carried out a project on CML, approaching a haematologist at my local hospital for guidance. Books such as One Renegade Cell by Robert Weinberg have increased my understanding of genetics beyond the syllabus. Economics has improved my knowledge of the financial challenges facing the NHS and possible solutions that might increase its efficiency.

Universities applied to:

➢ Cambridge: Offer
➢ University College: Offer
➢ King's: Offer
➢ Nottingham: Interview + Rejected

Good points:

Diverse background and varied work experience. The student clearly has spent a lot of time and effort preparing them for the demanding course of medicine, widening their horizon and acquiring new skills that go beyond the school syllabus. The student's starting point for studying medicine is also well formulated and provides a good idea of individual preferences. The paragraph on work experience at Meadow Wood School is particularly interesting and relevant.

Bad points:

The writing style of the statement is somewhat choppy; this lets down the content as it makes for less continuous reading. The student at times also remains very superficial, providing only limited insight into lessons learned and skills acquired during particular periods of work experience. Whilst the interest in economics that the student raises towards the end of the statement can potentially be a very strong point, it is sold somewhat under value due to the superficial nature of elaboration. In general, a bit more detail for most aspects of work experience would have been beneficial.

Overall:

An average statement that has some strong points and some weaknesses. Overall, it is a little let down in quality by the lack of detail as well as the writing style. Some aspects provide a very interesting basis for interview discussion, but as they stand in the statement, they are somewhat incomplete.

NOTES

Statement 10

Several months ago I saw my own heart beating on an echocardiogram, as I had volunteered at a medicine open day to be the guinea pig. There was nothing wrong with it, but it was still incredible. Prior to that, I had the opportunity to volunteer at a HIV charity in South Africa for a fortnight, working with the local people - again an experience I profoundly enjoyed. I would like to study Medicine because it brings together the two aspects of these experiences that I love - science and people. Science has always intrigued me - I turned eggs green at the age of 12 using red cabbage juice as a pH indicator, and have previously developed an interest in model rocketry. However, it is the human biological side of science that captivates me the most.

My scientific background has let me appreciate the awesome complexity of the human body, and the diverse range of chemical interactions that take place inside it, that are affected by so many different factors. It is this intricacy that scientifically draws me to medicine. Wanting to learn more, I have read around the subject, taking the initiative to regularly read the Scientific American, Student BMJ, and the BBC Health section, preparing me for the lifelong career of learning as a doctor. I also take part in biology and chemistry extension classes, which look at extra curricula material and introduce more difficult concepts. Recent work experience has furthered my desire to study medicine, after I shadowed members of a plastic surgery department for a couple of days at a local hospital. Their organisation and teamwork, as well as their practical ability, knowledge and caring nature made me realise how important the role of a doctor is, and how much of an impact they have on a patient. One patient, who had suffered from rhabdomyolysis and had subsequently lost large swathes of muscle, was in for fairly major skin graft reparation surgery. These injuries were managed, but it was also explained to me that the surgery would be ineffectual unless they could help her come to terms with what had happened in ways that she could understand and accept. Alongside that, it was incredible just to be able to see the range and extent of injuries that can be fixed with surgery. Whilst in South Africa, I went into the townships with community nurses to do basic health examinations and HIV tests. Patients were counselled before the HIV test, as previous patient reactions had been as extreme as wanting to commit suicide given a positive result, in which case they would not be tested. This opened my eyes to the reality of life, how fragile it actually is, and the good you can do in the healthcare profession.

Outside of academia, I am involved in several sports - martial arts, running, and climbing. All of these I enjoy, but they also help me to relax - a good outlet after the likely stressful days as a medical student. I recently led an Explorer Scout unit for six months, allowing me to demonstrate leadership, teamwork, and communication ability, skills I have further developed as a worship leader at a local church. This past year I undertook World Challenge, which required ingenuity and time management in order to raise over GBP3000 in the year of my AS levels. This culminated in an expedition to Nicaragua, during which I was the group translator. This showed me the importance of clearly explaining things in a way that people understand, a vital skill for doctors, especially when talking to patients. For the past three years my family have fostered young children, during which I have helped and cared for them. This has allowed me to see the positive impact that good care can have on someone from a neglected background. Since deciding to study medicine, every experience I have had of the medical profession has furthered my desire to become a doctor. I feel it is a lifelong career that I would enjoy, be good at, and something that will make a real difference to the people I come into contact with.

Universities applied to:

> Sheffield: Offer
> Manchester: Offer
> Newcastle: Interview + Rejected
> Leeds: Rejected

Good points:

The student demonstrates a great interest in the scientific basis of medicine which is important as appropriate and up-to-date knowledge is essential for safely practicing medicine and a good understanding of scientific core principles is essential for successful medical studies. The student also demonstrates diverse work experience undertaken to further broaden their horizons in a manner independent of academia.

Bad points:

The writing style of the statement is somewhat borderline in appropriateness. Some of the formulations are too familial which considerably decreases the quality. Appropriate language is equally as important as relevant content. In relation to the content, the student focuses very much on the academic side of medicine, almost ignoring the human aspect of medical care. This is a pity as some of the work experience placements, in particular the HIV attachment in South Africa, certainly offer themselves to reflect on the impact of severe diagnoses such as HIV on patients. It would also offer itself to reflect on the skills demanded of the doctor to appropriately communicate and explain complicated diseases such as HIV to patients from various educational backgrounds.

Overall:

A statement with good potential, let down by an inappropriate writing style and a lack of reflection on lessons learned during work experience. This is a pity as the student seems to have a very diverse background with regards to work experience and other non-academic experiences that would provide ample material for a very good statement.

NOTES

Statement 11

I cannot imagine a greater privilege than to improve the quality of people's lives which is why I am passionate about medicine. I spent five weeks on a Nuffield Bursary this summer with a cardiovascular team researching the effects of perivascular adipose tissue on mouse mesenteric artery contractility using a wire myograph. It has shown me the interdependence of clinical and academic medicine and the complex techniques involved. It improved my dexterity and practical skills, and utilised my ability to absorb technical information. I proposed a theory which will be published in an abstract and contribute towards a scientific paper and have been invited to enter my project for a Crest Gold Award. I have subsequently followed the debate regarding weight-loss surgery versus the long-term cost of obesity to the NHS.

I am inquisitive and love to explore new ideas so am excited by a career that demands lifelong learning. After being diagnosed with a brain tumour when I was 15, I was exposed to the reality of life as a doctor, teaching me the importance of communication and the need to be mentally strong as well as caring. My A-levels have enriched my ability to study Medicine; Biology explains how the body works and Chemistry supplies the reasons why. I particularly enjoyed dissection as it is a practical application of my knowledge. Maths has developed my logical and analytical skills which will be essential in clinical situations.

Having helped in a Care Home since February I am learning to communicate more effectively with elderly people and gaining an insight into the diversity of care that they require. This has inspired me to read about mental health in 'The Man Who Mistook His Wife for a Hat' and the Student BMJ on issues such as organ donation. I shadowed an Anaesthetist for a week, spending time in most departments including A&E, theatre and ICU and was struck by the diversity of hospital work and the spectrum of people involved in each patient's care. A week on a Gastric Ward with an F1 highlighted the concerns that patients raise and facilitated discussions on the realities of medical school. Volunteering for a year in an Oxfam shop, I worked in a diverse team where patience and clear communication were vital. Recently I ran 10km and raised £1500 for Christies Hospital and in October I am helping on an activity course for children with multiple disabilities at The Royal School for the Deaf.

Whilst academic success is very important to me, I have always had a wide range of interests. I enjoy the physical challenge and team element of sport and in recognition of my enthusiasm and dedication to the school teams I have gained colours in hockey, athletics and tennis; playing in orchestras provides a different team environment. My Duke of Edinburgh group won the outstanding team award for our enthusiasm. At MUN conferences I have enjoyed speaking on human rights, chairing debates, improving my public speaking and organising a large event. I like taking responsibility and have been chosen as a Senior Prefect, House Captain and First Form Friend after rigorous selection procedures. The House Captain's role is particularly demanding, balancing participation and success across all age ranges. I have represented the school in Team Maths Challenges at Intermediate and Senior level, where we came first and second respectively and I am the only pupil in my year to have won an academic prize each year. I have enjoyed making friends outside school whilst taking part in dance and pilates classes and horse riding. As I have always participated in numerous activities and set myself high academic standards, I have learnt to organise my time efficiently.

I am excited at the prospect of the challenge of medical school and eager to develop my knowledge to enable me to help others. My experiences to date have confirmed that not only do I want to be a doctor, but I want to be the best doctor I possibly can.

Universities applied to:

➤ Cambridge: Offer
➤ Leeds: Offer
➤ Newcastle: Interview + Rejected
➤ Birmingham: Rejected

Good points:

Well-structured and well-written statement providing good insight into the student's interests and academic achievements as well non-academic activities undertaken to further develop skills necessary for being a good and successful doctor. The student demonstrates a wealth of academic achievement including numerous awards and medical research interests, which is important in providing a sound scientific basis for future studies.

Bad points:

The statement lacks information of non-academic skills acquired and how these can be applied to support a successful medical career. Whilst the student touches on some lessons superficially, further in-depth discussion of the relevance for medicine would be desirable. Additionally, parts of the statement read almost like a simple list of achievements without much connection to the relevance for medicine. Whilst academic excellence certainly is a good basis for studying medicine, it can be assumed that the vast majority of students applying for medicine will have a history of academic excellence.

Overall:

A good statement with strong points and a good basis of content. It is clear that the student has a great interest in academia and research which is highly relevant. It is important however not to ignore the non-academic side of medicine that requires skills that cannot necessarily be learned from text books. These skills include communication skills as well as soft skills such as empathy and approachability. They are vital as a doctor needs to not only possess the theoretic knowledge, but also needs to be able to use this knowledge in a patient-friendly manner

NOTES

Statement 12

My motivation for Medicine stems primarily from appreciating its evolving nature, realising that ground breaking discoveries and techniques continually advance the field. This was typified during my work experience where I observed a laparoscopic cholecystectomy and was inspired by the surgeon's manual dexterity. This encouraged me to undertake an EPQ, researching the latest surgical advances. Also, I felt privileged to see in action the multi-disciplinary approach by healthcare professionals to deliver effective patient care.

In order to gain a realistic insight into a medical career, I organised work experience at a hospital where I appreciated the significance of team-work and communication between members of the healthcare team. This was emphasized when doctors had to ensure critical information about patients was exchanged. Conversations with junior doctors stressed the importance of sound reasoning in reaching valid clinical conclusions and communicating with patients in an empathetic, yet comprehensive manner. This was exemplified when a patient refused to have a CT scan, so doctors skilfully explained the potential risks of this yet allowed him to arrive at a personal decision. This enabled me to understand that a medical career will involve emotional hurdles, so as part of my development, I took a counselling course. I have also worked at a GP surgery, where I was involved in routine tasks essential to the smooth running of a clinic. While shadowing the GP I saw the trust and confidentiality between doctor and patient, and I valued the sincerity toward each patient

I keep abreast with current research, and recently read an article in the BMJ about using a Cytosponge to diagnose Barrett's oesophagus which could potentially provide a method of early detection. Reading 'Trust Me I'm A Junior Doctor' has helped me to understand that doctors must work effectively under pressure. More recently, I found 'Musicophilia' by Sacks to be a stimulating read; I was amazed by his interpretations as to the impact of music on the brain.

Throughout my A levels I have been committed to reaching my highest potential, pursuing my passion for science as well as acquiring analytical skills through AS history. Attending Medlink, where I met speakers ranging from students to surgeons, enabled me to gain a better idea of the exhausting yet gratifying life of a doctor. Recently, I attended a Master Class on Genetics at the University of Cambridge, which enabled me to engage in a stimulating discussion on the use of genetics in forensics.

Responsibilities, from mentoring younger students to being a prefect have developed my leadership and interpersonal skills. I teach maths and science, on a weekly basis at a Kip McGrath Centre, to children of all abilities including SEN, which can be challenging yet hugely rewarding to see them progress. I am a Biology Rep allowing me to constructively convey the views of my peers to teachers. Attending a medical ethics club has raised my awareness of issues such as transplants. I have successfully fundraised, most recently for 'Wings of Hope' and have been a member of our school Amnesty International group which involved communicating with MP's to promote human rights. I have represented my school on many occasions including heats of 'Top of the Bench' by the RSoC and received the BA Crest Award for making a pinhole camera, the Combey Award for 'Best Scientist of 2009' and the Jack Petchey award for outstanding achievement.

I have a passion for cooking, designing and baking celebration cakes. I also enjoy outdoor activities including cycling and walking which have proved purposeful for relaxation and time management.

I would deeply welcome this opportunity to apply my intellectual curiosity and passion in a highly stimulating profession. I feel that my instinctive desire to care and provide hope for people in a compassionate and personal way will support me in becoming a successful doctor.

Universities applied to:

➢ Cambridge: Offer
➢ University College: Offer
➢ King's: Offer
➢ Birmingham: Interview + Rejected

Good points:

A very well-written and well-rounded statement. The student provides an excellent narrative of their personal development both, academically and socially. The statement reflects a wide range of interests and abilities, all of which will provide useful for a future medical career. The student demonstrates initiative and self-directed improvement. The student also shows a history of academic excellence and well though through work experience with purposeful reflections.

Bad points:

Very few, if any. The statement could be improved by providing detail into the precise purpose of the counselling course undertaken in response to the challenges met on work experience. It could further be improved by an insight into how activity for organisations such as Amnesty International has impacted the student and provided them with skills valuable for medicine.

Overall:

A very strong statement with few minor flaws. It is well-written and easy to read and provides a wealth of information about the student's development, both at school as well as in the private, individual realm. It gives a good insight into personal interests of the student and reflects a good understanding of the role of doctors and the challenges of medicine, both as a career as well as a subject.

NOTES

Statement 13

When I was eleven, my best friend was diagnosed with a brain tumour. Fortunately she was treated and discharged within a month; I admired the speed with which the doctors helped her make a full recovery. What interested me further were conversations with her afterwards in which she described her post-operation frustrations, as she was unable to actually say some of the words she was thinking of. I later learned that this was a result of the meningioma affecting the parietal lobe, and therefore her speech. I was fascinated by how the intricacies in her body directly affected her life, thus my interest in medicine was triggered.

My interest in medicine was strengthened by my more recent experiences. On a trip to Singapore I took the opportunity to volunteer at Sunlove Care Home. I was able to adapt well to the different culture and overcome language barriers by using expressive gestures. Working with dementia patients sparked my interest in the condition; one man was able to repeat stories to me several times, with no recollection of having told them previously. Whilst researching, I was surprised to find that the root cause of dementia is yet to be discovered. Reading "The Man Who Mistook his Wife for a Hat" by Oliver Sacks has developed my curiosity into memory deficits. The stories based on unfamiliar diseases that Sacks comes across opened my eyes to the sheer enormity of medicine.

Due to my interest in mental health, I arranged a work placement at a psychiatric hospital. It was clear that building a close rapport with the patients was essential for the psychiatrists to fully understand symptoms, and make a diagnosis. By shadowing a GP, I recognised the importance of teamwork in the successful running of a surgery. I also learned about the dedication required to ensure the highest standard of care, and was moved by the devotion shown by one doctor, who chose to work from 6.00am to 10.00pm on his day off. I volunteer weekly at an after school society for children with special needs. Though emotionally challenging, this experience has developed my ability to use my initiative, whilst trying to engage reticent children in group activities. I also volunteer for the British Red Cross which has developed my self-confidence when working in a team of new people.

Studying Psychology has increased my ability to understand people, and English Literature has provided me with good analytical skills. Moreover, Biology and Chemistry have developed my passion for science, increasing my desire to study medicine. I help to run the school's science club, as I want to pass my enthusiasm on to younger students.

In my spare time, I enjoy playing the piano, in which I have passed my Grade 8 exam. I find this to be a good method of coping with stress and improving my manual dexterity. Last year, I was the pianist at school for our House Drama play, which required perseverance and good time-management as I was engaged at short notice. The commitment I showed led me to be appointed as Vice House Captain, which will involve co-directing the next play. I have completed the Bronze Duke of Edinburgh Award, which has helped me to practise my teamwork skills; I was able to encourage my group to overcome the demoralisation of taking a wrong turn, helping us to complete the course.

The continuous learning I will be faced with in medicine will keep me ever-absorbed. This is a subject which will combine my love for science with exciting opportunities to work with a range of people. I strongly believe that my well-rounded nature gives me the potential to be a very successful medical student.

Universities applied to:

- University College: Offer
- King's: Interview + Rejected
- Sheffield: Interview + Rejected
- Southampton: Rejected

Good points:

Good statement showing insight into the wealth of necessary skills for proficiently practicing medicine. The student demonstrates that they has spent time and effort into paving the way to a successful career in medicine. The student's fascination with mental health is particularly interesting as it provides a direct example of interest, which is valuable as it provides the examiner with a good entry point into the student's motivation to becoming a doctor.

Bad points:

At times the statement remains somewhat superficial stopping just short of developing an idea to its full potential. Whilst in some areas the student's intentions become very clear, in others, it is difficult to determine how a specific experience is relevant to the study of medicine. Whilst the student lists a good variety of non-academic work experience, they fails to properly reflect on lessons learned and the application of these lessons to medicine. Some of the experiences, in particular the work with children with special needs offers a wealth of skills that are highly applicable for a future career in medicine, most importantly communication skills.

Overall:

A good statement that addresses some very important and relevant aspects of medicine. Unfortunately it sells itself a little under value by omitting some important lessons that will make a big difference in the later stages of medical studies as well as being a practicing doctor. This is a pity, as the student's work experience provides many opportunities to improve medically relevant skills such as communication and empathy.

NOTES

Statement 14

To be a part of the developing, exciting, and challenging world of medicine is my goal. I will work as hard as necessary to become a doctor.

I am a keen scientist and seek academic challenges. My A-level studies and further reading have developed my knowledge and I have found studying the complexities of the human body and its processes fascinating. 'The Man who Mistook his Wife for a Hat' describes some of the problems that occur when specific parts of the brain are damaged. Ben Goldacre's 'Bad Science' Guardian articles have shown me the importance of scientific integrity as well as scrupulous analysis of data. Spanish studies and a Madrid exchange trip have improved my language and communication skills. Mathematics A-level with Statistics has helped me develop an analytical approach to problem solving. I have enjoyed being a member of the Maths and Science teams in interschool competitions. My desire to study medicine was enhanced when attending a RSM conference.

Shadowing respiratory and general surgical teams at the West Suffolk Hospital I witnessed multidisciplinary teamwork - each member of staff using individual skills to provide the best possible care. I gained insight into the huge logistical operation of running a hospital. On ICU I saw a 23 year old with organ failure caused by an E Coli infection. Researching his haemolytic uraemic syndrome was fascinating and left me eager to learn more. In contrast I saw elderly patients whose care involved difficult ethical decisions. Two weeks in a GP practice gave me insight into the variety of primary care. On reception and in the dispensary I liked interacting with patients of diverse backgrounds. Two days at a dental surgery taught me the importance of putting patients at ease and how manual dexterity is vital in surgery, as is confidence to make decisions quickly and correctly.

For 6 months I have visited a residential care home weekly; serving 'Sunday drinks' and entertaining residents. It has been satisfying and enjoyable. One lady I've helped is profoundly deaf - I learnt to use body language to communicate with her. She struggles to eat and drink due to Parkinson's disease; it is great to be able to lend a hand, helping her drink or making her smile by dancing with other residents. I am moved by the dedicated, caring people I work with there.

I was part of a small team in a week-long project teaching children with learning difficulties. It was a challenge to engage them in a way that accommodated and excited them; for a term I tutored yr 10 Spanish students at school. These experiences gave me confidence in my teaching ability, which I can transfer to a medical setting. I am really looking forward to working for 6 weeks next summer at a play scheme for severely disabled students.

I love sports. I played county U17 hockey, and play for my town's men's 1st team, whilst captaining the U18's. I captained a Sunday league football team for 8 years and now am captain of my 6th form team. As well as the physical benefits of sport, I enjoy the rewards of leadership. I represented my school at basketball, tennis, cricket, and athletics. I plan to contribute to university sports to the full. My other interests include Fair Isle knitting, reading, and playing rock drums. I taught myself to unicycle, which needs determination and self-belief! Work as a waiter and gardener has developed my self-discipline and time management. While completing Duke of Edinburgh awards I learnt to work as an effective team member and to value other peoples' strengths. I have served on the school council, allowing me to influence actions taken and initiate positive changes.

I have the motivation, hunger and scientific enthusiasm to be a great doctor. Through work experience I have seen how rewarding it is to care for others. I love to communicate with people using my positive approach to life to influence theirs. I would feel privileged to make a contribution to society by taking on this role.

Universities applied to:

➢ Oxford: Offer
➢ Cardiff: Offer
➢ Birmingham: Offer
➢ King's: Rejected

Good points:

Good, well-written statement that conveys a large amount of information about the student. The student gives a good account of some of the different experiences that shaped him during his academic career as well as outside of a school environment. The student demonstrates a wide range of non-academic experiences to further his preparation for his medical degree. Many of the experiences the student describes in his statement, have direct value for studying medicine by providing the student with valuable lessons for his future career in medicine. The student also provides good insight into his motivation for studying medicine and his particular interests.

Bad points:

The student provides good insight into non-academic interests and gives an idea of what fascinates him about medicine. There are only very few weak points, mainly related to the structure of the statement. It could be improved by addressing individual components of relevance one at a time.

Overall:

A good statement with very few weaknesses and many strong points. It conveys a large amount of information about the student and gives a good insight into the personal and academic development of the student leading up to his application for medicine. The statement is well-rounded in regards to academic and non-academic experiences.

NOTES

Statement 15

If asked why I want to study medicine, my honest would be that I cannot imagine myself doing anything else but being a doctor. I am enthralled by the science behind human health and the drastic deviations from good health to disease. Equally, I am passionate about the personal interaction with patients and will be driven by the responsibility to people at their most vulnerable, willing to divulge their weaknesses to a stranger.

Medical work experiences have exposed me to a spectrum of emotions from overwhelming satisfaction to helplessness and desperation. Whilst shadowing a haematologist, I was astonished to find drug developments such as imatinib could successfully treat diseases such as chronic myelogenous leukaemia. It was heartening to see a 51 year old male returning for a check up, 7 years after treatment with imatinib, showing no signs of relapse. My fascination with how new drugs can lead to vast improvements in quality of life, encouraged me to explore the history of medical developments in the 'Little Book of Big Ideas – Medicine' (Aldridge, 2009). During a biomedical laboratory placement, I discovered that I am a keen scientist, but it is the application of scientific theories to diagnosing and treating patients which truly excites me, illustrating that I am suited to clinical medicine. I observed several surgical procedures during an ophthalmology placement and was perplexed to see the dexterity with which surgeons performed glaucoma and cataract surgeries. I also witnessed the care of patients transitioning from diagnosis to treatment at the inpatient clinic. Following Medlink, where I gained further insight into studying and practising medicine, writing a research paper on Alzheimer's, enabled me to explore an area of applied science independently.

Currently, I volunteer weekly on the Acute Medicine ward at Stoke Mandeville Hospital. One of the highlights is the pleasure I get from talking with patients, many of whom are extremely old with no remaining family. This close personal interaction has enabled me to gauge patients' first hand opinions of the NHS and in turn, critically question my perspectives on the healthcare system too. Volunteering at a hospice shop for over a year has taught me to deal with dissatisfied customers, providing valuable grounding for a future doctor to deal with distressed patients. It also involved working with older people, which will be increasingly necessary for a doctor in an ageing population. Working with primary and lower school pupils as a trained peer and drugs mentor, I have further developed the ability to adapt my body language and content to work effectively with a range of ages.

On my placements, I noticed that while doctors need to be able to work well in multidisciplinary teams of hospital staff, in emergencies, it is essential for doctors to assess situations quickly and assert leadership. Through coaching at a summer cricket academy and my role as a senior prefect, I have developed strong leadership skills. I strive towards balance of collective responsibility and assertiveness vital for teamwork through playing cricket for the school and a local club and the Duke of Edinburgh Bronze and Silver awards.

I have been a drummer for 5 years and have played in several bands. As an avid reader of New Scientist, I am able to keep up to date with scientific developments. Human rights being a passion, I am a member of my school's Amnesty international group and was selected to be a member of the national Amnesty youth advisory panel, representing several youth groups from across the country.

Medicine is more than a naïve childhood dream for me; it is an informed career choice I am prepared to devote the rest of my life, time and hard work towards, in exchange for one of the most satisfying and rewarding of careers.

Universities applied to:

- Cambridge: Offer
- University College: Offer
- King's: Offer
- Birmingham: Offer

Good points:

The student shows a great range of previous experiences in regard to hospital work. The examples provided by the student are very interesting and varied and clearly taught the student many lessons relevant for their pursuit of a career in medicine. Good exposure to the practical aspect of medical practice is a great quality and very important in order to bet set apart from other students. The statement demonstrates that the student is aware of the challenges of modern medicine and the role of medical development as well as its direct impact on patients.

Bad points:

The statement purely focuses on work experience and ignores any academic context. It gives little insight into the scientific background of the student, even though they specifically stresses their interest in the scientific component of medicine. This somewhat weakens the statement as a very relevant aspect of medicine is ignored.

Overall:

A good, strong and well-written statement that provides a wealth of information about the student and about the student's motivation for studying medicine. It gives good insight into what the student considers important about medicine and about their strengths making them a suitable candidate for the study of medicine. The student provides evidence for a wide range of hands-on clinical experience which is a valuable asset in setting themselves apart from other applicants.

NOTES

Statement 16

I have an interest in human anatomy and physiology and I am fascinated by the amazing world of medicine. My first encounter with medicine was a couple of years ago when I took a first aid course. During this course I learnt basic medical skills and I realized the importance of techniques such as Cardio-Pulmonary Resuscitation (CPR). I decided to dig deeper into this field and so last summer I worked at the King Hussein Cancer Center (KHCC), where I worked one to one with cancer patients and their parents. It was one of the most rewarding experiences, a feeling of self satisfaction ran through me when I saw smiles on the patient's faces. I love to scuba dive, but diving into operation rooms, where I watched a craniotomy surgery, was an even more exciting experience. Before the operation, I was excited and at the same time nervous. When I first saw the patient on the operating table, four years old, scared and in tears, I felt with her. However, once the anaesthetists started working I was amazed by the whole process. When the surgeon got to her brain I was awe-struck by the beauty of such a complex organ. Observing this surgery made me more determined to pursue my dream, I realized that these doctors are working together to save people's lives and I hope to become just like them.

I got several opinions regarding my entrance into this field. Some of my family members are proud and happy that I might be the first doctor in the family. On the other hand, other family members discouraged me from going into this field; they referred to the fact that it is more difficult for women to become doctors in our society as they have certain responsibilities. The main female concern of my country is marriage and bringing up a family. The long years of study might prevent women from such responsibilities. However, I am determined to enter into this field and get a degree in Medicine, no matter how long it takes. I believe I have what it takes to be not only a successful doctor but a great one.

In the future after I complete my studies I plan to specialize either in oncology or psychiatry. I have also thought of working in war-torn areas in order to help the wounded. Living in Jordan, the areas that surround my country are blighted with strife and I have pictured myself working in such areas helping the victims. Here in Jordan, many people are misfortunate and ill-educated about health issues. I hope someday to be able to spread awareness among them concerning hygiene and the prevention of diseases.

I am a hardworking, motivated person who always aspires for the best. I care for other people and I am a good team member. I believe that I have many things to offer to society and that I can make a difference in people's lives. I already have experience helping for I am an active participant in such activities as, helping the disabled, working with orphans and raising money by working on our annual charity fairs. I also travelled to Moshi, Tanzania where I worked on renovating schools and building classrooms. I also worked closely with the children and ended off my stay by climbing Mt. Meru. My active participation in the MUN has helped me better understand the problems of poverty and areas that need change. My experiences have taught me many of life's lessons; to help others who have less than I; to be grateful for what I have; to be willing to work extra hard to achieve what might seem unattainable at first.

I think it is worth mentioning that I am fluent in Arabic, English and French with an understanding of Spanish. I believe my proficiency in these languages will help me in my further studies, while also assisting me later in my practice of Medicine to better interact and communicate with patients who speak different languages.

All of these activities have changed and affected my life and they have transformed me into the person I have become. A person who likes to help other people and wishes to have a wider perspective of life and through pursuing a career in medicine I will be able to fulfill such high aspirations in life.

Universities applied to:

- Leeds: Offer
- Birmingham: Offer
- Leicester: Offer
- Edinburgh: Offer

Good points:

A well-written and strong statement that gives a good understanding of the student and what motivates them to study medicine. It is interesting to read about the challenges the student faces in the pursuit of their studies. The drive to overcome these challenges will probably provide a great motivation to the student to do well. The student also provides a good overview of their previous work experience and the lessons they learned on these attachments. It is also a strong point that the student already has a general idea of where they hope their studies will take them in the long run. This gives insight into the student's interests as well as providing an idea of other motivating forces behind their choice of career.

Bad points:

The statement is well-written and structured in most areas. Some parts however seem somewhat out of place and less relevant for the study of medicine. This for example includes the passage related to the student's language skills. It would also be interesting to learn more about academic interests and qualifications the student has acquired in preparation for her medical degree.

Overall:

Good statement. Well-written and well-structured. It gives very good insight into what motivates the student to study medicine as well as her previous experience of the profession. The statement also shows a rough outline of what the student envisions for their future which is interesting as it provides further insight into her character.

NOTES

Statement 17

I want to study Medicine as I believe it will allow me to utilise my aptitude for the biological sciences. I am fascinated by physiology and human biology and would like to explore their practical application in the clinical context. For me, the greatest attractions of a career in Medicine are its unpredictability, both on a day-to-day basis and through the breadth of career paths it offers, and the opportunity given by clinical practice to interact with a great variety of people and play a crucial role in their wellbeing.

This attraction has been reinforced by my volunteer work. My work on the main reception and with the porters at the John Radcliffe Hospital took me to many different departments, where I witnessed first-hand the range of activities that a doctor can be involved in. When viewing a number of endoscopies in the Gastroenterology Department, I was struck by the level of skill, experience and dexterity that it requires to be a doctor. My work mainly consisted of delivering notes and specimens around the hospital, as well as aiding disabled patients.

I observed surgical outpatients, an arthroscopy of the knee and the workings of the Pathology Department. These experiences have all confirmed my intention to pursue Medicine as a career. In addition, when with a General Practitioner for a week, I helped him with an audit to determine the diagnostic and surgical precision of his skin excisions of suspected basal and squamous cell carcinomas. My role was primarily data collection from patient notes and data entry into Excel.

At the Great Western Hospital an encounter in the Acute Assessment Unit with a patient with metastatic pancreatic cancer made a great impact on me; by her own admission, the doctor grew close to tears at the bedside, yet she maintained her professional objectivity. This really helped me to understand the importance that a doctor is compassionate while maintaining a level of emotional detachment. I met more people with terminal illnesses in the year I spent volunteering at Sobell House Hospice where I saw the value of conversation with patients, listening in particular, and the importance of the doctor's role in ensuring the patient's health in mind, as well as in body.

The importance of maintaining good communication skills for a career in Medicine was a crucial influence on my choice to take history at A-level, as well as choosing to do a 5000-word extended study on a historical topic: 'Republicanism and Humanism in Renaissance Florence'. I have continued to read outside the biology and chemistry A-level curricula so, for instance, Dawkins' Selfish Gene has allowed me to investigate aspects of genetic biology; I am fascinated by the idea of the relative immortality of successful genes and the process of natural selection. I have also attended a series of lectures on medicine and biochemistry by Oxford University professors. Not only was I awed by their ground-breaking medical research, but also by the passion that they had for their subjects. I feel I have already shared in this somewhat through the areas of biology that have enthralled me, and I aspire to a career where I can pursue this.

At New College School, I was awarded the Old Boys' Prize, chosen for the boy 'with whom you would most like to cross the Sahara Desert'; selection criteria being qualities such as reliability, sociability and resourcefulness. In my free time, I enjoy sports and have become a strong skier, scuba diver and yachtsman. In addition, I have represented my school at 2nd XV level in rugby for two seasons and hold a green belt in judo. Training for these has provided me with a stamina, determination and ability to be a team player that will equip me for study at medical school.

Universities applied to:

➤ Cambridge: Offer
➤ University College: Offer
➤ Birmingham: Offer
➤ Bristol: Rejected

Good points:

A well-written and varied statement providing insight into an interesting path leading up to the application for medicine. It demonstrates good work experience and a wealth of lessons learned from reflection on the interaction with patients and the challenges faced by both, doctors as well as patients in the everyday practice of medicine. The experience of hospice work is particularly interesting as it will confront the student with important and emotionally challenging questions such as palliative care and end of life questions. Being aware of the limitations of modern medicine can be a very shaping experience contributing to the emotional development of the student. The student also demonstrates a varied academic interest that includes non-scientific subjects.

Bad points:

The statement is generally very strong and has very few weaknesses. It could be improved by providing further insight into the student's motivation to his pursuit of a career in medicine. It would be interesting to learn more about what motivates the student other than scientific interests in anatomy and physiology.

Overall:

Good statement, well-written and a wide range of information about the student. It gives a good idea of what the student considers important and valuable in the pursuit of medicine. The statement is generally very strong and well-written with some minor weaknesses that do not reduce the strength of the statement.

NOTES

Statement 18

My interest and enthusiasm for science along with a pragmatic and compassionate nature led me to look at careers in healthcare. Following the rapid decline of my grandmother's health during my GCSE examinations, I was exposed to a critical care environment; my family believed that this may diminish my desire to become a doctor. However, instead of being discouraged, these events increased my motivation to follow a medical profession. Organising a variety of work experience for myself has allowed me to explore different fields of medicine. Spending a week in a General Practice surgery with a walk-in centre illustrated the need for effective communication and improved my ability to deal with difficult, aggressive and emotional patients. A week at a local hospital offered a range of opportunities, though the stand-out moment came in a theatre observation when the patient had a blood pressure crash. Watching the team of healthcare professionals coming together under the leadership of the consultant highlighted the importance of teamwork and respect for the lead surgeon.

Another week at a specialist neurological hospital demonstrated the importance of palliative care, as the majority of patients had terminal conditions. I realised that the work of a doctor is not only curing patients, but often it is about improving the quality of life. Spending time with one memorable patient with CJD, presented possibly the most challenging aspect of healthcare for me. Though very upsetting, I found that I was able to remain composed whilst supporting the patient. Over the past year I have volunteered at a local nursing home; a placement that I secured myself. For two hours each week I chat and provide activities for residents. Although difficult at times, as the majority have dementia, it is also very satisfying and has given me a better understanding of the condition and its impact.

For the past thirteen years I have swum at a local club and as soon as regulations allowed, I volunteered as an in-pool teacher. Throughout the three years, I have worked with children of all ages; helping those with Down's syndrome and other disabilities has enabled me to improve my skill in adapting explanations to suit the individual. At sixteen I qualified as a fully trained lifeguard and have worked for my club on a voluntary basis ever since; being responsible for the safety of everyone in the pool. My reliability earned me paid work for an associated diving club. Having been awarded a Nuffield Research Project, I completed four weeks of research on X-ray diffraction in August, for which I received a Gold CREST award.

This opportunity allowed me to expand my scientific knowledge, whilst also helping to improve my independent study skills and time management. I was interested to read more recently, an article from the MRC explaining how X-ray crystallography has helped to identify an antibody that may be used in treating diseases like CJD. I am enjoying extra responsibility within the school community as a prefect and a senior house prefect; being a role model for the younger students and showing leadership during house events. As a member of the school hockey team for six years, I have been awarded commitment and players' player of the season awards. Hopefully my approach to the sport inspires others to participate in school events. My hockey and swimming help to relieve stress; however, I also find playing piano is a great way to unwind. Mountain biking gives me an escape and helps me to keep fit.

At a young age I took up RC model flying and showed quick progression of ability, winning club competitions; I still support the club by providing help for newcomers and technical support for others. I look forward to learning in greater depth about a field that genuinely interests me and know that the diversity of medicine would continue to challenge and stimulate me throughout university and a future career.

Universities applied to:

- ➤ Sheffield: Interview + Rejected
- ➤ Liverpool: Rejected
- ➤ Leeds: Rejected
- ➤ Leicester: Rejected

Good points:

A vey varied and well-structured statement with a good range of clinical exposure. The student demonstrates a good approach to the challenges of the medical profession and demonstrates an ability to reflect on the impact of individual experiences. This ability is a definite strength that will come in handy during the training as a doctor and later on whilst working as a doctor, where much of the professional development relies upon self-reflection. The student demonstrates that they has had the opportunity to hone communication and organisation skills in a variety of environments. Furthermore, the student demonstrates good academic potential and commitment to research supporting a good understanding of scientific method.

Bad points:

The statement is somewhat short of practical hands-on experience. Whilst the student demonstrates having witnessed medical care, there is little evidence of previous active experience, going beyond the mere observational stage. It would also be interesting to learn more about the student's understanding of the pathology of CJD since it seems they has a particular interest in the disease.

Overall:

A good statement with many strong points providing good insight into the student's characteristics and giving evidence of a wide range of medical, academically and non-academically experiences, all of which have relevance for work as a doctor and setting the student apart from other applicants.

NOTES

Statement 19

Living in Ghana for part of my life, I was exposed to the horror of diseases and how good clinical support makes a difference between life and death. Witnessing endemics like malaria filled me with empathy and encouraged me to pursue a medical career that someday I may be able to make a difference. The blend of scientific theories and the discipline of practical work in laboratories led to my interest in medicine. Reading Matt Ridley's Nature via Nurture revealed the versatility of science and philosophy to me. The virtue of approaching theories like evolution holistically, rather than accepting single explanations, became apparent; as Ridley noted: 'Similarity is a shadow of difference'.

At a Cambridge residential, a lecture which was particularly interesting was on the nervous system and dendritic spines and how they are linked to memory formation and creativity; how things as abstract as memory and creativity are implicated in more tangible elements like brain tissue and receptors. Enthralled by this new information, I decided to read about Alzheimer's disease and how it offsets this balance. Being able to merge its chemical and biological aspects independently was crucial for my understanding. I was chosen for a master class at Queen Mary London where I was privileged enough to visit the dissection centre to handle dissected cadavers. The organs were like nothing I have seen before, sharply contrasting with the mundanely coloured images in textbooks. A surgery enrichment scheme also familiarised me with suturing.

My current studies provide a solid basis, from the valuable skills of data analysis and laboratory work in Chemistry, to the vital ethics of experiments in Psychology, giving me the skill of debating the pros and cons of research. The discipline of Maths makes me confident with numbers, interpreting graphs, and solving problems with different approaches. I took part in a Chemistry enrichment programme lasting for five weeks; I was required to perform experiments autonomously. It tested my ability to cope with unfamiliar exercises and to follow protocols precisely to get accurate results. We worked at Imperial College London during the last session to test our samples with advanced equipment including Nuclear Magnetic Resonance Imaging. I gained useful laboratory experience as well as interpreting complex graphs.

During the summer, I worked for the Olympics and Paralympics and was absolutely blown away by the experience. I reaped from it good communication skills, teamwork and creativity. I won an award for an innovative idea I devised which created a more organised and time saving system. The Paralympics showed me how medical intervention allowed people with disabilities to unlock their full potential - something which may have been inconceivable in previous years. I was trusted with the sole supervision of a co-worker who was a dyslexic introvert and I developed a very good relationship with him - which I am proud of.

Being part of my college football team improves my teamwork and time management. I was selected to be a student representative for the Chemistry Department. I attend meetings with staff to discuss effective ways of teaching, as well as bridging the gap between students and staff; demonstrating my ability to be a leader. I volunteered to tutor and mentor GCSE Additional Maths students which improved my confidence as well as valuing confidentiality in the aspect of mentoring. I volunteer in a Cancer Research shop allowing me to work well with peers and relate to elderly people, giving me good communication skills with a variety of people. I am working towards the Duke of Edinburgh Award as well as my Church Choir and Youth Club where we carry out debates and recreational activities such as outreaches which enhance my interpersonal skills.

All these experiences have increased my desire to become a medic and reinforced the fact that medicine is the career I want to pursue for the rest of my life.

Universities applied to:

> University College: Offer
> Cambridge: Interview + Rejected
> King's: Rejected
> Bristol: Rejected

Good points:

Well-written and well-structured statement. The student demonstrates a varied academic career. They also provides information on a variety of non-academic experiences, undertaken to further their preparation for medicine as well as broadening their horizons. The student offers a well-balanced and well-structured overview of their work experience as well as providing insight into skills and lessons learned during these attachments. Particularly important are skills such as communication, handling challenges and unfamiliar situations as well as creative thinking to overcome challenges.

Bad points:

The student provides a lot of information about themselves. In this context, some information can be left out in favour of more details about other pieces of content. This is only a minor negative point, as the statement is generally well-rounded.

Overall:

Well-rounded statement with some minor weaknesses. In general, whilst it is tempting to put as much information as possible into the statement, sometimes it might be easier to pick a shorter list of characteristics and experiences and develop them in some more detail. In this statement for example, it would be interesting to know more about the student's role and experience during the Olympics as well as during his time in dissections.

NOTES

Statement 20

I have a passionate interest in medical science; as I continue to study science in greater detail, and am enthused to read further, I am certain I wish to pursue a career in medicine. Some books I have particularly enjoyed include 'Understanding Medicine' (Whiteman), which gave me a good introduction to the principles of clinical practice, and 'The Value of Life' (Harris) which I found thought-provoking as it presents many views for consideration. I also find some online resources informative such as 'Student BMJ' and the 'BMA' website.

Through work experience at the Countess of Chester Hospital, I have gained some insight into the value of teamwork whilst observing the liaising of staff at outpatient clinics in plastics and ENT departments, and also during a ward round. The hand injury clinic was particularly interesting as I saw many examples of specialist treatments. By being present as both Board of Governors' and Directors' meetings, and as a youth member of the Hospital's Foundation Trust, I have acquired greater awareness of the many difficulties facing the NHS. Some examples include the well-publicised problems of long waiting times and hospital infection, and also the less obvious, such as minimising the incidence of adverse drug reactions and the difficulty in meeting the needs of medically ill mental health patients. During a day spent at the occupational health centre at a large company, I learned something of the role the department plays in ensuring optimum health for its workforce through regular screening and observation of working practices. I was also able to gain a perspective of primary care by organising to shadow a GP. I realised the vital importance of effective communication to establish an accurate assessment, such as when a patient presented with abdominal pain, and how, with empathy, the doctor was able to put patients at ease. My varied experiences, together with the opportunity for some interaction with patients have strengthened my determination to study medicine.

I sing in four choirs at school, and have participated in music since joining the school aged eleven. I have taken part in more than one hundred performances – highlights include a concert tour to Paris, participation in BBC 'Songs of Praise' and recording a Christmas CD. Motivation and reliability are essential as I usually attend six rehearsals each week. I also enjoy playing the piano. Throughout my time at school and now, as Head of Library team, I am working hard to continually improve the library's services – this work has enhanced my organisational and collaborative skills. As a Senior Prefect, I am involved in helping the School in many areas, including mentoring two first-year students. As a qualified football referee, I have been awarded the district "Young Referee of the Year" award for last season; I am also the youngest member of Cheshire FA Referees' Academy, selected for excellent enthusiasm and potential for promotion. Refereeing requires strong communicational skills, attention to detail and the ability to remain calm under pressure; it has developed my confidence and independence. I hope to continue pursuing my current interests at university, and also look forward to new opportunities.

I am very keen to commit to the hard work and lifelong learning required of a doctor, and would find the challenge of applying scientific knowledge for the benefit of patients exceptionally rewarding. I am especially fascinated by the complex processes of degenerative diseases, which present an immense challenge for twenty-first century medicine. I am excited by the medical innovations which have the potential to revolutionise both diagnosis and treatment during my career such as in imaging, regenerative medicine and minimally-invasive surgery: I would love to be a part of this intriguing future.

Universities applied to:

- ➢ Cambridge: Offer
- ➢ Nottingham: Offer
- ➢ Newcastle: Offer
- ➢ Bristol: Offer

Good points:

Well-written and well-structured statement. The student provides insight into a varied personal and academic history that is likely to have provided many interesting lessons and experiences. The student seems interested, not only in medicine and the scientific basis of the profession, but also in the inter-human challenges of medical practice. The student also briefly addresses some of the challenges faced by the NHS, which demonstrates the student's interest in current events. It would have been interesting to hear a little more about this, but it provides good material for conversation during an interview.

Bad points:

Whilst it is interesting to read about academic and non-academic achievements and awards, they provide little information about the student other than showing their competitiveness. They would provide more information and value for the statement if they were tied to specific skills acquired that are relevant for the medical degree. Purely relying on a list of awards will carry little value in a personal statement.

Overall:

A well-written statement. It provides a variety of information about a student that is clearly dedicated to academic and personal development. The student demonstrates a wide range of work experience and extra-curricular experiences that all contribute to the acquiring of skills helpful for studying medicine.

NOTES

Statement 21

I am often asked why I want to embark on the challenge of becoming a doctor. To me it is simple. To someone who is fascinated in the way the human body works, has a genuine interest in people and an inquisitive nature, no career could be more worthwhile.

During a week's work experience at the John Radcliffe Hospital, I spent time in many departments, including endoscopy and SEU. I saw how the whole hospital works together as a multidisciplinary team – doctors, nurses, porters, social workers – and I became very aware of the huge variety medicine has to offer. I particularly enjoyed an afternoon in clinical neurophysiology where I was shown video clips of inpatients fitting and how these fits related to their Electroencephalograph.

I visited wards and sessions in physiotherapy and occupational therapy in further work experience at Abingdon Community Hospital, along with a memorable day at the Alzheimer's club. I saw clearly how simple games and songs brought temporary relief and genuine enjoyment to the sufferers. I subsequently decided to volunteer at the club and have spent two hours a week since February with them. Whilst I find this extremely rewarding and fun, there have been moments that have been emotionally difficult because of the close bond I have developed with many of the people there. These experiences have inspired a curiosity in neurology and brought me to read 'A portrait of the brain' by Zeman and 'The man who mistook his wife for a hat' by Sacks, as well as articles about recent research in the BMJ in an attempt to understand this increasingly common disease.

Communication is an important factor for all doctors. To develop this skill I regularly visited Kingfisher School for children with learning difficulties. The children I worked with were only two years younger than me so I found it difficult initially to find the balance between the need to show authority but also be supportive and helpful. I had to learn how to deal with aggressive behaviour and how to understand those struggling to communicate. In a GP surgery I experienced first-hand the relationship between professional and patient, the trust people place in their doctor and the necessity of clear communication in difficult situations – both medical and ethical. I sat in on patient-doctor appointments, attended sessions with nurses and health visitors, as well as making a few home visits. I also helped out on the reception where I really enjoyed the high levels of interaction with both patients and staff.

Another crucial element in medicine is problem solving. The ability to make wise decisions and prioritise tasks is a necessity in finding the best solution. As a school charity representative our team organised a fete for over six hundred people. During the course of the day we faced many problems which needed to be solved quickly and calmly despite the pressure of ensuring the day ran smoothly.

I am interested in genetics and have read books such as Ridley's 'Genome' and Dawkins 'The blind watchmaker'. As an insight into the scientific and research side of medicine I spent a week at the Wellcome Trust Centre for Human Genetics. I assisted with the preparation of DNA by GluRa genotyping for experimental psychology.

I have the determination, energy and organisational skills necessary to study medicine. I organised the schedule for my school's junior admissions interviews and am working towards grade 8 on both the piano and the saxophone which has developed my own personal discipline. Playing 1st saxophone in a concert band has shown me the need to listen to others in order to produce the best outcome. After receiving my junior sports leader award, I know I have the necessary skills for being a strong leader from running a dance club for those aged 9-11.

Through work experience, volunteer work and academic studies, I feel I have a real grasp of what is required to be a successful doctor, the positives and the negatives. I'm ready for the challenge.

Universities applied to:
- King's: Offer
- Birmingham: Offer
- Cardiff: Offer
- University College: Rejected

Good points:
A statement that demonstrates many interests and provides interesting insight into the student's character. The student demonstrates a well-balanced experience of clinical care during their work experience. This is important as the more diverse the medical exposure, the better the understanding of some of the challenges of modern medical care. Their work at the Alzheimer's Club is particularly interesting as it provides a good insight into the emotional challenges associated with medical care and with incurable diseases as well as the very specific challenges that come with Mental Health disorders. It is interesting to read about the student's response to the challenges witnessed.

Bad points:
Whilst the statement contains many strong points and a lot of good information, some points raised are less valuable for the overall quality of the statement as they add little to the overall content. For example in the last paragraph the student almost seems to overvalue the relevance of some of their experiences. Whilst the paragraph on genetics is interesting, it is too superficial to appropriately contribute to the quality of the statement.

Overall:
The statement is well-written and well-structured. It is generally very strong content wise. The few minor weaknesses make little difference for the overall quality of the statement, but they could improve the statement if they were replaced with further information about lessons learned from work experience or skills acquired that are supportive of success in medicine.

NOTES

Statement 22

Caring for my grandmother through her knee replacement, and later through breast cancer brought to light the various complexities involved in medical care; vital decisions regarding a suitable course of treatment, as well as the ethical dilemmas posed by them. These experiences reinforced not only my belief that medicine is both science and art, but also my desire to pursue such a diverse career. The academically and emotionally challenging nature of medicine, combined with an opportunity to benefit others, is what drives my passion to pursue the subject.

I have always enjoyed studies that challenge me intellectually and logically, reflecting my choice of A Levels. The topics of health and disease have been of particular interest to me in Biology, combining my knowledge of the structures of systems in the body with the actions of pathogens. This, coupled with an opportunity to observe orthopaedic surgery in sufferers of rheumatoid arthritis, sparked my interest in auto-immune disease to extend my studies. Organic Chemistry has allowed me to apply molecular principles to biological situations; to broaden my insight in this subject I attended a Salters' Chemistry Camp at Imperial College, applying my existing knowledge to new situations and developing my thinking skills. Finally, the study of Spanish has enabled me to appreciate cultural diversity and build interpersonal skills through mentoring younger students.

My enthusiasm for learning led me to complete an Open University module on Molecules, Medicines and Drugs, developing my motivation towards independent study. Furthermore, my recent involvement in the anaesthetics audit project at my local hospital has alerted me to the application of my mathematical studies in medical research, as well as helping me to develop time management skills and the etiquette required of a professional setting.

I have been a regular volunteer at a residential home for the last two years. Whilst learning about the daily care of those affected by chronic illnesses, I have been able to empathise with the elderly and support their needs. Having also organised a week's work experience at my local hospital, I observed both diagnostic and surgical procedures including angiograms and the insertion of stents, and shadowed doctors as they attended to patients on wards. Overall, I appreciated the significance of teamwork and good communication in every area, ensuring rounded patient care. I also observed clinic-based medicine, building a strong doctor-patient relationship, similar to what I had already encountered in my experience at a GP practice.

As a well-rounded individual, I enjoy a variety of interests which I wish to maintain at university. As a member of the school orchestra, I enjoy playing the Piano and Viola to grade six, - particularly the thrill of performing in concerts with fellow musicians. My pursuit of public speaking enabled me to compete at regional level, whilst providing me with essential communication skills and the ability to deliver an articulate argument with confidence. My determination and resilience during the Bronze and Silver Duke of Edinburgh Awards led to my selection for the school's World Challenge expedition to Kenya and Tanzania. This greatly improved my independence and leadership skills, as well as allowing me to work as part of a team to make decisions and overcome tough physical and emotional challenges. Part of the expedition was spent at an orphanage in Malindi - a humbling experience. I sensed the gratitude expressed by children receiving care, and realised that my love of science together with my compassionate nature could eventually lead to making a difference to the lives of others.

Medical innovation, alongside the increasing expectations of clinical excellence necessitates continuous learning; I am confident that I have the motivation, ability and thirst for knowledge which will enable me to succeed in this ever-evolving field.

Universities applied to:
➤ Oxford: Offer
➤ University College: Offer
➤ Birmingham: Offer
➤ Nottingham: Rejected

Good points:

This student demonstrates that they has been spending a lot of time and effort in the preparation for their medical career. The statement provides information on a wide range of different interests and work experiences, all of which helped further the student's knowledge and insight into the subject field. Particularity valuable is the direct exposure to chronic disease in the form of volunteering in a care home as well as the interest in medicines and drugs represented by the Open University course. This demonstrates initiative and a desire to excel which is very helpful for a medical degree. Exposure to chronic disease also has the added bonus of exposing the student to potentially challenging emotional situations and furthering their communication skills.

Bad points:

Generally, this is a good statement. There are some minor weaknesses mainly related to the writing style which in some instances is somewhat clumsy. This applies in particular to the paragraph addressing extra-curricular interests.

Overall:

A good and well-structured statement, providing good insight into the student's interests and some insight into the student's character and into their priorities and interests in studying medicine. It is clear that the student has spent time and effort in gaining as much experience as possible in preparation for their degree.

NOTES

Statement 23

Throughout my childhood I became increasingly captivated by the way the human body works; how various elaborate systems give rise to an intelligent, fully-functioning organism. My interest in medicine stems not only from my passion for science, but the delight I find in interacting and engaging with people. Medicine will provide me with the opportunity to fulfil my desire to have a unique, challenging career which uses my interests to the benefit of others. Whilst I am aware of the reality of the career and the challenges being a doctor would entail, I am confident that my level-headed nature would allow me to overcome any obstacles I could meet.

Observing and talking to doctors during my week of work experience within the A&E department and a ward of a local hospital made me aware that being a doctor can be taxing and difficult, however the experience gave me insight into the medical profession and a stronger determination to pursue my goal. Within A&E I observed patient examinations, electrocardiograms and X-rays and gained insight into the pressure a medical team faces with patients in critical conditions. Shadowing a consultant in a ward allowed me to observe alternative side to hospital medicine, where I learnt the importance of ensuring palliative care is provided to those with terminal illnesses. This inspired me to become a volunteer for a local hospice where I am responsible for providing patients with company and care. Working at the hospice has shown me the extent to which palliative care ensures a better quality of life. Whilst at first I found it heart-rending to see people with severe illnesses, it helped me become familiar with the fact that there are emotionally challenging situations when a doctor can help, but cannot cure the patient.

Taking part in a pilgrimage to Lourdes was an enjoyable experience where my duty was to help feed, transport and care for the sick. My confidence developed as a result of the time I spent helping and talking to the pilgrims and I discovered the importance of faith and religion to the emotional welfare of some patients. Additionally, as a residential volunteer for the charity Vitalise I was taught to care for people with disabilities, such as Cerebral Palsy and Muscular Dystrophy, and I improved my interpersonal skills and skills communicating with those who have communication difficulties. I am also becoming a Biology mentor for my college's Year Twelve students to share my understanding for biology with students who need support, within this I will be required to have a patient and sensitive attitude in order to provide students with the support they need.

My developing interest in the science behind every-day compounds has inspired me to begin an Open University course in Molecules, Medicines and Drugs. So far this has taught me about the meticulousness of drug development and clinical trials and the mechanisms of pain-relief drugs. The course requires a lot of self-motivation and time management; however I believe these qualities are essential for studying Medicine. Additionally, I attended an international student summit on Darwinism; a deeply fascinating conference which outlined the importance of the understanding of evolutionary biology to developing cures and understanding diseases. I am also enthusiastic about rowing as a part of my local rowing club; which allows me to improve my stamina and willpower. Furthermore I adore reading classical literature, the study of which develops the vocabulary and writing skills I require for University and for my career.

I believe my attributes of being patient, compassionate and empathetic are important qualities for a potential medical professional. My part-time job has allowed me to build my team working and social skills required to be a good doctor, and my experiences volunteering have made me certain that Medicine is right for me and my qualities are right for such a demanding vocation.

Universities applied to:

- University College: Offer
- Leicester: Offer
- Newcastle: Interview + Rejected
- Aberdeen: Offer

Good points:

Well-written statement that addresses several important aspects of the medical profession. The student identifies and addresses several key disciplines that are highly relevant for becoming a doctor (communication, empathy, compassions, curiosity, discipline and determination) and provides examples of situations and experiences where they has been able to learn these skills and get familiar with these disciplines and their role in medicine. The student also provides insight into experiences they perceived as particularly challenging, such as the confrontation with end of life questions during experiences of palliative care. This is good as it reflects positively on the student's ability to learn from situations and analyse them for their challenge and value in order to learn from them. A quality that will be frequently drawn upon during medical training.

Bad points:

Some of the experiences listed in the statement such as the summit on Darwinism, are interesting but add little to the overall quality of the statement other than providing further evidence of the student's academic interests. This is due to the lack of contextualisation of the experience to make it relevant for medicine, which is a pity since evolution is an important driving factor in for example antibiotic resistance.

Overall:

A very good statement with some minor weaknesses and flaws. These flaws do not reduce the strength of the statement as it is well-rounded and well-written as a whole, providing good insight into the student's interests and character.

NOTES

Statement 24

There has been no defining moment in my life or past event that has prompted my decision to study medicine. Throughout secondary school I have become increasingly interested in human physiology and the mechanisms of disease. This enthusiasm for biology has been important in defining my aspiration to study medicine; yet it is also the compassion and social interaction involved in the diagnosis and treatment of patients that have been the impetus of my ambition to be a doctor.

A week of work experience in a Cardiology Unit and a further week in a GP surgery gave me insight into a career in medicine. When observing procedures in the Cardiac Catheter Lab and shadowing the junior doctors on the Cardiac Unit I saw how emotionally demanding a career in medicine can be when treating acutely ill patients. However the optimism, motivation and teamwork displayed by the doctors left a lasting impression as they appeared genuinely fascinated by each case. In a diabetes clinic at the GP surgery, it was enlightening to see the significance of the psychosocial aspects of illness and how the management of chronic diseases greatly improved the patients' quality of life, disproving the glamorous image in the media of medicine as being solely about saving lives. When shadowing the GP on home visits, I saw how an approachable empathic manner was crucial when the GP had to break bad news to the relatives of a patient with dementia about her prognosis and resuscitation status. In both clinical environments I saw how rewarding and stimulating it was to be able to diagnose and treat across a whole range of medical conditions.

At GCSE, I was awarded the Physics and Chemistry prizes for achieving the highest GCSE marks in my school year. Due to these achievements and my contribution to the school community I was selected for a school expedition that raised £50,000 for the Ghana Education Project and visited schools in Nkwanta. After visiting a rural hospital, I was struck by the poor availability of treatments for HIV and TB and how contracting these diseases led to alienation of the patients in their communities. Reading Kenneth Kiples' "Plague, Pox and Pestilence" provided further understanding of the history of global infectious diseases which inspired me to base my AS biology coursework on the prevalence of multidrug resistant TB in the UK. This involved researching the mechanisms of antibiotic resistance and the methods for preventing resistance, including Directly Observed Therapy. By carrying out this project I have learnt that bacterial resistance is an increasing problem and during my work experience, it was interesting to see the precautions taken to reduce the rates of hospital acquired infections such as MRSA in hospital wards.

Since 2010 I have volunteered for Kent VSU which involves looking after children with learning difficulties, such as autism and ADHD, for two hours a week. This experience has taught me how to interact with young people who find social situations difficult. I have benefited from the responsibility this has entailed as it has been rewarding to see the children progress over the three years. The impact of debilitating neurological diseases on children and their families was further demonstrated during my two week work experience at Young Epilepsy, a school for children with epilepsy in Surrey.

Aside from my studies, sport and music are very important to me. I have represented my school and Sussex County in hockey and have run for the Kent Schools Cross-Country Team; working towards grade 8 in guitar is my current musical venture after achieving grade 7 in piano last year.

The prospect of developing my scientific knowledge over a lifetime combined with the opportunity to diagnose and care for patients, greatly excites me. I am fully aware of the level of commitment required to pursue this profession and I believe I have the determination, compassion and academic ability to excel in a degree and career in medicine.

Universities applied to:
> Oxford: Offer
> Newcastle: Interview + Rejected
> Leeds: Offer
> Edinburgh: Rejected

Good points:
A well-structured and honest statement, presenting the student as well-balanced and reasonable. The student demonstrates good clinical experience, with a good selection of specialties, providing good insight into the workings of a career in medicine as well as the challenges that arise with different frameworks for medical care. The student also provides evidence of good non-medical experiences strengthening soft skills such as communication skills and organisation skills. Being exposed to the challenges of working with children with learning difficulties will have provided the student with a good opportunity to adjust to the challenges of more complicated communication.

Bad points:
The student chooses to include results from their GCSE exams, which is somewhat a waste of space since the achievement has little to no relevance for the statement itself as it lies too far in the past. To a very limited extent, it reflects academic performance, but that is not enough reason to include it here. It would be more relevant to read about the student's experience in Ghana and their experience of the challenges of medical care in poor regions.

Overall:
Good statement that provides adequate insight into the student's interests and abilities. Generally, it is a strong statement with some minor weaknesses. These weaknesses do not reduce the strength of the statement significantly, but omission would improve the quality by adding more relevant information.

NOTES

Statement 25

Change, in medicine, is inevitable. New diseases develop, incurable illnesses are eradicated, and improved treatments are developed. This is what makes medicine so riveting: the field is constantly refined and challenged. As someone who enjoys acquiring new knowledge, this aspect of lifelong learning greatly appeals to me. When my grandfather was diagnosed with cancer, I spent hours in the hospital observing the medical professionals as they treated him. This made me develop a profound respect for them. I understand that medicine is a demanding career, but believe I am a suitable candidate for the vocation as I have passion and commitment for understanding how to best care for the sick. I read scientific magazines, such as the 'New Scientist', and am always eager to learn about new medical discoveries. Medicine has been at the forefront of my academic journey for many years.

I have taken the opportunity to research Obsessive Compulsive Disorder for my Biology coursework, which helped both my problem-solving and evaluation skills. Completing an EPQ on elective caesareans has taught me to broaden my mind-set and be open to constructive criticism. As one of the Biology Representatives at my school, I worked within a team to promote the subject. Further Mathematics has developed my logic and helped me become more sensible and reasonable. A week spent work shadowing at both a family clinic and womens' clinic in Singapore has further fuelled my ambition to become a doctor. Not only did I experience how healthcare was provided to a range of patients, from infants to the elderly, but I saw, first-hand, how doctors have to communicate both professionally and sympathetically to patients to gain their trust. I also volunteered weekly for a year at an elderly carehome. This showed me that medicine is not only about finding cures, but also about providing palliative care. Although several communication barriers were present, I managed to get through to most of the elderly patients, developed friendships and learnt about how they each developed different coping mechanisms for their various conditions.

Recently, I have become fascinated by the topic of epigenetics. Reading several books on the field including 'Nature via Nurture' by Matt Ridley and 'The Epigenetics Revolution' by Nessa Carey have convinced me that it is a key part of the future of medicine. Understanding how our environment and genes both play a part in determining our eventual characteristics will enable us to recognise individuals more predisposed to develop terminal illnesses, and take preventive action

In my free time, I enjoy film photography. I have taught myself how to shoot with analog cameras, leading me to become a devoted member of the Photography Club in my school. I have developed an observant eye, winning several competitions, including one held by Lomography for the most creative essay and photo submission. I was nominated Head of IT in my Young Enterprise team, and was able to think creatively and explore my aesthetic side. In addition to this, I swim regularly and was part of a synchronised swimming team in Singapore. Good time management skills and a strong work ethic have enabled me to balance my time well between work and recreation. I strongly believe that I will thrive at university, as it is an intellectually stimulating environment.

I have a strong sense of independence and can work on my own initiative, which I hope will support and encourage my learning journey. A cure for malaria, treatment for Parkinson's and prevention of hepatitis have all been discovered. There is still a long way to go, with AIDS cures to be developed and a need to better understand how tumours form. New challenges will constantly be presenting themselves, but I am not afraid of a challenge. Medicine may be seen as an evolutionary struggle, but in reality, it is a battle, and one that I feel I am ready for.

Universities applied to:
➤ Birmingham: Interview + Rejected
➤ Edinburgh: Rejected
➤ Leeds: Rejected
➤ Oxford: Offer

Good points:
Stylistically well-written. The student demonstrates a great interest in the ever-changing nature of medicine and acknowledges that medicine is a field under constant change. This curiosity is definitely a strong attribute when it comes to being a successful doctor. The student further demonstrates a history of academic scientific interest and creativity.

Bad points:
There are some areas of the statement where the student contradicts themselves. This begins in the introduction with the eradication of incurable diseases. The entire problem with these diseases is their incurable nature and without cure it is next to impossible to eradicate them. Furthermore, the statement lacks discussion of practical experiences. It would be interesting to read more about reflections on the work experience spent in the Singapore hospital. Working in a women's and family clinic certainly provided ample material for discussion and reflection.

Overall:
Average statement that demonstrates a wide range of professional interests but in some areas sells itself short by lack of detail or contextual contradiction. Some aspects raised in the statement serve little purpose without tying them to their value for medical studies.

NOTES

Statement 26

From a young age I have had a passion for the workings of the human body. Medicine as a career entices me as it gives the opportunity for life-long learning applied to helping others on a daily basis.

To gain a realistic perspective about Medicine I organised various placements, which I found inspirational. In a London hospital I was humbled to meet Regina, a child from Africa, whose surgery to remove a lymphangioma had been funded by charity. The difference this surgery made to her life is one which I hope to replicate in my own career. The ophthalmologist's level-headed and compassionate approach showed me the importance of tailoring care to each individual patient, even during routine procedures.

Shadowing a neurologist and spinal surgeon helped me to realise the critical interactive relationship between many departments in delivering the best possible care, often under intense time pressure. The multi-disciplinary approach to problem-solving in making diagnosis was intriguing. The vital role of each health professional was evident in the PCHT I visited this summer. It also showed me how a GP's trusting relationship with their patients can greatly benefit the service they can give and how medical care comprises of so much more than just medical intervention. I was fascinated by time spent in the dermatology department at the John Radcliffe. I was struck by how skin conditions can reflect disease within the body, as well as profoundly affecting a person's psychological wellbeing. I have since conducted further research on skin complaints such as psoriasis and pruritis.

Volunteering at a Care Home has helped me to comprehend the obstacles presented by old age. I really admired the nurses who integrated skill with the care needed to keep dignity intact. As well as this, I truly experienced how simply giving of your time can greatly benefit others.

A fortnight volunteering at a children's home in Argentina was an incredible experience. Gaining the trust of the children was rewarding and taught me invaluable skills to overcoming language barriers. The necessity for confidentiality was highlighted through meeting a 13 year old diagnosed with HIV whose relationship with the other children would have been compromised had confidentiality not been upheld. I saw how the suburbs of Buenos Aires had very poor hygiene levels, and how this, coupled with a lack public health education, was leading to an increase of disease incidence and transmission.

Reading beyond my A level syllabuses has prompted me to investigate further into the polypill, a controversial primary prevention strategy for cardiovascular disease. Its potential benefits to individuals and the health economy, as a whole, need to be balanced against its cost, possible side effects and the ethics of prescribing drugs to a healthy population. It shows a shift in medical practice, in that doctors now often focus on prevention rather than treatment of disease.

As a School Prefect and 1st XI Hockey Captain, I utilise my communication skills to the full, motivating myself and others to strive for a positive outcome, whatever the situation. I particularly enjoy representing the younger pupils' concerns to the staff in the school as well as empathising with their issues. I also enjoy representing the school in the Tennis and Netball 1st teams. I have captained my county Hockey side and participated in Regional Hockey and Netball Teams. In addition to this I play the Clarinet to Grade 8 standard and partake in many bands. I am currently gaining my Gold Duke of Edinburgh Award, during this I have learnt how vital commitment, stamina and determination are in reaching goals. With such a busy schedule I have learnt to balance my time, still enjoying myself and striving to improve. I believe my skills are well suited to a life in medicine and look forward to the challenge that it will bring.

Universities applied to:

- ➤ Birmingham: Offer
- ➤ Oxford: Rejected
- ➤ King's: Rejected
- ➤ Cardiff: Interview + Rejected

Good points:

A well-written and well-structured statement. The student provides good insight into a variety of different work experience attachments and reflects efficiently on their value for his career as a medical student as well as a doctor. The choice of specialties for placements demonstrates a varied interest in medicine and a well-balanced preview of what medical care consists of these days. Briefly addressing the future of medical care regarding prevention rather than treatment is also an interesting point to raise. Being exposed to emotionally challenging experiences such as the children's home in Argentina are further strong points of the statement as they further support the diverse interest in the human, non-academic, side of medicine.

Bad points:

Very few. The statement is somewhat light on detail regarding academic and research experience as well as active hands-on experiments of medicine. It would be interesting to see if the student had any chance to supplement their observed experiences with practical application of knowledge. Furthermore, information regarding academic performance is highly relevant as they provide instant access into the student's work ethics.

Overall:

Good statement. Well-written and well-structured. Some minor weaknesses. The student's main focus clearly is the application of knowledge in a medical environment. This is generally fine, but medicine also requires academic commitment before application is possible, and for this reason it would be helpful to read/know more about the student's academic interests.

NOTES

Statement 27

My desire to pursue a career in medicine stems from a fascination with the anatomical and physiological intricacies of the body, the social interaction between doctor and patient, and how the chemical balances of the body can fail and be manipulated, leading me to follow these interests through my studies and spare time.

Studying Chemistry has given me valuable scientific knowledge and practical skills: recently I particularly enjoyed synthesising aspirin. Through learning more advanced Maths, my problem solving ability has improved and I feel that Spanish offers me a contrast by developing my communication and language skills. Biology has introduced me to some current medical issues and epidemiology. Learning about the heart in the AS course, and a talk about organ donation, encouraged me to pursue work experience in cardiology. In December I will shadow a heart transplant consultant at Papworth Hospital.

I undertook two weeks work experience with students who had severe disabilities such as cerebral palsy. At times it was difficult to communicate; I had to persevere with understanding the individual's needs and their own ways of expressing their views. However the reward of their recognition, or even a smile, was worth the effort. I also completed a day's work experience at a leading fertility clinic. Witnessing a live ICSI fertilisation was incredibly thought provoking. I was also present during a consultation where a patient was notified she was very unlikely to conceive; seeing the discussion at first hand really helped me to empathise with both the patient and the difficult position of the medical professional breaking such news. I spent two days shadowing in the dementia ward at New Cross hospital. Many of the patients were at the end of life and, although upsetting, it was interesting to see the procedures undertaken by the hospital to ensure good palliative care, such as the Liverpool Care Pathway and the partnership with social workers. During my week's work experience at the Leeds General Infirmary I shadowed consultants in different specialities; it was surprising to see how interlinked different fields of medicine are in the care of a patient, for example the relationship between cardiological and vascular aspects of many conditions. Volunteering at the EAU at Addenbrooke's hospital for 12 weeks as a ward helper highlighted the roles that all hospital workers play, and it gave me an opportunity to talk to some of the patients about their illnesses. I have also been volunteering at the Hertfordshire MS Therapy Centre since November 2010, an interest sparked by my mother's secondary progressive multiple sclerosis. Seeing her deteriorating but knowing I can do nothing to help has been incredibly difficult, but has given me an insight into how chronic illness impacts the life of a patient and their family. It has been interesting exploring the alternative therapies available; the centre offers oxygen treatments and reflexology and although these treatments clearly have an impact on sufferers, I personally remain unconvinced as to whether or not this is a placebo effect.

Attending lectures given by doctors at College and at Addenbrooke's hospital has furthered my interest in medicine, and as an active member of my College's medical society I help out at college events, working as part of a team to encourage other students to pursue medicine. Outside college I regularly run, tutor GCSE Spanish and have reached grade 5 theory on the flute. I have also completed Duke of Edinburgh and World Challenge awards. Throughout these I worked as part of a team and as team leader, which on occasion was difficult, but vastly rewarding.

I have tried very hard to make myself aware of the demands of a career in medicine; and having been introduced to its constant challenges and changes, I cannot now think of a profession of which I would rather be a part.

Universities applied to:

- ➤ Oxford: Rejected
- ➤ Brighton & Sussex: Rejected
- ➤ Leeds: Rejected
- ➤ Birmingham: Offer

Good points:

This statement is well-written and provides a wealth of information about the student. The individual's motivation for purusing a career in medicine is important and interesting for the examiners to read about. The student demonstrates good reflection in issues surrounding chronic and incurable disease, probably also in part due to being personally affected by this. The work experience placements the student chose demonstrate a wide range of interests and a good exposure to different types of clinical practice and medicine as a whole.

Bad points:

At places the student remains too superficial. This is particularly obvious in the passage related to their experience of MS treatment where he attributes effectiveness to the placebo effect. Whilst this is an interesting idea to address, it needs appropriate reflection and contextualisation in order to provide strength to the statement. The student does not fulfil these criteria in this context. There are other areas where information provided does not seem to serve any other purpose but to list achievements. This provides little support for the quality of the statement as most students applying for medicine will have a history of awards and academic excellence.

Overall:

Good statement providing good insight into a diverse clinical interest. This is a definite strong point. In areas, the statement is let down by superficial argumentation and rash judgement which somewhat weakens its overall value.

NOTES

Statement 28

Medicine involves a lifetime of learning and I would thrive in an environment where I am constantly expanding my knowledge, discovering new challenges and making a difference to people's lives. Witnessing a woman recovering from a miscarriage was the moment that confirmed medicine was the career for me. The compassion and empathy shown by staff was incredible and by combining their professionalism with a caring nature they were able to comfort her at such a tragic time. It made me appreciate that medicine is not always about positive outcomes but the ability to offer help and support in some way.

I strive to achieve to the best of my ability and attained the highest grades at GCSE and AS in my year, receiving a prize for academic excellence, as well as five subject awards. Biology and Chemistry A levels have developed my independent learning, my practical skills and given me an analytical approach to problem solving. The complexity of the human body intrigues me and I have enjoyed studying biological molecules; this improved my understanding at molecular level and demonstrated the way different scientific disciplines link together. I enjoy the logical nature of Maths, whilst French has improved my communication skills and made me appreciate the importance of a second language.

Medlink and a medical taster day enabled me to explore the career paths within medicine. During work experience at a hospital, I visited Fracture and Haematology Clinics, A & E, Theatre, ICU, and Obstetrics and Gynaecology. This highlighted the value of teamwork between departments and staff. The hard work, communication and resilience that is vital for medicine was clear. Their optimism showed me that medicine is a rewarding career and a sense of humour is needed to get through the toughest days and although physically, emotionally and academically challenging, it is definitely worth it. As a volunteer at a residential home for the elderly, I observed care in a community setting, found that I had a natural empathy with the residents and genuinely enjoyed the experience; whether preparing drinks, meals or chatting.

I support students at the school science club instilling in them an enthusiasm for science through practical and fun activities, including rocket building and dissections. This has enhanced my confidence and ability to communicate my ideas to others, as well as my passion for science. I was proud to be elected House Captain and a member of the school and house councils, where I act as a role model, student voice and an ambassador for the school. I have organised charity events, interviewed prospective teachers and umpired netball matches, all of which required me to act in a trustworthy and impartial manner.

I enjoy sport and have represented my school at football and captained the netball and rounders teams. It has taught me the worth of teamwork, communication and I have enjoyed motivating my fellow players. Completing a Sports Leader's Qualification and D of E Award has developed my leadership skills and improved my proficiency at organising people and equipment. At Rainbows Girl Guides I was responsible for arranging activities and providing advice and guidance, which I thoroughly enjoyed. Studying the saxophone and piano to Grade 8 required commitment and determination, my dedication gave me the opportunity to mentor younger musicians. I participated in the Labour Party Conference, attending seminars on medicine and science, enabling me to see the value of healthcare in the community. My part time job in a shop has enhanced my work ethic, teamwork and flexibility and I have improved my time management and taken on more responsibility.

Medicine is a diverse, demanding profession offering a variety of career paths. I feel that my conscientious, dedicated and positive attitude would suit medicine. Despite the challenging workload, I am both academically and emotionally prepared and will relish the opportunities medicine will offer me.

Universities applied to:
- Newcastle: Interview + Rejected
- Birmingham: Offer
- Leeds: Rejected
- Oxford: Interview + Rejected

Good points:
Well-structured statement. The information provided gives insight into the interested and curious but also dedicated and disciplined nature of the student. Drawing on experiences learned during team captainship as well as political engagement supports the well-rounded impression of the student. The work experience placement described seems to have confronted the student with a variety of clinical specialties, providing good insight into the intricacies of medical care in a hospital setting. Furthermore, providing a compelling example for the student's motivation of studying medicine, adds to the overall quality of the statement.

Bad points:
The main weak part of the statement is the lack of a link between academic interests and the student's motivation for studying medicine. Claiming to be motivated by the ever-changing and academically challenging nature of medicine necessitates a more in-depth discussion of academic interests than the one provided by the student.

Overall:
Good statement with some weaknesses. This statement demonstrates the importance of balancing non-academic achievements with academic achievements in regards to the content. Both aspects are important in providing an adequate image of the student's interests and abilities as well as their suitability for the challenges of a medical career.

NOTES

Statement 29

I have never doubted that I would pursue a career in science; in Medicine I can combine this ambition with my ability to work with and benefit others. The functioning of the body has always amazed me: the dramatic ways in which its systems can fail and the science behind recovery. At the Bodyworlds Exhibition I was intrigued by the intricate detail of the plastinated specimens and the way all the components fit together.

I enjoy dynamic situations and thrive in an environment where I am constantly being challenged academically and emotionally. I learnt this at Selly Oak Hospital where I shadowed doctors in the Military and Burns wards. I saw young patients who had been through traumatic events, had lost limbs and suffered severe psychological scarring. Coping in these situations made me confident that I will be able to handle medicine as a career. I also observed a hospital environment in Virginia Beach, USA where I spent a few days with consultants in contrasting specialties from a radiologist to an orthopaedic surgeon. These experiences impressed upon me the efficiency of the multidisciplinary team working together with one aim in mind: to cure or alleviate the patient's condition. Seeing doctors and nurses take a holistic approach to the people, rather than just the medical cases, has ignited my aspiration to be a part of this profession.

While staying in Botswana last year I volunteered at a local nursery where a third of the children were AIDS orphans and most of the volunteers suffered from the condition. I took the opportunity to further my knowledge of the disease, learning about the difficulty of treatment due to its ability to mutate and the relative ease of transmission. Each morning we checked children's bodies for abuse; the necessity for this was troubling but sadly I know I will have to become accustomed to it. I was struck by the dramatic differences in terms of attitudes to life and behaviour between the children in Botswana and those at a local Wiltshire nursery I had been at a few weeks previously. I plan to expand my cultural horizons by taking a gap year working in a hospital abroad where I can immerse myself in another society whilst increasing my medical knowledge and experience.

My desire to read medicine has been developed by a range of talks on the Medlink course and presentations including a memorable lecture at the Royal College of Obstetricians and Gynaecologists. I have recently become engrossed in books recounting medics' stories such as Nick Edwards' 'In Stitches' from which I have come to understand something about the realities of working for the NHS. I have been able to observe two completely contrasting healthcare systems, both of which have their faults. While the UK's ageing population may be a burden on the NHS, the retired can be assured of good healthcare, whereas many of America's elderly are forced to continue to work to be able to afford even the most basic of medical attention.

Volunteering at a local Multiple Sclerosis Centre and at an autistic school has helped me develop patience and the communication skills vital in any caring profession. During my Duke of Edinburgh Gold expedition in the Brecon Beacons each of us in turn reached a low point and became reliant one another: this made me recognise the importance of teamwork. This skill also played a part in my role as Managing Director of a County Cup winning Young Enterprise team, through which I appreciated the significance of leadership and delegation. My role as Head of House gives me a considerable responsibility to set a good example to the younger girls and represent them in school council. I am organising various charity events which, along with my work and other commitments requires time management and organisational skills.

I am enjoying studying sciences at A level but I am really looking forward to specialising in those aspects of science that are directly related to Medicine, and to a career of lifelong learning.

Universities applied to:

➢ Imperial College: Offer
➢ Southampton: Offer
➢ Edinburgh: Rejected
➢ Cambridge: Interview + Rejected

Good points:

Well-written and well-structured statement. The student demonstrates an excellent variety of work experience and manages to put these experiences into context with important lessons and reflections they drew from these experiences. The diverse nature of the student's work experience is a definite strength as it provides insight into a variety of healthcare settings, ranging from a third world level of care to experiences made in the developed world. In addition, the student's experiences will also allow them to compare contrasting healthcare systems which are likely to influence their perception of healthcare in general.

Bad points:

The student could improve their statement with a further exploration into their own feelings and reflections from different experiences. In particular, this would be interesting in relation to the work in a military and burns unit but also their experiences in Botswana. Finally, it would be interesting to learn more about what the student's impression is of the reality of working in the NHS. They claim to have gained some insight- but unfortunately don't share it with the reader.

Overall:

A good statement that provides a wealth of information about the student's character and personal development. It is due to this great variety of experiences to draw from that in some aspects the statement remains somewhat superficial and could be strengthened by elaborating in some more detail.

NOTES

Statement 30

A dramatic incident occurred during work experience in Somaliland, in the Horn of Africa. I witnessed the tragic stillbirth of a baby due to hand presentation, a sharp reminder of how critical timely medical intervention is to the preservation of life. My aspirations remain firmly to serve the health needs of others and I will make the greatest effort in pursuing this vocation.

Work experience at Edna Aden maternity hospital in Somaliland was unique. Mothers had travelled from rural communities and urban slums and it was here that I recognised how vital good doctor-patient relationships are. I had an entirely different experience on my two-week placement at King's College hospital. Days spent in the hectic A&E department made me even more determined to be a doctor. Amid endless queues of patients and critical cases, I realised my ability to work well under pressure would be of great value. Observing the joy the doctor found in each individual's recuperation, showed me the reward that comes with responsibility.

I have really enjoyed volunteering for two terms at a local primary school once a week. Whilst learning transferable teaching skills, I had the opportunity to work with and support individual children with special needs. For two years I have also served as a Sunday school helper, acting as a role model to many younger children.

I am a curious and open-minded scientist, decisive and diligent in my approach to work. With a passion for understanding new scientific concepts, my favourite Chemistry module was 'What's in a medicine?' I particularly enjoyed the experimental side of learning, which included making our own penicillin. Within Biology, I was fascinated to learn about the body's response to infection and I hope to further my biological knowledge with an Open University YASS course on Genetics and Health. Being an able and keen problem solver, Mathematics has extended my logic and analytical skills. Religious Studies made me look at problems with a different perspective. I developed the understanding of how ethics applies to daily decisions and reading Tony Hope's 'Medical Ethics' has focused this interest whilst challenging my views on arguments such as assisted euthanasia.

As well as my commitment to learning, I enjoy contributing to school life. I am honoured to have received the Cathedral Parish Voluntary Service award from school. Within Medics' Society I have especially enjoyed 'doctor-patient diagnosis' exercises, as well as our trip to the Medsim conference at Nottingham University. Here the stimulating keyhole surgery practical has made me eager to join Dissection Club as it begins this term.

Playing the flute for the school orchestra has been a pleasure, giving me the chance to meet new people and improve my listening skills. I find playing the piano a useful relaxation exercise which also provides the opportunity for public performances, thus increasing my confidence. I enjoy keeping busy and active, running and dancing regularly, yet always maintaining a high standard in academic work.

This summer I took part in a World Challenge expedition to Morocco, a demanding experience which increased my independence. I was able to work both as part of a team and to develop leadership qualities. As leader, I enjoyed including team ideas in making final decisions. I had to manage responsibility on a daily basis, be it coping with a vigorous trek or dealing with group budgeting. When some unexpectedly fell ill, we carried extra bags and even people! Such a physically and mentally challenging experience revealed my ability to cope in intense circumstances.

As it is such a vital profession, it would be a privilege to work as a doctor. I believe my academic capability, personality and drive are suited to this career. I am a well-rounded person, equipped to deal with the inevitable challenges and dilemmas. I look forward to a vocation in Medicine and making the most of university life.

Universities applied to:

➢ Birmingham: Offer
➢ Manchester: Offer
➢ Glasgow: Offer
➢ Bristol: Offer

Good points:

Excellent entry into the statement that is well connected to the student's motivation to pursue a career in medicine. The entry is memorable and provides a good impression of the student's willingness to face challenges and overcome difficult situations. In general the student demonstrates an excellent work experience background, drawing from many different types of experience, all of which are well-reflected on with regard to lessons learned and personal changes triggered by them. Being able to contrast between medical care in developed vs. less developed countries and reflecting on the challenges this causes for medical professionals in either situation is a great topic for interviews. The student also demonstrates some hands-on experience.

Bad points:

Few. The statement could be improved by even better focus on contrasting experiences and lessons learned from those experiences. Whilst it becomes obvious that the student is a compassionate and empathetic individual, there are further personal qualities that could be devolved. The more insight into the student's character, motivation, and ideas the statement transports, the better.

Overall:

A strong, well-written statement with many very good points and few minor weaknesses. The student manages to provide a good representation of previous experiences and their impact on their life. This could be developed further in some places.

NOTES

Statement 31

I believe Medicine is largely about problem solving. In order to fix something that is broken, knowledge of how it works is fundamental. My passion for understanding biological processes and how their interactions affect the workings of the human body is the basis for my long held desire to study medicine.

I have completed 15 days of work experience: 5 in a hospital home and 10 with a Consultant Surgeon at St Richards Hospital. Whilst at St Richards I experienced many different aspects of medicine, including the observation of laparoscopic and open surgeries, endoscopic procedures, an outpatient gastroenterology clinic and multiple ward rounds by various physicians. One of the surgeries that particularly interested me was an Anterior Resection lasting 5 hours performed on a lady with a primary cancerous tumour in her large intestine that had further metastasised to her lungs and kidneys. The importance of aptitude and concentration required by surgeons under such demanding circumstances was readily apparent. Contrastingly, in the gastroenterology clinic, the necessity for strong interpersonal skills was obvious when the consultant colorectal surgeon I was shadowing was required to deliver bad news to patients. This experience has reinforced the need for the honesty, respect and empathy doctors must show at all times.

Volunteering for over 100 hours at St Richards over the past year has further developed my abilities to communicate confidently, work as a member of a team and to empathise with patients. My main responsibilities involved working alongside the housekeeper providing breakfast for patients and assisting the HCA's and nurses with their daily routines. The rewarding nature of the work far outweighed the physical and emotional demands involved. Many patients on the ward were without friends or family and easily became isolated or lonely which could hinder their recovery; therefore I sought to brighten their day with cheerful conversation.

I enjoy reading about the frequent, exciting discoveries being made that provide doctors with the knowledge to help solve today's problems. I was particularly interested to learn that two independent American research groups recently found evidence linking Fusobacteria to the development of malignant colorectal tumours. Experts hope this discovery will lead to earlier diagnosis of the disease thus prolonging patient's lives. This research was of particular interest to me having witnessed during my work experience the devastating effect this type of cancer had on many families. I am excited to think that I could soon join a profession that is improving the outlook for patients of the future.

My GCSE grades and predicted A Level grades highlight my academic ability and work ethic. My A Level choices reflect enthusiasm and aptitude for problem solving and analytical thinking. I particularly enjoyed the human biology aspect of AS Level Biology, during which we delved deeply into the complicated, yet captivating workings of the heart and lungs.

An avid golfer for over 8 years, I have spent the last season taking on the many responsibilities of Junior Captain. Strong leadership, appropriate confidence, integrity and responsibility are all necessary skills to ensure that the Junior Team performs to a high standard. These attributes are essential in doctors who are part of a wider healthcare team. I also enjoy playing tennis, snooker and the clarinet. I have successfully completed Bronze and Silver Duke of Edinburgh awards. This ability to balance my extra-curricular activities with significant academic commitments has taught me effective time-management and hopefully keeps me well-rounded.

I relish intellectual challenge and enjoy developing meaningful relationships with patients. I firmly believe that I have the right attitude, personality and skill set to undertake a medical degree in order to follow my chosen career path. Consequently, I submit that I am well suited to the medical profession.

Universities applied to:

➢ Oxford: Rejected
➢ Bristol: Offer
➢ Birmingham: Offer
➢ Southampton: Rejected

Good points:

Well-structured statement. Good exposure to the surgical practice of medicine. Having an idea of how surgical procedures work and what attributes are required for a good performance in the field is very beneficial. Volunteering work adds to the general aspect of patient exposure. This is a strong point as it is likely to demonstrate to the student the challenges of medical practice and it will also allow the student to reflect on relevant skills needed in order to be a successful doctor.

Bad points:

Medicine is more complex than a merely almost engineering-like profession. The interaction with the patient is significantly more demanding than a simple recognition of physical manifestation of disease. Whilst it is true that recognising certain physical manifestations in order to make a decision regarding diagnosis, the fixing component of treatment needs to address more complex needs such as patient opinion and preference as well as side-effects. Not to mention that sometimes physical manifestations of psychological issues. Whilst the student underlines the importance of empathy and human skills later on, the initial statement is a significant over-simplification that reduces the overall strength of the statement. Also, the academics paragraph of the statement does not deliver any relevant information, particularly since A-level subject choice is very restricted by course requirements.

Overall:

Average statement. Good general potential, but let down by overarching claims that promote a wrong perspective of medicine. It is essential to recognise that medicine is both a science as well as an art and existence of one without the other will necessarily make for a bad doctor. Do not ignore the relevance of inter-human skills.

NOTES

Statement 32

During pregnancy, my mum suffered pre-eclampsia and I was born seven weeks premature; without the rapid response from a team of medical professionals it is unlikely I would have survived. This together with my love of science, thirst for knowledge and desire to help others in the same way have been the driving factors in fuelling my ambition to pursue a career in medicine. Studying medicine will be an exciting challenge and the thrill of knowing that we still do not fully understand the complexities of the human body inspires me.

My scientific acumen was recognised at school when I received the trophy for excellence in GCSE Physics and the AstraZeneca science award having displayed "a genuine passion for the pursuit of scientific learning". I was also fast tracked into completing A Levels in Maths and Further Maths to A* grade. I am self-motivated and able to grasp difficult concepts quickly and think logically.

To experience what it might be like to work in a hospital and caring for patients, I undertook a six month period volunteering at a local geriatric ward. My role was to assist staff at supper times serving food and drinks to the patients. This helped me to recognise the importance of working in a team and understand how all medical staff play a part in the everyday running of a ward. I enjoyed meeting and conversing with a diverse range of patients, and crucially I learned how to communicate with vulnerable people who were suffering from diseases such as dementia and cancer. I now fully appreciate the importance of being an empathetic listener and speaking clearly to avoid confusion. At a practical level, I learned how the risk of hospital-acquired infections can be minimised through good hygiene.

More recently, I attended a work observation programme at Leicester Royal Infirmary where I shadowed a number of surgeons and anaesthetists. During this time I was able to witness lengthy surgical procedures such as the removal of a fatty plaque blocking a section of the carotid artery in an obese man and the removal of a tumour from the bowel of an elderly woman. This experience gave me the opportunity to see how doctors and theatre staff work as a team, particularly in the way they communicate effectively in stressful situations and also how they have to deal with limited resources when treating patients. It also highlighted to me the pressures currently facing the NHS such as treating an ageing population, cancers, diabetes and circulatory diseases. A visit to a vascular outpatient clinic allowed me to gain insight into the doctor-patient relationship.

I enjoy cooking and have combined this with my passion to care for people by volunteering as a kitchen assistant at Rainbows Hospice, which provides palliative care for children and young people. This role requires me to be compassionate and sensitive to both the patients and their relatives. Mentoring a GCSE student, being a science classroom helper and managing merchandise stalls for the hospice have allowed me to develop my organisational, communication and leadership skills. At Rainbows, I was part of a team that raised GBP5k and I found this very rewarding. Playing tennis for a local club allows me to keep fit, socialise and de-stress. I am also a keen 100m sprinter and regularly attend training sessions at Charnwood Athletic Club. I have represented my school in Senior Maths Team Challenges. We achieved second place in two regional finals; success in this competition relied heavily on organisation, team-work and thinking under pressure for sustained periods of time. Being well-travelled has given me the opportunity to meet people from a variety of cultures.

I have learned through my experiences that medicine is not just a career choice but rather, a way of life. I have the drive, ambition, enthusiasm and sense of humour required to rise to the challenges posed by a medical career; I look forward to the prospect of a lifetime of learning.

Universities applied to:

➤ Birmingham: Offer
➤ Keele: Offer
➤ Liverpool: Offer
➤ Edinburgh: Rejected

Good points:

Very diverse and shaping work experience. Being able to witness surgery as well as the challenges faced by patients with chronic and very debilitating diseases, provides a good insight into the day-to-day challenges faced my health-care professionals, both in a hospital setting as well as in the community. The student also states a history of academic excellence and interest which is valuable for satisfying the requirements for academic foundations of medicine. It is also a strong point that the student reflects on the challenges faced by the healthcare system in response to changing demographics and disease patterns.

Bad points:

The student's account of their experiences is somewhat let down by imprecise and sometimes even sweeping statements that reduce the strength of reflections on experiences made. Particularly relevant in this context is the comparison of dementia and cancer. Whilst both are very debilitating diseases, the experience by the patient is a fundamentally different one, not least due to the different manifestations of the disease. This type of undifferentiated statements reduces the strength of arguments made. Also, the student's pre-mature birth and their mother's pre-eclampsia seem a little far-fetched as motivators for studying medicine.

Overall:

An average statement with strengths and weaknesses. It demonstrates the importance of concise formulations and the necessity to be very clear in the development of one's ideas. Finally, achievements that lie too far in the past such as at GCSE level have little strength for a personal statement.

NOTES

Statement 33

I've always had the innate sense that being a doctor is what I want to do with my life and so it has only ever felt natural to pursue a vocation in medicine. From my experience on the maternity unit, to ward-rounds on the CCU, I have witnessed both the excitement of birth and the critically ill with heart-failure, gaining an insight into human life and its progression, and this first-hand exposure to medicine has motivated me further to read this fascinating subject at university. My grandfather's struggle with blindness and leukaemia was what originally inspired me to volunteer in a care-home, which I've committed to for the last fifteen months, and despite the grittier side to medicine this environment has revealed, I treasure the relationships I've built there. While it has, at times, been difficult to observe the incapacities of the elderly, my emotional stamina has strengthened considerably, something I hope will enable me to better manage the emotional strain promised by a medical career.

Aside from the elderly, I volunteer weekly with disabled children and have especially enjoyed the challenge of teaching myself Makaton, so as to involve myself further with the group. I also organise and assist with the running of Rainbows on a weekly basis, proving my acceptance of responsibility and eagerness to lead, qualities I realise will be vital as a doctor, where cooperation and multidisciplinary integration are essential. Similarly, my waitressing job of two years has left me well-accustomed to dealing with difficult customers, and no stranger to hard work; I hope my experience of long-shifts and spending hours on my feet will stand me in good stead for a medical career, as I realise the physical demands of the profession are intense. Gaining my ASDAN International Award and Young Language Leader Award also required a great deal of commitment, as I had to coordinate a series of language tutoring sessions for primary school children - and volunteering with this age-group has since inspired potential consideration of a career in paediatrics.

Studying Spanish has heightened my appreciation of culture, and I hope my bilingual ability to communicate will enable me to embrace medical aid work abroad. My flair for languages extends to literature, and I channel stress into writing novels; I hope to combine my love of words with medicine, potentially writing for the BMJ in the future. I currently journal my own medical blog, alongside further reading, and have recently finished In the Midst of Life by Jennifer Worth, which explores the progression of medicine from 1950s to present-day, as well as differing approaches to death. Since engaging with this, and On Death and Dying by Elisabeth Kubler-Ross, the ethical difficulties doctors now face, such as the increasing prospect of litigation, have fascinated me. In my free time, I enjoy acting and even received an award for my most recent performance; my self-confidence has improved greatly, and I hope the ease with which I adopt different roles on stage will prove useful as a doctor, where adaptability is essential in forming relationships with patients and colleagues. Also, as a black-belt in karate, giving-up is a foreign concept to me.

Eight years of the sport has provided me with the discipline and self-control I hope will enable me to practice as a competent doctor, while evidencing my commitment and determination to succeed. I have been dancing non-competitively since 1998 and I'm also a dedicated member of the school choir and a rotary-run association raising money for charity, where I recently helped organise a charity fashion show, applying my communication skills in order to contact suppliers and make the evening a success. I understand that medicine is a challenging profession, though a privilege, and one that will enable me to combine my desire for life-long learning with the hands-on practice and demanding altruism the profession requires.

Universities applied to:
➤ Birmingham: Offer
➤ Cardiff: Offer
➤ Keele: Offer
➤ Bristol: Offer

Good points:
Well-written and well-structured statement. It provides good insight into the student's interests. The experiences described from their lengthy placement in a care home provide good evidence of their exposure to the challenges and necessary skills of medicine and in particular of caring for an ageing population, where frailty and chronic disease are becoming increasingly common. Having had time to experience these challenges and reflecting on the best way of handling them is definitely advantageous. In addition, some of the organisation skills the student describes further support their application in a positive way as the ability to handle resources to reach a specific goal is becoming increasingly important.

Bad points:
The entry is somewhat cliché, is not per se a bad point, but there are many different ways of starting a personal statement as this sentence really does not add anything to the content. The passage concerning the student's interest in writing is generally good as it contributes to the understanding of the student as an individual, but the part about write for the BMA journal is again somewhat cliché. Unless there is a precise piece of work that already exists, there is little point mentioning this as it does not contribute to the content.

Overall:
An average statement that addresses some of the core qualities of doctors and also provides a good insight into the student's interests and their character. There are some points of weakness, which is unfortunate as the statement had the potential to be very good.

NOTES

Statement 34

Since Key Stage 3 I have held a great curiosity into the science that underpins the human body. My specific attraction to medicine was inspired during my two-week placement at a local hospital. I spent time in a number of departments including orthopaedic pre-assessment and fracture clinic, where I observed how radiology is so critical to the work of doctors. One of the most poignant moments during my time there was when I helped a physiotherapist to physically support and encourage a wheelchair-bound man to walk. Despite only making a few steps, his delight at his achievement was self-evident and I saw the impact that I had made. In theatre, I saw minor operations including the removal of skin cancers, where I observed how a surgical team worked to maintain a sterile environment and prevent infection.

I am currently shadowing a GP in his surgery, and have been struck by the wide range of conditions a GP may encounter, from schizophrenia to lymphedema. I have learnt that relationships and effective dialogue are crucial to ensuring the best possible outcome for a patient. For example, a victim of assault was initially prescribed one drug; however upon discussion with the patient about her previous history and lifestyle, it became evident that another was more appropriate.

Having studied Frankenstein at GCSE, I became inspired to research Freud's model of personality, and to question whether it is mainly our genes or our environment which influence the way we think. I encountered this also through self-study of AS Psychology and I have further explored my interest in psychopathology by reading excerpts of the 19th Century 'People's Medical Adviser'. What I found intriguing was the contrast between archaic theories such as phrenology and the diagnostic approach that we use in the 21st Century. Reading Oliver Sacks' 'Migraine' opened my eyes to the varying experiences that are had by patients even with the same condition, such as the 'aura' ascribed to classical migraine and the ongoing research behind its origins. Studying news articles surrounding potential treatments of migraine including Botox and transcranial magnetic stimulation, has given me an insight into the competitive and compelling world of medical research.

I have spent 10 months volunteering with the charity InterAct, which provides support for young adults with learning difficulties. Playing a part in assisting a young person's wellbeing has been very rewarding, and this was most profound when a shy member of the group approached me personally for support. I was able to listen, show empathy and provide reassurance, and my experience with InterAct has allowed me to develop these skills.

Since April, I have been the Head of Student Voice in my school, with responsibility for directing School Council meetings and chairing student interview panels for prospective teachers. I am also involved in the Charities Committee and Medical Society at my school.

I work part-time in my local Argos store, where my ability to interact with people from a range of diverse backgrounds has led me into working on the public side of the business. I enjoy being a part of a working team, and I also relish leadership roles; I have had the opportunity to lead as part of my Duke of Edinburgh Silver Award and during my World Challenge expedition to Costa Rica. I love sport, in particular tennis, squash and table tennis. For five years I have played tennis at my local club, and more recently represented them in our regional league.

My greatest motivation for choosing a career in medicine is the rewarding prospect of helping others together with continuous learning, as doctors have a responsibility to stay current with medical research. My experiences to date have shown me that medicine is a challenging career, and one I feel will greatly suit my enquiring and caring nature.

Universities applied to:

- ➤ Cambridge: Interview + Rejected
- ➤ King's: Interview + Rejected
- ➤ University College: Offer
- ➤ St Andrews: Offer

Good Points:

Well-rounded statement that provides good insight into the personal and professional development of the student triggered by their academic career as well as by the different work experience attachments. The student demonstrates that he/she reflects well on their experiences and aims to put them into context with regards to the value for a career in medicine. The student demonstrates a good understanding of the soft skills required for medical interaction and also shows exposure to a wide range of medical care environments, both in primary and secondary care. The student presents themselves as well-versed and aware of the challenges of medical practice as well as some of the relevant skills and abilities.

Bad Points:

It would be interesting to learn more about the student's understanding of the psychological impact on physiological disease. Having researched Freud, it is likely that he has come across this issue, at least, to some extent. Proper reflection on this connection would significantly improve the overall quality of the statement as it is an often overlooked link.

Overall:

Well-written and well-structured. Generally, a good statement with a lot of opportunities to be great and to set the student apart from other applicants. Unfortunately, some of the more challenging issues are only discussed superficially which prevents the statement achieving its full potential.

NOTES

Statement 35

Watching three surgeons urgently try to stop a haemorrhage and anaesthetists replenishing blood back into a patient through a blood recycling unit after losing 4 litres of blood; I knew this was the job for me. Three separate weeks at the RD&E hospital gave me a wide insight into the NHS. I saw many fields from mobility to radiology, lab work to surgery; showing how crucial constant learning is due to continuous medical advancements such as the blood recycling system. I have shadowed a radiologist learning what an eclectic role it is, entailing medical equipment, patient contact and surgery, showing the importance of a wide skills base. Practicality on my placements, whether learning to wash hands, suture, take blood or blood pressure, confirmed my enthusiasm for hands-on work and a First-aid qualification through leadership awards has supported these basic foundations. In addition, The PreMed course at Imperial College gave me a chance to see various aspects of medicine. I learnt from speaking to the doctors what a tough yet rewarding career medicine is. Volunteering at the MS centre in Exeter highlighted how teamwork amongst the staff is critical in ensuring holistic treatment of a patient. Whilst observing informed consent in vascular surgery, I noticed how building rapport with the patients helps them gain trust in you as a doctor. However reading 'The Immortal Life of Henrietta Lacks' by Rebecca Skloot revealed how this trust could not always be obtained.

A2 Chemistry and Biology fascinate me, whether studying amino acid structure and peptide linkages or heart diseases. My studies of blood vessels came to life when talking to patients with vascular disease in clinic and when my Nan was diagnosed with angina. After questioning how these diseases develop and learning about obesity in AS P.E I decided to further my studies in an extended project: 'Should the NHS provide gastric bands to obese people in the UK?' which I find demanding and stimulating.

Travelling to Ethiopia was a life changing experience. Leading sports was challenging due to language barriers but rewarding as I could see how my fundraising had helped. The trip broadened my geographical knowledge of development, inspiring me to work in overseas countries. Discussing issues with Ethiopians about contraception and access to healthcare proved how fortunate Britain is with the NHS.

Leading a science workshop with primary students and teaching sexual education to year 9 taught me how adapting styles of communication to suit an audience is vital. My part time job at Lloyds TSB has confirmed I can build rapport with people of all ages and work under pressure. It has also shown me how confidential information should be handled, as I had to abide by strict regulations and training, similar to medicine.

As a house leader at my school and an Olympic ambassador for East Devon schools; my ability to cope with varying circumstances has improved, such as when the projector failed during an assembly on the government cuts to sport or taking charge of an inter house competition when the leader fell ill. Organising an athletics festival in the East Devon leadership academy enhanced my presentation and communication skills. I had to balance delegating my peers and controlling primary students; testing my interpersonal skills. Voluntarily coaching children tennis and a paired reading scheme demonstrates my commitment and reliability. I'm proud to have represented Devon at Badminton and of completing the 35 and 45 mile Dartmoor Ten Tors endurance event. This tested my physical boundaries, concentration during fatigue, and importance of a strong team bond.

Reading 'the man who mistook his wife for a hat' by Oliver Sacks, and esteemed journals such as 'Biological Sciences review' taught me this career can pose new challenges and provide discoveries every day such as that pericytes are a form of stem cell. It is this constant buzz and challenge that entices me to medicine.

Universities applied to:
- ➤ Birmingham: Offer
- ➤ Cardiff: Offer
- ➤ Nottingham: Interview + Rejected
- ➤ Southampton: Rejected

Good points:
Well-structured statement. The statement demonstrates an appropriate amount of work experience relevant to the study of medicine. The student seems to have gathered a good experience of the challenging nature of medicine and the limitations as well as the possibilities modern medicine offers in the treatment of disease. Furthermore the student demonstrates a wide range of practical skills that will come in use during his studies and that also sets them apart from other students applying for medicine coming with less hands-on experience. The student also describes a variety of non-medical experiences teaching him valuable skills for the study of medicine, in particular this includes the organisational skills for, event organisation as well as the sense of responsibility coming from a paid job at a bank.

Bad points:
The statement has some weaknesses. Firstly, some parts of it are stylistically poor, reducing the overall positive impression somewhat. This is particularly the case for the beginning. The style improves throughout the statement- it becomes increasingly well-written towards the end. The statement also has some structural weakness- it almost seems like the student ran out of space towards the end, causing some of the final points to be very superficial and poorly developed, which is a pity as some of the points raised have the potential to be very beneficial for the statement as a whole.

Overall:
Good statement with some weaknesses. There is plenty of very good information to draw from for the composition of the statement, but it is let down quality wise by a somewhat poor choice of priorities. This statement demonstrates that sometimes it is better to, focus on fewer aspects but develop them to the full.

NOTES

Statement 36

A doctor's role in society is not only to diagnose and treat patients' physical symptoms, but to support them emotionally and psychologically. This was reinforced by my observation of a consultation where a distressed psoriasis patient confessed that his debilitating condition had forced him to resign as a prison chef. I felt that his employer's ignorance of the disease had rendered his time there intolerable. Improving the patient's quality of life necessitated not only prescribing more suitable medication, but also corresponding with his employer and educating him about the condition. This experience furthered my conviction to study Medicine and has taught me the importance of treating the patient emotionally as well as physically. Volunteering at a care home specialising in dementia every week for the past year has been an equally eye-opening experience dealing with both the residents and their families.

The Alzheimer's Society has published that 1 in 3 people over 65 in the UK develop the disease therefore it is important to find ways to halt the deterioration. A current preventative treatment is memantine. Memantine blocks receptors for the neurotransmitter glutamate, which is released from the synaptic clefts in excessive amounts when brain cells are damaged by Alzheimer's disease, thus avoiding further brain damage. Through reading articles that complement my Biology A-level, I found that lifestyle choices and other diseases, such as type 2 diabetes, can lead to Alzheimer's disease. Therefore a healthy diet and regular exercise may reduce the risk of its development. Attending a series of science lectures including 'Science and the Media' have been enlightening, supplementing my knowledge of alternative medicine gained from reading 'Bad Science' by Ben Goldacre. I am fascinated by the use of controversial treatments such as homeopathy and acupuncture which may have the ability to appease the patient's mind, producing a placebo effect which may alleviate their symptoms. It could be interesting to see if these treatments have any influence on the treatment of Alzheimer's.

Through attending Medlink I became aware of the many branches of medicine, and to test my skills in time management I wrote a paper on Stem Cells for which I gained a merit. I enjoyed the research aspect and found producing Induced Pluripotent Stem Cells from fibroblasts and alternatives to embryonic stem cells particularly interesting. Aside from in-depth scientific knowledge, I consider compassion and integrity to be qualities any good medical practitioner should possess. These traits were evident during my work experience in Gloucestershire Hospitals where I observed a lady who had undergone IVF numerous times receiving upsetting news about her foetus' engorged bladder. I was impressed by how the doctors kept the patient calm and well-informed whilst waiting for a confirmation of the diagnosis and prognosis.

Given the responsibility of Chair of the Charity Committee at our school by staff, I have to use my initiative when organising charity days involving the whole school. Communicating effectively with staff and pupils is of the utmost importance and having genuine respect for the charities we support are vital to succeed in the role. Volunteering at my drama school allowed me to work with younger children, the skills I developed were helpful for when I became a mentor in maths and sciences for pupils lower down in the school.

Being fluent in Farsi has allowed me to share elements of my Persian culture through language festivals, helping me gain the Language Leaders Award. Achieving a distinction in my grade 7 LAMDA and participating in the Debating Society have challenged me and developed my communication skills. I take pride in my tenacity and know that I can sustain this course as I am firmly committed to a career in Medicine. I do not hold any misconceptions about the challenges that lie ahead; in fact, I believe I will thrive on them.

Universities applied to:

➤ Birmingham: Offer
➤ Cardiff: Interview + Rejected
➤ King's: Rejected
➤ Sheffield: Rejected

Good points:

This student bases their personal statement on a specific disease and uses it to exemplify their interest in medicine as well as their previous experiences in the field. This is a powerful tool to provide insight into their academic interests and abilities as well as the soft skills they have learned. The choice of dementia is generally a good one in this context, as it includes a very diverse clinical field and many different specialties as well as playing an increasingly important role in modern healthcare delivery with an ageing population.

Bad points:

Some aspects of the statement are factually wrong. This is particularly bad as the statement hinges on the one disease the student chose to make the foundation of their statement. Not only does this weaken the content as a whole, it also reflects poorly on the student's ability for research. The most striking example is the passage addressing the treatment of Alzheimer's. The drug mentioned in the statement is not preventative, but rather a form of treatment for mild Alzheimer's once the disease has set in. To this day, there is no prevention of Alzheimer's. In addition, diabetes only represents one of many risk factors that are known and there seem to be many more that are still unknown to us. Unfortunately, this factual error significantly reduces the quality of the statement and distracts from the good points raised further down.

Overall:

A statement with a lot of potential due to the student's diverse background. Unfortunately, the quality is significantly reduced by factual errors that reflect poorly on the student's academic abilities. Factual errors like this should be avoided at all costs, especially grave ones like this one.

NOTES

Statement 37

Studying the human body, I am amazed that though the body is resilient, it also succumbs to disease. This was reinforced when I shadowed doctors in the infectious disease ward in the University Malaya Medical Centre (UMMC) where I saw a patient suffering from gastrointestinal problems due to drinking contaminated tap water. It highlighted the fact that in some areas, little is being done to prevent diseases that are easily preventable: I am determined to play a part in restoring health to patients who live in areas where disease is rampant but medical care is limited.

During clinics and ward rounds at UMMC, I saw the importance of effective and reassuring communication in good medical practice especially when trying to get the cooperation of the patient. I witnessed a palliative biliary bypass where I observed teamwork between the surgeons and nurses. This notion of teamwork was cemented when I attended a radio conference meeting where I saw doctors from different specialities analysing patients' scans and their subsequent care plans. Attracted by the meticulous research at UMMC into the prevalence of H. pylori in the population, I conducted my own study on HIV/AIDS as I realized the importance of research in improving medical knowledge and thus better quality care. I applied to PT Foundation (a non-profit which provides HIV/AIDS support) to learn how the virus is dealt with in Malaysia. Here, I realised the importance of preventative medicine and education in public healthcare to reduce transmissions and stigma and wrote an article that promoted awareness on the issue. Developing a stronger interest thereafter, I read about research involving deletion mutation of the CCR5 gene that provided resistance to HIV. Volunteering with Reach Out, a charity that feeds the homeless and the UNHRC to teach Burmese refugees English, has allowed me to develop my interpersonal skills and empathy despite the language barriers. While working with the British Red Cross as a peer educator, I had the responsibility of creating a language game and my colleagues commented that I was able to highlight the struggles of refugees through the game. I also volunteer at Charing Cross Hospital to serve meals and feed patients. Talking to the patients I realized that the understanding, patience and bedside manners of doctors and nurses, so crucial in providing quality care, have made the hospital a bit more bearable and homelike.

At school, I was awarded the Prefect Award for leading a team to organise an event that raised £40,000 for paediatric surgery for children with congenital heart defects. I am a founder of the Malaysian Youth Programme that increases learning opportunities for students and through this my leadership has improved to cope with a team 6700 miles away. Participating in Model UN (I am my club's President) and debating-my team was ranked 11th in the country-have both developed my confidence in presenting cases. I enjoy books like The Big Picture by Dr Ben Carson which describes his surgery to separate conjoined twins. It was fascinating to read that a combination of hypothermia, circulatory bypass and deliberate cardiac arrest was used to preserve brain tissue. Equally impressive was the carefully coordinated teamwork required. To relax and improve my stamina, I train with the Imperial College Fencing Team and represent my state in squash. I have completed my Gold DofE Award and I serve on the Gold Award Forum as an Ambassador and a mentor for new leaders in the programme.

Having been in medical care settings in UK and Malaysia, I have learnt that the profession is challenging and ever-changing. To bring medical care to people with no access to it drives my decision to pursue this career. I believe that I have the necessary spirit, skill and stamina to become a good doctor.

Universities applied to:
> Cambridge: Rejected
> Nottingham: Rejected
> University College: Rejected
> Birmingham: Offer

Good points:
A strong statement that demonstrates a wide range of practical experience drawn from both national and international sources. This comparison, and recognising the differences between healthcare and the challenges arising from the different economic situations, is important and a good reflection on the student's horizons. The student also demonstrates a good scientific interest and an interest in the academic side of medical research. In combination with voluntary work, this reflects as an intelligent and dedicated student. The student also underlines their experiences of the importance of soft skills such as communication and team work.

Bad points:
The writing style of the statement is challenging at times, making it confusing to read. This makes it more difficult to appropriately appreciate the student's experiences and ideas. This is a pity as they has a wide range of very varied and valuable experiences. The introduction of the statement could also be significantly improved. Disease is usually a lot more complex than failing resilience. Also, the connection between the student's interest in H. Pylori and their HIV research is somewhat unclear. If the interest is infectious diseases, it would be more suitable to make that clear.

Overall:
A good statement with strong points and interesting aspects and some weaknesses. It provides an interesting basis for a future interview and also provides a good insight into the student's character and their particular interests in medicine. It would be interesting to learn more about their understanding of pathology.

NOTES

Statement 38

Imagine having a conversation with someone whilst they operate on your brain. This is what I watched, transfixed, on a documentary when I was eleven years old. Throughout the procedure, the patient was asked questions to ensure his communication was not damaged, giving the surgeon the boldness to proceed without removing vital components of the brain. With a passion for science, medicine was always a natural choice for me, but it was this experience which confirmed in me an ambition to also become a neurosurgeon. Last year my closest friend developed idiopathic epilepsy. Frightened and concerned I sought to understand how this could suddenly happen. Whilst on a work experience, I visited the Clinical Neurophysiology department at the John Radcliffe Hospital and observed several EEGs. I was amazed by how each patient was so entirely different, a puzzle to be solved using extensive knowledge gained from a lifetime of learning. I know I can be the one responsible for making these life-saving decisions.

Spending time in a GP's surgery gave me the opportunity to ask questions of the doctors and to witness the routine of the more familiar face of our healthcare system. I was intrigued by the different way in which each doctor communicated with their patients. Those with a good sense of humour, used appropriately, seem to connect and empathise well. Being involved with an ambulance service for several days also gave me an insight into the need for urgency and quick decision-making. A week on a geriatrics ward in Swindon Hospital taught me some unglamorous realties of healthcare. Whilst aiding nurses in giving bed baths and helping patients to use the toilet, I was struck by the vulnerability of the very elderly and how it is our duty to protect their dignity as they become more dependent on others. This is increasingly important as the aging population grows. Since starting sixth form, I have volunteered at my local community hospital, once a week. After a tiring day at school, I am sometimes reluctant to go, but without exception I always leave with a sense of achievement, and it continues to be as fulfilling as the first day. Unable to do much more than make cups of tea, it is still uplifting to simply provide company to an elderly patient who may be feeling lonely or depressed. It is difficult to know how much help I am, but I have learnt the importance of commitment and the significance of dedicating my time to each patient separately, seeing each person as an individual, not just a hospital bed.

I play the oboe and the piano and have taken part in various orchestras including the Oxfordshire County Youth Orchestra. Both instruments require a high level of manual dexterity. Tours across Europe have heightened my attraction towards travelling and experiencing different cultures. As well as enjoying music the experiences have improved my ability to work in a team both as a leader, for example taking the role of section principal, and follower. I also teach piano to young children which is rewarding yet has taught me the importance of patience and communication. At school I have participated in dramatic productions, student council and am a prefect at Sixth form. My study of art enables me to express my creativity and has developed my research skills. I particularly enjoy photography, and find printing my photos in the darkroom helps me unwind from my busy life, as does using a treadmill.

The neurosurgeon who first inspired me so much was Henry Marsh. Though one of the most highly commended surgeons in the country, he spends his time attempting to improve the medical system in Ukraine. Henry does not charge patients for consultations; he goes out of his way to help people in need. As a Christian and with my determination, stamina and ability to take on what seems an impossible challenge, I hope to become an altruistic doctor like him, as in his words: "What are we if we don't try to help others? We are nothing - nothing at all."

Universities applied to:
- ➢ Cambridge: Offer
- ➢ University College: Rejected
- ➢ Southampton: Rejected
- ➢ Imperial College: Rejected

Good points:

A very personal and very individual statement that draws on personal experiences to demonstrate the student's motivation for choosing a career in medicine. Exposure to medicine in a primary and secondary care environment provided the student with good opportunities to experience medical care in practice and under real life conditions. This allowed them to experience the challenges and opportunities a career in medicine presents whilst providing insight into many of the necessary character traits and abilities required for a doctor. Being exposed to the emotionally challenging experience of caring for the frail elderly will help the student appreciate the relevance of chronic disease and appropriate support in an ageing population. The student's description of their extra-curricular activities completes the impression of a balanced and hardworking personality.

Bad points:

At some instances, the statement has a tendency to slip into the cliché. This weakens the content somewhat as it tends to diminish the overall value of the presented information. One example of this is the introduction where the student describes their amazement at watching a documentary about brain surgery at the age of 11 which then triggered the decision to become a neurosurgeon due to the student's passion for science. It seems somewhat unlikely that an 11 year old would be able to differentiate this far and come to these conclusions.

Overall:

A generally good statement providing a good representation of the student's interest and their motivations to becoming a doctor. The student provides good evidence of a clinical experience putting them in contact with medical care in order to demonstrate to them the reality of today's medical practice. The overall impression of the student is that of a hardworking and interested individual that aims to perform well and is likely to do well in their pursuit of a medical degree.

NOTES

Statement 39

I thrive on challenge and this has led me to pursue a career in medicine. I feel very privileged to have obtained an Army Scholarship to study medicine at university and look forward to life as an Army doctor. My determination to follow this career has been further strengthened by my work experience and research into gene therapy as the subject of an extended essay.

A week at a General Practice gave me insight into the process of diagnosis and the role the doctor plays within a community. There was a particularly interesting case where I followed the GP as they completed a part 2 cremation form and then visited the family of the deceased. The patient was a Jehovah's Witness in his late fifties and had suffered from lymphedema. He had refused a blood transfusion because of his religious beliefs and this had caused considerable upset for his family, who did not share his beliefs. His wife spoke about how she had pleaded with him to consider the transfusion and the doctor offered reassurance and consolation. This was a humbling experience that exemplified the difficulties doctors face and the importance of understanding and tact. During a further week in the John Radcliffe Hospital, I saw how specific departments function and interact. A highlight was the time spent in the cardiology department, using ECGs and Echocardiograms to diagnose patients' problems. During AS Biology it was interesting to learn how electrical waves in the heart help control the activity of the heart muscle, and as a result dictate blood flow around the body. Studying the sino-atrial and atrio-ventricular nodes helped me understand the conditions of the patients I had seen.

My extended essay explored the ways in which gene therapy could be used in the treatment of cancer. I enjoyed the opportunity to research using medical journals and textbooks such as Knowles and Selby's 'Introduction to Cellular and Molecular Biology of Cancer'. One particularly interesting aspect of the research was the potential use of apoptosis (programmed cell death) to kill cancerous cells, by activating, inactivating or changing the number of oncogenes and tumour suppressor genes and hence triggering oncogenesis. In particular I looked at P53, a tumour suppressor gene that is absent or mutated in over 50% of all human tumours.

Research into how the genetic material could be delivered helped me understand why the process is so difficult, but medical advances in this field could result in gene therapy becoming a successful treatment for many cancers. This treatment would have more benefit to the patient than many of the current treatments which have severe side effects. I have become very aware of these side effects through volunteering at a hospice for terminally ill cancer patients. I have found this a very rewarding experience, particularly meeting one of the younger patients at the centre who unfortunately passed away recently after battling with two brain tumours and continual chemotherapy.

I am proud to be the Head of School; through this I have demonstrated leadership, organisation and the ability to liaise between pupils and senior management. I am also the Under Officer for the CCF, leading the cadet force and instructing younger cadets. This summer I was selected as one of 12 British cadets to attend the 6-week Rocky Mountain Leadership and Challenge course in Canada, and was selected as the top British cadet. I am a keen sportsman: vice-captain of the 1st XV rugby and captain of the 1st XI football at school. This year will be my third season as a qualified football referee, officiating men's football most weekends.

My busy life at school will be good preparation for the rigours of a Medicine degree and I am hugely looking forward to the chance to learn more about medical theory and practical procedures.

Universities applied to:

➤ Birmingham: Offer
➤ Manchester: Offer
➤ Newcastle: Offer
➤ Sheffield: Offer

Good points:

Excellently written and well-structured. The structure helps greatly to guide the reader through the content in a coherent fashion. The student demonstrates a wide range of academic and non–academic experiences, biomedical and non-medical. He provides good insight into lessons learned and skills acquired during his attachments and his non-academic extra-curricular activities. The student presents himself as disciplined, well-organised and dedicated- all qualities well sought after in doctors. His reflections on the challenges of the medical profession are very valuable as well. Furthermore, his research work demonstrates a fundamental interest and understanding of scientific research methods and clinically relevant topics.

Bad points:

There are no major weaknesses in this statement. The only point of complaint would be the passage addressing the patient the student saw. The context makes it sound like the patient died of lymphedema and refused a blood transfusion for the treatment of this, which would be incorrect.

Overall:

A very good statement with much strength and only some minor weaknesses. Well-written and structured and good choice of topics selected. The statement gives adequate insight into the student's interest and their character. The statement is structured very clearly which ensures efficient communication of relevant points.

NOTES

Statement 40

From the miracle of birth to the miracle of life, the human body is astonishing in its complexity, the development of intricate anatomical systems such as the heart and the brain truly fascinate me. To be able to understand and restore these systems is one of the foremost reasons I want to study medicine. The diverse nature of medicine, its continual evolution and breadth of knowledge would provide a constant challenge to satisfy my academic curiosity regarding anatomy and physiology.

On work experience at a neurological clinic, I had the opportunity to examine MRI scans and to learn about epilepsy and motor neurone disease, I also met the individuals with these disorders and I discovered the deep compassion and care that doctors have for their patients. This experience sparked my interest in the brain and prompted me to research further into genetics and neurology. Consequently, I read "The Man Who Mistook His Wife for a Hat"; in which I found the cases of idiot savants in particular quite thought-provoking as, despite being deemed unintelligent by society, they have awe-inspiring talents in music and calendar calculation for reasons still poorly understood. An enthusiasm for learning about physiology encouraged me to read "Life at the Extremes" by Frances Ashcroft, a book detailing the limits of human function and survival; this fascinated me as I enjoy rock climbing and so the restrictions caused by altitude in particular captured my interest. I also like to read the BMJ to keep up to date with news concerning recent medical innovations and breakthroughs to further my knowledge of medical studies. To further my knowledge of medicine as a career, I attended the Medisix conference in Nottingham. I have had work experience in several fields such as Geriatrics, Plastic surgery and Orthopaedics in a number of hospitals; I also spent a day in A&E. My most memorable moment of work experience was observing a Coronary Artery Bypass Grafting operation; this thrilling experience reinforced my desire to learn more about the heart and encouraged me to research further into cardiothoracic surgery which I look forward to studying at university.

I completed an EPQ regarding the issues of prescribing medication to children/adolescents with psychiatric disorders. From this, I learned how to develop my opinions as initially I thought medication may have been forced upon young people as way of avoiding of dealing with real psychological problems and that therapy alone would be appropriate, however through research I realised that this was not the case but that medication is necessary in conjunction with therapy to offer the best form of treatment. From this experience, I have improved my time management, my ability to work efficiently under pressure and my use of critical analysis and reliable sources. An interest in psychiatry inspired by my EPQ motivated me to seek relevant experience and I was able to find an opportunity to volunteer at SeeAbility, a home which cares for blind people who often have an accompanying psychiatric illness. Through volunteering, I have come to realise that I genuinely enjoy talking to and working with the residents and that I would like to do more to help the people in my community.

I thoroughly enjoy dissection and being a part of the Medical Society at school has allowed me to pursue this interest as well as have the opportunity to hear the views of medical professionals each week. Dissection is one of my many interests, amongst rock climbing, badminton and reading. I am a member of the hockey and netball teams at school in which I have acquired vital teamwork and leadership skills. I am excited to begin university and to meet new people, but most of all to begin studying medicine. My passion for medicine has been reinforced by my work experience and extra reading and yet, despite what I have heard and read about the rigors of medical training, I am certain I will make an excellent and compassionate doctor.

Universities applied to:
➤ University College: Offer
➤ Edinburgh: Rejected
➤ Imperial College: Rejected
➤ Bristol: Rejected

Good points:
The student provides some insight into their interests and their work experience. Addressing mental health in their research project is an interesting choice that has great relevance for a career in medicine, particularly due to the general ignorance of the relevance of mental disorders. In addition, it provides a good opportunity to hone communication skills and become aware of important issues such as stigmatisation and social isolation. The student demonstrates other essential lessons from this experience such as time management and stress resistance.

Bad points:
The statement has a somewhat impersonal and removed writing style, which produces an artificial distance between the student and their hospital experiences. This artificial level of distance reduces the overall strength of experiences described in the statement. In their discussion of medical literature, the student remains too superficial in his reflections. It would be very interesting and relevant to read more than half a sentence about the student's thoughts regarding his hobby of rock climbing and the physiological effects on the human body as this is an opportunity to demonstrate the ability to apply learned knowledge to a real life scenario.

Overall:
Average statement mainly challenged by the student's writing style. It is also somewhat limited in regards to clinical experience and clinical reflection which is a pity. The interest in mental health is very interesting and will provide a good basis for discussion at the interview stage, in particular due to the increasing public focus on mental health.

NOTES

Statement 41

The harsh reality of disease was made clear to me when I spent a week at a residential home for people with severe dementia. Speaking to the residents who have struggled to manage life with a degenerative illness, I realised that medicine is far more complex than merely offering lifesaving cures to those in need. Over and above being an academic science, medicine encompasses the art of dealing with people compassionately, considering both their emotional and physical needs. It is this that sets medicine apart from other scientific subjects.

I have always found human biology the most intriguing aspect of my studies. Visiting Dr Gunther von Hagens' 'Body Worlds' exhibition and seeing the plastinated prosections of human cadaver provided me with a fascinating insight into the complexity of human anatomy and the devastating effects that disease can have upon it. Furthermore, from reading 'The Emperor of all Maladies,' I have gained an understanding of the importance for doctors to be able to critically evaluate and analyse the work of others, a skill that I have begun to practise and develop through my A-level Religious Studies course. Reading Mukherjee's account of Mary Lasker's 'war on cancer' led me to consider the relationship between medical research, politics and the public. This is a theme that I am currently developing through my EPQ on the efficacy of alternative medicine, a phenomenon I find interesting due to its perceived opposition to evidence based medicine.

However the role of a doctor is not merely confined to the analytical diagnosis and treatment of disease as medicine is essentially about people. Observing a psychiatrist at Coventry hospital, I gained appreciation for the diverse demographic that a doctor must interact with, each patient facing their own difficult situations. Whilst shadowing a cardiologist at Warwick hospital, I gained an insight into the vast numbers of professionals that a doctor must work with on a daily basis. Experiencing the seemingly chaotic and busy ward round enabled me to understand the pressures that a doctor faces in order to respond to each patient's needs, making decisions within restricted timeframes. Following a placement at Shakespeare's Hospice, I was further inspired, having seen the genuine relationship between the nurses and their patients. This reaffirmed my belief that it is the importance of working sensitively with others that makes medicine distinct from other academically demanding vocations.

I have already started to regularly face the challenges associated with working with the general public through my part time job in a cafe. Learning to be adaptable in my communication skills, I have found working and engaging with people both worthwhile and rewarding. This is one reason I took on a position as a mentor at my school, where I lend time to listen to and support my younger mentee. For the past three years I have also volunteered as a young leader at my local Brownie group. By helping to run sessions I have improved my leadership and organisational skills. These attributes helped when faced with having to work to tight deadlines in my role as the administrations director in a Young Enterprise company. Although challenging, the result of our team reaching the regional finals having successfully written, printed and marketed two children's books was an immensely gratifying experience.

Team work, again played a key role this summer, when for my Gold Duke of Edinburgh Award, I acted as a crew member on a ship that voyaged across the North Sea. I was swiftly required to bond as a team with people I had just met and learn new skills in adverse conditions. Through a vocation in medicine I would expect to be physically, emotionally and academically challenged, but ultimately I am certain that to be a doctor will be a worthwhile and incredibly rewarding career.

Universities applied to:
- ➢ Oxford: Offer
- ➢ Sheffield: Rejected
- ➢ King's: Interview + Rejected
- ➢ Leicester: Offer

Good points:
The student provides a well thought through and realistic perspective on their future as a doctor, acknowledging the challenges and difficulties of the profession whilst also putting them into perspective with the many benefits and satisfying aspects. This demonstrates that the student has an inquisitive and reflective character and also tries to analyse information presented for their impact on his choices in order to make the most informed and relevant choice possible. The student furthermore recognises the importance of team-work and other soft skills such as compassion and communication besides the obvious relevance of academic excellence and security in applying scientific principles to the diagnosis of disease.

Bad points:
The student describes a keen interest in human biology and anatomy, in this context, it would be relevant to know if the student has any other exposure to this area of medicine other than visiting a prosection exhibition. It is also relevant in this context to address the controversial aspects of von Hagen's exhibition when it comes to issues such as confidentiality. Being aware of the ethical connotations of this is highly relevant.

Overall:
A generally strong statement, that benefits from a clear structure and a good writing style. There are some weaknesses that do not necessarily weaken the statement as a whole, but that could be improved nonetheless. The student gives good insight into their individual motivation. They succeeds in presenting themselves as a suitable candidate for the pursuit of a career in medicine

NOTES

Statement 42

Seeing the anatomy of the human body while watching an autopsy brought my Biology studies into reality. The cause of death was a heart attack. After this I was determined to find out more about the varied and fascinating life of a doctor. The medical profession had grabbed my attention, specifically with regard to how we diagnoses and treat illnesses. When a family member was diagnosed with type 2 diabetes mellitus, I had a strong desire to learn more about this interesting and complex disease. I took an interest in how this chronic disease is managed and the different conflicting dietary advice.

My work experience first started in a Histopathology laboratory. This is an interesting area where I learned how a small biopsy sample when looked at under the microscope can provide extremely important information such as whether a patient has cancer or not. It was captivating to look through the microscope myself and attempt to identify cancer cells, on the few occasions I succeeded it was very satisfying! Watching an autopsy fascinated me and it became apparent that a great deal of information can be gathered from the dead to more effectively treat the living. The consultant explained to me that the autopsy has been used for hundreds of years to make important discoveries about diseases and collect vital statistical data. Orthopaedics was next on my rotation. In this area I learnt about fractures and joint diseases and how they are treated. I was surprised to see large felt tipped markers being used on patients to identify the correct operation site to avoid a mishap as has happened in the past. Watching hip and knee replacement operations and seeing the improvement in the patients' quality of life was amazing. I also spent time in radiology learning how important X-rays and particularly MRI and CT scans have become in patient management. This was coupled with a session in oncology and radiotherapy where doctors spend a lot of time planning personal treatment plans for cancer patients.

I balance my academic work with several outside activities. Since a young age I have taken part in recreational gymnastics. I started volunteer work at the centre, initially as part of my Duke of Edinburgh bronze and silver award and now have an enjoyable part-time job working 7 hours a week with young children, some of whom have special needs. The sports centre is sponsoring me on a level one training course in Kent which has already provided me with additional skills for teaching, training and leading groups. In addition I have volunteered to undertake charity work with a local organisation called "Out and About" and spend time with an autistic boy, James, taking him into the community on a regular basis; it is a pleasure to assist him in increasing his social skills, independence and confidence. It has taught me to be patient with people and give positive encouragement and I believe I have made a small but significant difference to his life.

My charity trip to Namibia was to help school children improve their school. I found this an exciting experience and was amazed at how a small amount of interest from outside organisations can make a big improvement to these communities. This experience helped me enhance my team-work and leadership qualities by organising events for a group of 15 young charity workers, including myself, sorting out daily activities. In my leadership role I learnt to be fair and all inclusive and to ask people to undertake manageable tasks with support if necessary. I have several interests which include playing local and junior Essex league tennis; dinghy sailing, having completed up to level 3 Royal Yachting Association sailing courses. I also competed in county trampoline competitions at junior level. Skiing, high board diving and horse riding are activities I enjoy with my family. My favourite hobby is cake making and decorating. These activities give me a chance to relax, relieve stress from working and meet a variety of people.

I believe that I am a well-balanced, self-motivated person with a strong desire to succeed and feel that medicine is the one profession that provides lifelong challenges with the opportunity for continuous learning and development to better treat illnesses and to improve the health of individuals and communities.

Universities applied to:
- Nottingham: Rejected
- Brighton & Sussex: Interview + Rejected
- Birmingham: Offer
- King's: Rejected

Good points:
Good statement with a variety of interesting experiences, some of which have a good relevance for the student's pursuit of a career in medicine. The student provides good accounts of their work experiences and how the time spent there has helped them improve skills relevant for being a good and successful doctor as well as succeeding on an academic level. The student's reflection on their experience demonstrates a good ability to analyse experiences for their value for individual development. This is a useful skill for future doctors as a career in medicine will require continuous self-improvement. The student also provides account of some non-academic experiences they experienced as useful and stimulating for their personal development. Organising events and teaching children provides valuable soft skills with regard to communication, allocation of resources and organisation

Bad points:
The statement lacks a clear structure and in some areas lacks conciseness. This somewhat reduces the quality of the statement and also consumes space that could be used to provide more relevant information about personal experiences relevant to medicine.

Overall:
A good statement with many strong points and some minor weaknesses. These weaknesses do not significantly impact the overall quality of the content, but could be improved. The statement provides a good representation of the student's experiences and interests.

NOTES

Statement 43

Learning about the body and all of its complexities is absorbing, whilst applying the knowledge can be lifesaving. I am inspired by the opportunity to spend my working life contributing to the health of the public whilst always being challenged to call on my faculties to ensure the effective care and treatment of patients.

Over a six month period, I volunteered at a care home. The experience helped me to appreciate the immense emotional and physical strain placed on healthcare workers when putting others' needs above their own. However, the humility I witnessed weekly from the nurses furthered my dedication to contribute to people's lives in such a way.

As a ward volunteer, I am aware of the realities of hospital life. Being in this environment has highlighted how the quality of care of the patient relies on the teamwork between the different healthcare professionals, requiring interaction on all levels. Speaking with many junior doctors made me aware of the pressure put on them, such as the unsociable hours they have to work. A doctor must therefore be committed and consistent, and with my strong work ethic I believe I could cope with the demands of the career. Observing doctors' relationships with patients highlighted the importance of sensitivity and empathy also. Psychological factors can affect a patient's recovery, sometimes more than the treatment. I realised it is vital to treat the patient as a whole.

For three months, I worked in a village in Bangladesh tackling issues such as poor access to healthcare and sanitation. Through raising awareness and partnering with key influential figures, we were sustainable in our approach. Working and living in a cross-cultural environment, whether it was teaching children English or running health camps, was challenging but invaluable for developing my confidence and communication skills. Working with very few resources, I realised the importance of flexibility and team-work as we used our varying backgrounds to work effectively. From volunteering, I have developed a strong sense of global citizenship which I could perhaps build on as a qualified doctor by looking into working with NGOs.

After having studied humanities at A-level, I am taking an access course. Learning about conditions like Down's syndrome on the genetic level, especially engages me. In broadening my scientific knowledge, I have enjoyed reading popular science books like 'The Selfish Gene' by R. Dawkins, as they have taught me to engage with ideas more independently. Additionally, Melvyn Bragg's BBC podcast on medical ethics furthered my understanding of how ethics forms a key aspect of a doctor's job. As medicine is widely described as both a science and an art, the balance requires the doctor to act in a way that puts the patients' best interests first. Sir Pratchett's documentary, 'Choosing to Die', introduced me to the ethical controversies surrounding euthanasia. Issues like these make it easy to realise that medicine intersects with many other areas of society and requires the doctor to be a moral, responsible and compassionate person.

I have been playing rugby for ten years. It challenges me to concentrate when under pressure and it keeps me in shape. In my spare time, I take great interest in producing and editing music. I have played various gigs over the past two years as a DJ. I find it liberating to be able to be creative with my music and I find it is a great way for me to de-stress. As a multi-lingual, I am also very keen on travelling and learning about the world's different cultures.

With a medical career come many benefits and limitations. It will be by no means easy, but my maturity, focus and drive give me the confidence that I will succeed, both, professionally and academically. I am inspired by the opportunity to pursue a lifetime of learning in which my skills and knowledge would help give people hope when at their most vulnerable.

Universities applied to:

- ➢ King's: Offer
- ➢ Leicester: Interview + Rejected
- ➢ Southampton: Rejected
- ➢ East Anglia: Rejected

Good points:

A well-written and well-structured statement providing good insight into the student's motivation for choosing a career in medicine. It also gives good insight into steps taken by the student to broaden their horizons and getting a good exposure to medical practice and the challenges that arise from dealing with patients of different walks of life. Having worked in a care home will have confronted the student with questions of end of life as well as teaching them valuable lessons regarding the needs of chronically ill patients as well as the importance of communication and a holistic approach to medical care. Further humanitarian volunteering demonstrates the student's interest in helping those in need and emphasise the student's compassion and empathy. Having the prospective of working for aid organisations upon graduation is an interesting motivator.

Bad points:

The statement somewhat lacks details about the student's academic career. They mention studied humanities at A-level, but don't provide further details for their choice of profession at this stage. It would be beneficial to include information regarding this as it can greatly enhance the overall perception of the student's motivation and character.

Overall:

A well-written and well thought through statement with some minor weaknesses. The student manages to present themselves as a well-rounded individual who is driven by the desire to help others and making a difference to people's lives- a very admirable motivation.

NOTES

Statement 44

Studying medicine has always appealed to me because of the way it is intrinsic to society and is ever-progressing; new discoveries are made each day which will inevitably affect each of us. An interest in the sciences from an early age has enabled me to explore beyond the A level syllabuses, and take interest in issues in the wider world through articles read in the student BMJ. An example of this is recent work I've followed on the measurement of blood pressure and prescription of drugs for hypertension following a Lancet paper. Research work by doctors and research scientists is showing better ways to manage health for diseases such as cardiovascular disease.

Not only does the academic side of medicine appeal to me but also the opportunity to communicate effectively whilst assessing a situation. This is a skill which I have been able to develop during work experience in a GP practice, and in my part time job in a pharmacy where I have worked for a year as a qualified Counter Assistant. In this role, I have completed the GPhC accredited Interact qualification. I have developed my communication and team working skills and ability to interpret patients' needs through the experience of working with people from different backgrounds in an NHS environment. This has been a fantastic opportunity to gain knowledge of a wide variety of prescription only and over the counter drugs, while working alongside the pharmacist as part of an efficient team. As part of my duties I am responsible for independently carrying out cholesterol and blood pressure monitoring sessions for patients. I am currently studying a YASS Open University short course in Molecules and Medicines, which has helped me to get used to undergraduate level study.

I independently arranged my Year 11 work placement at Northampton General Hospital, where I learnt about the efficacy of multidisciplinary teams. I spent a week in the Pathology department shadowing both biomedical scientists and Consultants. This enabled me to see how scientists, nurses and porters are vital in helping doctors to do their job. I am returning next month to shadow a Consultant Anaesthetist and to observe operations in theatre.

Leading on from this experience, I arranged a voluntary work placement in a local GP Surgery, which helped me to explore further the importance of Healthcare Assistants and Nurses in the NHS as I accompanied them on house visits and sat in on a smoking cessation clinic. However, the majority of my work was spent with a GP preparing and observing minor operations and consultations. This placement helped my understanding of the services provided by PCTs and confirmed my choice of a career in medicine.

I volunteered at my local Age Concern day centre for 3 months, which helped me to appreciate the profound effect degenerative diseases have upon not only the elderly patients, but also their friends, family and carers. I have attended conferences at Medlink and the University Hospital, Coventry to further improve my knowledge of the medical profession.

As part of my A level French study, I worked in Bordeaux in February 2011 in a book shop, where it was necessary for me to speak French for the week. This experience vastly improved my fluency in French, which I would like to make use of during the elective period in the 5th year of a medical degree.

I play the trombone and violin and played in a concert with my school Jazz band at Disneyland Paris. To relax I play regularly in a local badminton club and work out in a gym. I am a senior Prefect taking responsibility for younger students on a daily basis.

I feel that my flair for science, as well as my ability to work as part of an effective team will greatly benefit me while I am studying medicine. Carrying out work experience placements has strengthened my desire to become a doctor, and I feel that my skills combined with the experience gained thus far has confirmed that medicine is the subject to which I can apply myself best.

Universities applied to:
➢ Birmingham: Offer
➢ Bristol: Offer
➢ Leeds: Interview + Rejected
➢ Sheffield: Offer

Good points:
The student demonstrates a wide range of experiences and personal interests, some of which are relevant for medicine and lead to the acquisition of relevant skills such as communication and organisation skills and the ability to work as part of a wider team. The student demonstrates good exposure to clinical medicine as well as medicine in a communal setting. This experience contributes to the understanding of the different priorities and challenges of different care settings. Having been exposed to the challenge of degenerative disease is important and beneficial as these types of diseases will become increasingly important in an ageing population.

Bad points:
The introduction of the statement is somewhat clumsy. Whilst it is true that medicine is progressing, attributing a daily change is a needless exaggeration. Additionally, there usually is a significant delay between the discovery of new facts and their penetration into actual medical practice. Not acknowledging this reflects negatively on the student's understanding of research in a medical setting. Some of the aspects raised in the statement have little relevance for a study of medicine. Whilst it is interesting that the student has spent time working in France, the form in which this is presented in the statement does not demonstrate much relevance for the subject.

Overall:
Good statement with strong aspects and some weaknesses. The latter is mainly related to the presentation of the content and the writing style. The basic principles are good and provide a well-balanced image of the student.

NOTES

Statement 45

I am terrified of small talk. I feel crushed by the atmosphere of awkwardness, and I am so desperate to find something to say that I usually end up saying something stupid. I am not interested in the weather – why are we socially obliged to discuss it? As you can imagine, I was faint with fear when I began my work experience as a receptionist in the radiology department of Peebles Hospital in the British Virgin Islands. Being the main point of contact for an entire department was pressurising enough, let alone all the chitchat I imagined I would have to make over endless cups of coffee…

I was of course not entirely correct in my perception of what the work would be. Organisation was very important, whether it was sorting hard copies of scans or letters for patients to collect, or ensuring scans for patients were present on the PACS system. Conversation with colleagues was a bit awkward at first, but perfectly fine after I had gotten to know them – I even felt confident enough to ask to sit in on an ultrasound, where I was able to see the care and compassion which the radiographer and radiologist showed towards the soon-to-be mother, and how their strong relationship as professionals helped put the mother at ease and provide for her the best standard of care.

One downside to the work was dealing with difficult patients. I learnt how important it was to try and remain as calm as possible when patients grew angry that their documentation was not ready to pick up, how to admit when it was my mistake when something had gone wrong and how to explain to the patients that the doctors were very busy without aggravating them. I also learnt that it was important to remain compassionate as a patient may have gone for a mammogram and rightly be anxious about the results – would I not be just as angry in the same situation?
I also had the opportunity to sit in on orthopaedic clinics at the hospital. The skill with which the doctor diagnosed patients, and the balance of care and frankness which he explained these diagnoses to them, caused the patients to treat him with much respect. This taught me the importance of patient-centred care, as the patients seemed to appreciate and respond better to the doctor when he explained the situation to them and asked their opinion. It also showed me the need to constantly keep up to date with the current best standard of care and to think on your feet as you never knew what new case would come through the clinic door next.

In effort to attempt to understand the research that doctors are involved in, I conducted a research project on back pain in Sixth Form girls at my school. I gave a presentation to around sixty of the girls, followed by a questionnaire I had designed (asking about how they carried their bag, the location of any pain they had, how strongly they would rate the pain etc.). I compiled the results and did some rudimentary statistical analyses before writing it up in the style of a scientific paper, including a brief literature review. I would very much like to continue with such research in my future career and hope to one day be able to contribute something of value to the medical field.

When I am not studying, I enjoy participating in dramatic productions at my school. I feel this has increased my confidence enormously, and also helped me deal with pressure that comes from having to act in front of large audience. I also enjoy mentoring younger students, which I have been able to do as a Year 10 prefect and an English mentor to a Year 9 student – helping the girls get through all the difficulties I remember facing at that time is very rewarding. I also love to read, though I have so little time to properly become absorbed in a book that recently I have taken to reading poetry.

What draws me to medicine is how it takes scientific research and applies it with care and compassion, and the teamwork involved in this application. I look forward to a day when I can be a member of this team.

Universities applied to:

- ➢ University College: Offer
- ➢ Bart's: Interview + Rejected
- ➢ King's: Interview + Rejected
- ➢ Bristol: Rejected

Good points:

A very honest statement that openly admits to weaknesses and experiences the student predicted to be particularly challenging. This openness and the ability to face these challenges are admirable and demonstrate a high degree of dedication to the subject of medicine. The student's reflections show a great degree of maturity as they make insightful conclusions about the challenges of medical care. Appreciating the difficulty arising from dealing with a variety of patients, including angry ones, is an important lesson to learn. The research project also sounds very interesting and is likely to have provided good insight into the basics of scientific method and research.

Bad points:

Even though the student demonstrates an admirable willingness to face their dislike for small talk, it probably represents the biggest hurdle in their pursuit of medicine. Due to the very high relevance of communication and exchange with patients, it is imperative to feel comfortable in communication with patients from all backgrounds and all walks of life. It would also be interesting to learn more about the student's research project at school, particularly since it has orthopaedic relevance.

Overall:

A good statement demonstrating a good level of self-reflection and an excellent awareness of one's own limitations. This is very important as recognition of individual fallibility will prevent making mistakes as a doctor further down the line. The student's difficulties with communication are a real challenge, particularly since so much of medicine is based on good communication. It would be very interesting to assess this further during the interview stage.

NOTES

Statement 46

From the discovery of Penicillin to the decoding of the human genome, the ever advancing nature of medicine has never ceased to amaze me. Over the years I have endeavoured to further my understanding of it through reading, work experience and my A-Level subjects. I understand that the fatigue and long hours, accompanied by a lifetime of learning will involve many sacrifices. However, these sacrifices pale into insignificance when one can spend a lifetime in such a rewarding, highly respected career.

My work experience includes a week spent in a day-surgery unit where I observed many procedures, from the removal of skin cancers to a knee arthroscopy, where the surgeon removed a torn medial meniscus. The following week was spent in A&E where I witnessed a heroin overdose which encouraged me to relate my studies to real life situations. Observing seven cardioversions end-to-end for patients experiencing atrial fibrillation was captivating as this was an area of the Biology specification that I had found extremely interesting.

Additionally, being present at a hip replacement made me aware of the manual dexterity a surgeon requires. I had the opportunity to follow an elderly lady undergoing a CT scan after having suffered a stroke due to a cerebral haemorrhage. Studying how swiftly the doctor dealt with this delicate topic underlined the importance of communication skills whilst handling such sensitive matters; something I was able to develop whilst helping in an orphanage in India. I also worked at a general practice on a weekly basis for six months; here I was able to sit in with the doctor and observe consultations and treatments. I learnt a great deal about the personal rapport between doctors and patients and how to deal with sickness in the community. The orphanage alongside A&E made me aware of the less pleasant side of Medicine, which was to face many emotional challenges. Luckily, I have been able to develop my emotional intelligence through the orphanage, working as a teaching assistant at a primary school and assisting home-schooled students with Chemistry practicals.

To extend my knowledge, I have completed an Open University YASS course titled 'Molecules, Medicines and Drugs: A Chemical Story', for which I read far beyond my Chemistry syllabus and was able to apply what I was learning to modern day medicine. I also achieved a merit for an externally marked joint project on Alzheimer's. The task involved putting forward our own hypothesis on how to cure the disease, which required a great deal of research on the aetiology and symptoms of Alzheimer's. This inspired me to visit a psychiatric institute where I witnessed the effects of dementia first hand. Subsequently, I was inspired to read further into degenerative diseases, and Science in general. I have read New Scientist, the Student BMJ, Dawkins' 'The Selfish Gene', which deals with the gene-centred aspect of evolution, 'The Man Who Mistook His Wife For A Hat' and more.

As Head Girl, elected by my peers and staff members, I have had to arrange events, deliver assemblies and meet deadlines, along with being on the student council. Achieving five belts in Korean Karate and completing my Bronze, Silver and Gold Duke of Edinburgh Awards, show my dedication. In addition, I am an Award Scheme Leader, which involves educating the Bronze participants.

To relax, I go to the gym, attend dance classes and play the keyboard and guitar. I play the guitar at concerts and my dance group has performed at venues such as the Royal Albert Hall, and are to perform in Wembley Arena in 2011.

I participate in charitable activities, such as working at the British Heart Foundation charity shop and being Vice President of the Interact organisation at my school. Also, being one of the Heads of the student run Medical Society is a position which highlights my dedication to my chosen subject; the dedication I will most definitely show when presented with the challenges of my chosen career.

Universities applied to:
- Birmingham: Offer
- Cambridge: Interview + Rejected
- Kings: Interview + Rejected
- Imperial College: Rejected

Good points:
Well-written statement with good structure and appropriate writing style. The student provides a well-balanced and detailed account of her previous work experience as well as her reflections on these experiences and how these have influenced her and encouraged her to further pursue a career in medicine. The student provides an interesting account of her clinical experiences that cover a wider range of specialties and events. The contrasting nature of experiencing A&E and the less acute environment of a day surgery unit provides valuable insight into the challenges of medical practice, challenges that can be on a purely academic level, testing the limits of knowledge, but that can also be on an emotional level.

Bad points:
The statement's main weakness originates from an occasional lack of clarity related to the detail provided about the individual experiences. In some cases the student remains on a somewhat superficial level of reflection reducing the described experience to a mere listing. This does not provide much value for the quality of the statement as a simple list of experiences does not deliver any insight into the character of the student.

Overall:
Good statement with some minor weaknesses. The statement demonstrates that occasionally it is beneficial to rather reduce the amount of content in order to fully develop certain ideas, making them relevant to the topic itself.

NOTES

Statement 47

Since winning a science competition for my model of the human digestive system, I have been fascinated by the complexities and workings of the human body. My decision to study medicine stems from this fascination and a desire to use my scientific knowledge to treat illness and improve the quality of people's lives.

Through my work experience I have developed a realistic perception of a career in medicine and I have enjoyed seeing how the theoretical science I have learnt in my A Level subjects can be applied in the art of restoring and preserving health. At a breast clinic, I was involved in a deeply moving consultation in which a patient was told she had incurable breast cancer. I appreciated the limitations of medicine and it made me reflect on the emotional demands of the profession. I saw the further challenges of medicine in my 3 weeks work experience at an acute hospital. I saw the problems doctors faced controlling the antibiotic resistant strains of bacteria I had studied in biology such as MRSA and TB. Through reading the New Scientist I learnt about the use of genome sequencing to identify the type of MRSA. In theatre, I was fascinated by the use of infrared spectroscopy to monitor the breath of patients under anaesthetic, a technique I learnt about in Chemistry. I saw how the analytical and problem solving skills I have developed in maths must be combined with compassion and empathy to reach a diagnosis. I have taken blood, patients' histories and blood pressures linking theory to practice. In a neuroscience lecture I was excited to learn more about the neurobiology of schizophrenia and the multidisciplinary research attempting to understand brain function.

For the past three years I have worked at a dementia nursing home. Engaging with the residents has shown me the difference good care can make to quality of life. Spending time with people who are terminally ill has been emotionally challenging at times but has been invaluable experience inspiring me to pursue a career in medicine. Through shadowing a consultant specialising in medicine for the elderly and my voluntary work, I have seen the growing problem of dementia within hospitals and the community and I am currently researching the treatment of dementia for my EPQ.

As deputy head girl I have developed my public speaking and leadership skills through organising events and liaising with students and teachers. I teach karate to adults and children of all abilities and this has taught me the importance of communicating effectively at an appropriate level. I was head of sales in my young enterprise team and our effective team-work led us to win the spirit of enterprise and overall winners award at the county finals. I have developed these skills further through Gold Duke of Edinburgh's Award. As a member of St John's ambulance I have been able to put my first aid skills into practice. The British Sign Language course I completed has helped me to communicate with and support people in neuro-rehabilitation and with dual-sensory impairments in voluntary placements.

My effective time management has enabled me to maintain a range of extra-curricular interests as well as two part time jobs without losing academic focus. I enjoy drama, playing chess, athletics and netball. I am a black belt in karate and have been training with the England squad for the last four years. This requires discipline and motivation but it is also a great way to relax. I represented England at the world championships where I was thrilled to win two gold medals highlighting my ability to perform well under pressure.

The diversity of care I have experienced from looking after the elderly to observing lifesaving surgery has given me an insight into the career dedicated not only to lifelong learning but also to caring for others. I am fully aware a career in medicine will be demanding but I believe I have the motivation and compassion to become a successful doctor.

Universities applied to:

➤ Birmingham: Offer
➤ Cardiff: Offer
➤ Cambridge: Interview + Rejected
➤ Leicester: Offer

Good points:

An excellent statement. Well-written and well-structured, providing excellent information on the student's work experience, the skills acquired there as well as her interests and academic career. Throughout the entire statement each point raised is guided by an underlying skill or ability which makes the content highly relevant and clear. The student is able to demonstrate a wide range of academically relevant skills as well as soft skills such as communication and discipline, all equally important for performing well as a medical student and as a doctor. Throughout the statement the student maintains a clear line of argumentation not wasting any space on information that does not actively contribute to her representation as a good choice for a potential future doctor.

Bad points:

Whilst all the aspects of her experiences raised in the statement are very relevant and well-argued, some carry more value than others and could be developed further. Particularly beneficial would be to learn about any medically challenging experiences made during the student's time at the St. John's ambulance. Also interesting, would be her motivation for learning sign language as this adds an additional layer of depth to the statement.

Overall:

Excellent statement covering a wide range of very valid and relevant subjects and experiences. The statement greatly profits from its clear structure and purpose-lead design, giving every piece of information provided a specific purpose in regards to the whole of the statement.

NOTES

Statement 48

The intricacies and complexities of the human body have always fascinated me, not only the systems and processes, but also the driving force behind them: the emotions and aspirations of individuals. During a 5 day placement at a local hospital, I witnessed how doctors paid attention to both the physical and emotional needs of the patient, healing the body in a way that left the patient feeling they had been shown care, compassion and understanding. Though not all outcomes are wholly positive, the empathy of the medical staff was always vital. The reality of life as a doctor was made abundantly clear; the work was constant, challenging and tiring, but the doctors' professionalism and patience did not diminish, and the diversity of the illnesses and tasks meant it was never monotonous. I saw the importance of teamwork, the camaraderie between the staff enabling them to work together to give the patient the best possible care. However, it is the patients I spoke to who stand out; many were full of gratitude towards the doctors who strived to give them back their health and drive. Seeing this served to increase my determination to become a doctor.

A year ago, I arranged a weekly placement at a GP's surgery. Working on reception required me to communicate with many different people, which has increased my confidence and inter-personal skills, and when given the tasks of filing or inputting confidential medical data, I was keen to do so diligently. I enjoyed taking part in a medical terminology course and learnt a lot from it. Working in different areas of medicine, my appreciation for its many aspects has grown, motivating me to learn more about topics of particular interest.

Therefore, I am undertaking an EPQ on the effects and treatment of haemophilia during pregnancy and childbirth. This has required a great deal of independent research while studying for my A Levels, showing my organisational and time management skills allied to my capacity to carry a large workload. I am absorbed in the project and find it fascinating.

At Fairplay, I work with children who have special needs, taking them on trips and running activities. This requires a large amount of responsibility, and my understanding of a wide variety of conditions that affect young people has grown. Helping to run fund-raising events at a local hospice has developed my communication and organisational skills. Voluntary work at a nursing home for the elderly, where I talked to patients, helped them at mealtimes, and ran games and activities has given me valuable insight into the lives of older people who struggle with their health, and taught me how to handle delicate situations such as people living with dementia. I also spent two weeks in Lourdes, where I was responsible for looking after a disabled pilgrim. During talks with him and other pilgrims, I learnt about the importance of faith to sick people. The contrast between these roles has highlighted how people's needs vary according to not just their condition, but other aspects such as age and faith. However, a need for dedication and commitment were common to all, and each one made me feel privileged to help others.

During my free time, I enjoy developing my skills in French and German. Taking part in exchange visits to France and Germany, I adapted well to the new environments, made good friends and improved my communication skills. I feel that languages are an asset in life and that the self-motivation and dedication required to learn and maintain them are universally valuable skills. I also enjoy teaching myself Japanese, which I find relaxing.

It is clear that a career in medicine is immensely challenging, but I have always been determined to work my hardest to achieve my goals. The prospect of immersing myself in such an interesting area of knowledge, and of engaging with and connecting to many different kinds of people, is hugely motivating. I believe that medicine is absolutely the path I should follow.

Universities applied to:

➢ Sheffield: Offer
➢ Keele: Offer
➢ Nottingham: Offer
➢ Oxford: Rejected

Good points:

A very well-written statement with a wide range of clinical and volunteering experiences relevant for medicine. The student reflects well on all these experiences and puts the lessons they learned into perspective, judging how they serve them to improve their understanding of medicine, medical care and the realities and challenges of working with patients from different backgrounds and with different expectations of the healthcare system. Having worked as a GP receptionist is a very valuable experience, providing good insight into central ideas of communication, confidentiality and organisation. Working with disabled children will support the development of a sense of responsibility and maturity in the student. All these experiences contribute a great deal to the overall impression of the student being well-suited for a medical career.

Bad points:

The statement is somewhat short of academic interests. It would be interesting to learn more about this as the student seems to dedicate a very large proportion of their life to medicine-related subjects already. It would also be interesting to know more about the student's coping mechanisms and extra-curricular interests. This would greatly enhance the overall insight gained into the student's character.

Overall:

A good statement containing a wealth of information related to the student's experience in different settings of healthcare. The statement presents the student as a very proactive and interested individual that recognises the human aspect of medicine and displays curiosity about understanding the basic underlying principles of medicine. This student seems well-suited for the pursuit of a career in medicine as they seem disciplined, invested, and dedicated.

NOTES

Statement 49

Locked-in Syndrome: a fascinating yet tragic disease leaves an individual trapped within his own mind. For many years there was no hope for these patients, but now a tiny electrode inserted in the brain can detect activity and transmit data to generate vowel sounds by a computer. Jean Dominique Bauby's 'The Diving Bell and the Butterfly' was a revealing portrait of this condition which spurred me on to track developments in this syndrome with passion. Thus, I realised medicine is an ever evolving profession that is always at the forefront of scientific development to improve the life of a person for the better. This, without a doubt, stimulated a profound motivation in me to study this subject at university.

The pursuit to understand this career, led me to attend the Medlink Conference. Here I gained an insight into the dedication and passion required to become a doctor which I later saw being put into practice during my work experience. At Shrewsbury hospital, I shadowed a consultant Obstetrician in an ultrasound scanning clinic where he diplomatically told a couple that their fetus had Down's syndrome. Whilst informing them he was sympathetic, listened to their views and supported them to make an informed decision. This highlighted the importance of communication in order to establish a 'patient-doctor' relationship. I caught a glimpse of the extent to which smoking is a public health problem during my time at the Respiratory Department of Telford hospital. Here I witnessed how consultants, nurses and paramedical staff worked as a multidisciplinary team for the care of patients suffering from lung cancer and COPD.

During the summer I encountered the medical challenges of another continent while shadowing a consultant dermatologist in India. Apart from specific clinical problems, doctors there face overcrowded hospitals, illiterate patients and financial restraints. I had the opportunity to meet and support patients suffering from leprosy which was beyond the usual disease spectrum found in the UK. At the Neuropathology unit of Imperial College London I learnt how the examination of a small piece of brain tissue can lead to a life-changing diagnosis of a brain tumour. I was later moved by the impact such a diagnosis had on a patient who was informed that he had a curable tumour. On speaking to him, he explained how relieved his family and him were to go back home to enjoy the simple pleasures of life. Moments such as these drive me towards becoming a doctor myself; I want to make a difference.

At Mother Teresa homes in India I helped serve meals to the elderly and taught orphans English, Maths and football. Interacting with the children gave me a chance to listen to their problems and ambitions. This experience instilled in me a sense of gratitude and desire to help others. Over the past year I have volunteered at a charitable cafe located next to my local A&E where I could sense the emotions of patients and their families whilst being in the hospital.

I have been appointed as one of England's Young Sports Ambassadors. This prestigious role involves promoting sports in youth for the 2012 Olympics and gave me the opportunity to meet famous and inspiring athletes like Darren Campbell and Lord Coe. Moreover, I play badminton, cricket and table-tennis at county level and coach these sports to juniors at my school. Besides sports, I was the Finance Director of a Young Enterprise company which won 2nd prize in the regional finals. As a house captain and prefect, I execute leadership and communication in order to organise and participate in charity events, public speaking, Dance and Talent shows.

I am immensely intrigued by the science of medicine and amazed by the complexity of the human body. With the UK being such a multicultural society today, I feel that my ability to communicate in four languages alongside my determined personality gives me the cocktail of requisite qualities to become an accomplished doctor.

Universities applied to:
- ➢ Birmingham: Offer
- ➢ Sheffield: Offer
- ➢ Cardiff: Interview + Rejected
- ➢ King's: Interview + Rejected

Good Points:

The student demonstrates a well-balanced and very diverse picture of themselves. The described attachments of work experience demonstrate a good and varied exposure to different medical specialties as well as a wide range of valuable experiences. The student reflects well on their experiences, drawing appropriate conclusions regarding the challenges of medicine and relevant skills. Having experienced medical care in environments of different levels of wealth is a valuable experience, allowing for good appreciation of the complexity of healthcare today, including the great importance of appropriate funding.

Bad points:

Wrong presentation of locked in syndrome. Patients suffering from locked in syndrome are unable to communicate. They are not trapped in their own mind. This is a particular issue as the student claims to have a particular interest in the syndrome. Furthermore the writing style of the statement at times is too prose-like. This weakens the statement by reducing its clarity. Additionally, this type of language is unsuitable for a factual piece of work like a personal statement.

Overall:

Good statement that is generally well-structured. It suffers from some weaknesses that reduce the strength of the statement somewhat. The most significant weakness probably lies in the error relating to the nature of locked-in syndrome, mainly as this is the introductory statement.

NOTES

Statement 50

My gap years were chosen to give me a variety of experiences relevant to Medicine and at an early stage confirmed that Medicine was the right choice for me. Indeed, long before placements in an Indian and UK hospitals made a profound impact on me, I knew I was suited to this career. Passionate about science and good with people I wanted to use my talents to make a difference to people's lives. Shadowing doctors in India and at home gave me an insight into resilience: they were exposed to the full spectrum of life's sad and joyful moments during their hectic schedules.

I also saw at first-hand how a strong work ethic and skill enable doctors to compensate for limited resources and I learnt that while a command of theory and high level practical skills are essential, good medicine is about compassion. Meeting role models who viewed the patient as an individual who deserved the best quality care strengthened my resolve to become a doctor. I enjoy intellectual challenges and personal challenges. I won the Gold Crest Award for a Nuffield project which investigated a relationship between the linker length of dimethylaminopyridine compounds and the inhibition of choline kinase alpha in cancer cells. My research design included a literature review and I conducted a rigorous data analysis. My scientific understanding was enhanced and the high level of precision I attained in the experiments will be useful in future investigations. An extended period as a patient companion at Northwick Park hospital developed my confidence as I became an integrated part of the ward team. I understood the importance of teamwork and professionals' approach in communicating with patients, making them feel respected.

Observing a medical team during an Oophorectomy I learnt how important it was to synchronise individual technical expertise within teamwork. The careful coordination of complementary skill sets ensured successful patient outcomes. I was also able to build up a number of case studies which included a patient who was particularly distressed about her condition. I noted how her fears were visibly allayed by the doctor's confident attitude and sympathetic approach during the consultation.

Volunteering at a nursing home, where many of the south Asian patients were suffering from Type Two diabetes and paan-chewing increased the risk of mouth and oesophageal cancers, gave me an added perspective on the health service. Fluent in Guajarati and Hindi, I was able to promote the benefits of lifestyle changes to patients. I was able to establish a high level of trust even with clients who, according to the manager, had hitherto been reticent. This experience taught me that patients will only confide in care professionals if they have built up trust beforehand. I keep up-to-date with medical research and issues affecting the NHS.

My wider reading has included 'Medical Ethics 'by Tony Hope which emphasises how advanced technologies create new moral choices. Paid work at my school has been an invaluable experience as working for and alongside my former teachers gave me considerable confidence. I received very positive commendations as I worked hard, used initiative, and met deadlines by prioritising duties. I enjoyed tutoring students, preparing resources, handling data and helping in the preparation for Ofsted. Liaising with a wide range of staff and parents further developed my interpersonal skills. I know that my career choice requires a high level of stamina so I make sure I keep a balance between study and leisure. I attend a traditional Kathak dance class and play badminton. I believe my level of commitment and strong work ethic will support me in the demanding and dynamic medical profession. Gaining an insight into various medical career branches has helped me to recognise some of my personal strengths such as empathy and being able to collaborate in a team. I have a clear insight into life as a doctor and I am determined to attain my goal.

Universities applied to:

➢ Birmingham: Offer
➢ Liverpool: Offer
➢ Lancaster: Offer
➢ Bristol: Interview + Rejected

Good points:

A well-structured and very clearly written statement that presents a disciplined and dedicated student. The student provides evidence of different work experience placements drawing appropriate conclusions from the placements. The student demonstrates a well-balanced view of the challenges of medical practice and some of the key characteristics of a medical professional. The student addresses the challenges to medical care and the health system that arise from financial differences between countries. This international experience is beneficial on an additional level, demonstrating the student's well-rounded nature and their broad interests. In the statement, the student also gives evidence of a good exposure to clinical procedures.

Bad points:

Some of the content has little relevance in the way that it is provided in the statement in the sense that it does not serve to set the student apart from other students applying for medicine. One example of this is the student's claim to be following current events in the NHS. This is very much expected of an individual applying for medicine. Furthermore the student's claim that good medicine is only about compassion is somewhat misleading. Whilst compassion is very important, a good doctor also needs to be able to emotionally distance themselves from their patient to make the right decision, based on a strong basis of knowledge.

Overall:

Good statement with some little weaknesses. The weaknesses somewhat reduce the strength of the statement with regards to promoting the student to the best extent. The statement contains a good amount of very relevant information that presents a hardworking and interested student.

NOTES

Statement 51

The variety of work experience I have carried out has confirmed my absolute desire to enter the medical profession; from a day –hospital for elderly patients with mobility issues to home visits by GPs to check up on terminally ill patients I have been inspired by the doctors I have shadowed. I realise the importance of human contact for these patients is vital, and I would be privileged to help and emotionally connect with the most vulnerable people in our society as a doctor.

The most incredible medical experience I have had so far is watching twins being born by Caesarean section, at Royal Tunbridge Wells Hospital. Not only did I appreciate the surgical skill and teamwork of the doctors, but also the empathetic nature used to calm and reassure the expectant mother. Empathy is vital not only for the patients, but also their relatives as I saw when meeting a 12-year old suicide victim at Alder Hey Children's Hospital, Liverpool, who is now in a vegetative state. This case deeply shocked me but confirmed my ambition to treat patients experiencing severe suffering. At the Cheltenham Science Festival this year I thoroughly enjoyed taking part in a re-enactment of an emergency trauma admission to A&E and trying to resuscitate a new born baby by intubating it. I have found my weekly volunteering at a school for special needs children and a care home for the elderly to be invaluable experiences. Both of these opportunities have taught me how to communicate to people of different ages at a very personal level and also to cope with death, as the lady I spoke to at the care home died soon after I began visiting her.

In June I embarked upon researching the effect that caster sugar and artificial sweeteners have on the mass of caffeine released when tea bags are placed into boiling water for my Extended Essay. I carried out independent research, managed my time effectively when collecting data and critically evaluated my results. I also work well as part of a team, evident by my selection with two other girls to represent our school at the national finals of the Royal Society of Chemistry Analyst Competition. In Biology, I find it intriguing to learn about how the human body functions, and I extend my knowledge in this area by reading books such as "Human Instinct" by Robert Winston and "Proof of Heaven" by Eben Alexander .My passion for science has been demonstrated by becoming involved in a Chilli Research Project at my school. We are changing various factors that affect the growth of chillies and reporting our results to Oxford University. The group's results may then be published in an academic journal. In my role as an Academic Representative for Chemistry I hope to inspire younger pupils in the school to enjoy and become confident in their Chemistry lessons.

Studying the International Baccalaureate has taught me how to be reflective, both in my work and extra – curricular activities. When participating in Bronze, Silver and Gold DofE I cooperated effectively with people and managed the team when we were in unfamiliar surroundings. I am an effective motivator, and I believe this personal quality led to me captaining the U14, U15 and U16 netball teams at my school. Similarly, my organisational skills and hard work are reflected by my appointment as deputy head girl at College. Through this role I am in charge of helping to coordinate the curriculum and teaching throughout College. Also I am head of the Academic Society. I hope that this responsibility will help me to enhance my leadership skills further.

All the skills I have witnessed and learnt from my work experience have deeply inspired and motivated me to enter the medical field. I strongly believe I have the necessary commitment, skills and attitude to be a successful doctor.

Universities applied to:
➢ Birmingham: Offer
➢ Manchester: Offer
➢ Liverpool: Rejected
➢ Bristol: Rejected

Good points:

The student provides good insight into different experiences made during a variety of work experience placements. This provides a balanced view of the student's interests and the level of clinical exposure and personal development in the frame of medicine. The experiences described by the student are interesting and relevant and provided her with significant exposure to the emotional challenges of the medical profession. A wide range of extra-curricular engagement allows the student to hone her communication, organisation and management skills, all of which are relevant for a career in medicine. Being able to gather experiences in teaching are also a good distinguishing factor in comparison to other students, as teaching skills are becoming increasingly relevant for future doctors.

Bad points:

Some of the statement is somewhat poorly structured. This particularly applies to the passage addressing the experience of the care for a 12-year-old patient that attempted suicide. Whilst the student briefly acknowledges the emotionally challenging nature of this experience, within a sentence, she moves on to discuss experiences made during a science festival. Further reflection on the emotional relevance of is experience would greatly benefit the statement. The way this is presented in this instance gives the impression of a lack of appreciation for the emotional implications of the situation.

Overall:

A good statement with a solid basis of significant experiences and skills. The statement suffers somewhat from the unfortunate structuring of ideas leading to a potential misrepresentation of the student.

NOTES

Statement 52

The day that Kevin returned home, I realised that I would only be content with a career in medicine. I had been volunteering since January 2009 at Birmingham Children's Hospital, organising activities for the children on a cancer ward and Kevin was our most avid member, always first to join us when we arrived. Our craft sessions were a highlight of his week and his parents seemed to benefit from them too; we were able to build a strong relationship with them over the weeks and to support them through the most difficult time of their lives. Through this, I realised that whilst it is true to say a doctor must have sound scientific knowledge, they must also be able empathise with, comfort and support not just the patient but also their family to bring about the quickest and fullest of recoveries. I believe that I hold these vital traits.

In order for a doctor to make a swift and accurate diagnosis they must be able to communicate effectively with their patients. I have developed this skill through participating in a volunteer led group for housebound members of my local community providing them with hot meals and, more importantly, a chance to socialise. Through conversation with the members, I have improved my interpersonal skills, helping them to feel comfortable in my company. The importance of this cannot be overstated as helping a patient to relax during a stressful visit to the hospital can only aid the doctor in reaching a decision concerning the patient's ailment. Similarly, through volunteering in a geriatrics ward at Good Hope Hospital every week since February 2010, I have become more adept and confident in how I speak to people from older generations. A number of the patients suffered debilitating illnesses like dementia and initially I struggled to overcome the obstacles which arose as a consequence of these. However, over time I tailored my style of communication to suit each patient's unique situation. This experience shed light on the constant pressures faced by nurses and doctors alike when striving to care for people with mental illness.

The two weeks I spent in India only furthered my desire to become a doctor. I gained many valuable insights into the Indian healthcare system but my most memorable experience was at a leprosy clinic. There is still a strong stigma associated with the disease in India and, unfortunately, the country also has the highest leprosy rate in the world. The plight of these patients, nearly all of them disowned by their families, was very moving and by the end of the trip I was very conscious of the way in which we take the NHS for granted.

Through my extensive work experience I have come to realise the great diversity in medicine. Of the huge range of specialisms, oncology is of a particular interest to me and I have extended my knowledge through reading. Consequently, I now feel I have a growing understanding of the diagnosis, physiology and treatment of the disease.

I enjoy participating in a wide range of extracurricular activities. I am an enthusiastic musician, playing both the violin and piano to a high standard, and dedicating myself to 5 different musical rehearsals a week. I utilized my musical talents, recording, producing and selling a CD to help fund my trip to India. I have nurtured my leadership capabilities by accompanying the school choir. On the other hand I have developed my ability to integrate myself into a team by playing in large groups like the school big band or orchestra. In addition to my musical activities I enjoy badminton, having represented the school, and climbing which requires tenacity and a high degree of problem solving; it is demanding but as a consequence very rewarding.

Intellectually, I always seek a challenge. I believe that medicine is one of the only careers where I will be stimulated in this way while also having the opportunity to improve the lives of people on a daily basis, including children like Kevin.

Universities applied to:

- ➤ Cambridge: Interview + Rejected
- ➤ Sheffield: Rejected
- ➤ Nottingham: Interview + Rejected
- ➤ Birmingham: Offer

Good points:

A stylistically well-structured statement. The personal relationship to the patient described in the statement helps underline the importance of the relationship between doctor and patient. This relationship is central to the modern type of patient-centred care. The student further demonstrates a good range of clinical and non-clinical experiences providing examples for many relevant skills such as communication and organisation. Having experienced different environments for medical care, working in an environment of different financial freedom is a valuable, experience as it allows appropriate appreciation of the challenges that come with a shortage of resources and the role doctors play in an appropriate and efficient allocation of the resources available.

Bad points:

Oncology is not a disease. It is a specialty of medicine, dealing with cancers of almost all types and affecting a multitude of tissues in the body. Describing it as a disease demonstrates a fundamental deficit of understanding. This considerably weakens the quality of the statement.

Overall:

Good statement with many strong points and interesting facts about the student. The statement gives a good idea of the character and the motivation of the student as well as their interests in medicine and their appreciation of the challenges of the profession.

NOTES

Statement 53

I am fascinated by Medicine, not only for academic reasons, but also because of the interactive and social aspects of its practice. The intricate biological workings of the human body have so far been fascinating to learn, but it is the ability to diagnose and treat the ailments that afflict it that I find truly inspiring. From what I have seen and experienced, Medicine requires not only detailed scientific knowledge, but also the ability to forge trusting relationships with both other doctors and patients alike. It is this mix of scientific study and social exchange which attracts me to Medicine.

Within a broad interest in biology, I have a specific personal interest in Neurology. My mother was diagnosed with brain cancer four years ago and not surprisingly I wanted to gain a better understanding of her condition. As I learned more about the brain, I discovered how complex and vast the conditions are that Neurology encompasses both mechanistically and behaviourally. Several fascinating cases are detailed in 'The Man Who Mistook His Wife for a Hat' and 'Phantoms in the Brain'. The ability to diagnose such bewildering and varied cases is one that is highly impressive.

Carrying out a placement at Greenwich University showed me what research can be like. I worked on a short project on insecticide action in insects - highly concentrated work, but also a great lesson in how scientific research teams operate. In my upcoming gap year I have arranged to help teach HIV prevention in South East Asia. I hope to see first-hand how big an impact health education is having in developing countries, and how it can be used in frontline areas to stop the spread of disease. I also think it will be rewarding to play a role in enhancing the life of others. In addition to the obvious benefits that access to drugs and therapies provides, I am also aware of the long term psychological support that doctor-patient relationships can have on a patient's recovery. I arranged to spend a week shadowing a consultant neurosurgeon. During his clinical sessions, patients were sometimes told of their life changing conditions. Seeing first-hand some of their reactions was, at times, upsetting - but it emphasised the harsh realities of illness and showed that there is a limit to what medical care can do. In these situations the importance of personal relationships was evident, time and time again - but not just between doctor and patient. The nurses, doctors and other hospital staff were a supportive team. Seeing how effective this was, brought home to me the importance of communication and reliability within a medical environment.

This attitude of working as a team is also essential when I take part in extracurricular activities. As a member of our school's athletics, hockey and swimming teams, I realised how integral teamwork is in order to succeed. Being put under pressure to perform to the best of my ability is fulfilling and it gives me an impetus not to make a mistake. Singing has also played an important role in my life. I was head chorister of Jesus College choir in Cambridge, before singing as a baritone at Kings. Singing is not only a very enjoyable experience, it is also quite challenging. You are constantly aware of being part of the group and of the importance of practice, dedication, and pulling your own weight!

It is, and has been for a long time now, my desire to become a doctor. I fully understand there is a large amount of work involved, and realise the sacrifices I must make in order to achieve this aim. But I feel I am a determined individual who has the necessary personality to succeed in this field. I think I would respond well to the challenges that clinical practice presents, and would relish the opportunity to apply myself in this area.

Universities applied to:
- ➢ Cambridge: Interview + Rejected
- ➢ University College: Offer
- ➢ Edinburgh: Offer
- ➢ Bristol: Offer

Good points:
The student demonstrates a good interest in the academic basics of medicine. This is very important as it ensures an ability to understand and appropriately address all the scientific aspects involved in disease. Furthermore, an aptitude in academics will make it easier to grasp the many principles that underlie medical care. The student also demonstrates a good variety of work experience placements and succeeds in reflecting on their experiences during these placements, making them relevant for his/her choice of career and adding to the strength of the statement. Finally, the understanding of the relevance of team-work and shared responsibility is very helpful for a career in medicine, where much of the treatment of patients revolves around a multi-disciplinary approach. The student also gives insight into a very personal interest and motivation for studying medicine which gives the statement additional strength.

Bad points:
Whilst the student provides good insight into the reasons for their specific interest in neurobiology, it would also be interesting to learn more about how the literature they read influenced him/her in their understanding of the subject. In the manner it is presented at this stage, the literature contributes little to the overall strength of the statement.

Overall:
A good statement providing good insight into the student's character and interests. The impression of the student is that they are hardworking, dedicated, disciplined and interested in the challenges of medicine, supporting the idea that they is well-suited for a career in medicine.

NOTES

Statement 54

I have always been fascinated by science. Work experience has shown me that medicine will be my perfect career, enabling science to be applied in an empathetic and direct way which I think will make it more rewarding than other, often impersonal, scientific careers. Sitting in with nurses and doctors at a GP surgery I saw the importance of good communication skills. Especially striking were the techniques the doctor employed in order to take a complete history, obtaining information the patient often thought was irrelevant.

During my weekly visits to an elderly person's home I gained a personal insight into the complexities of dealing with patients as I reassured a woman with very poor short-term memory who asked the same question many times. Spending a week at the Royal Brompton in London I observed a paediatric cystic fibrosis clinic. I realised just how many people are vital to the treatment of the patient and how important teamwork is in medicine. I saw this again while spending time with a radiologist, when the discussion between radiologists and surgeons was often vital in planning future management. At the respiratory department at Southampton hospital I saw many patients but for me the most humbling was a man with severe allergy-induced asthma as it was clear it massively limited his daily activity.

I think a doctor must be able to analytically deduce an answer to a problem. My logical brain, which explains my love of maths, will help with this as it did with learning classical Greek. My academic scholarship enabled me to be stretched with discussion groups and I entered the Kelvin essay competition, discussing a quotation from Bernard Cohen on the importance of scientific ideas. I enjoyed the research opportunity and was delighted to be awarded a rare prize at school.

I have read a series of stimulating books. Richard Dawkins' 'Selfish Gene' challenged my view on ongoing interests, evolution and genetics. Reading 'Ancient Medicine', I compared the ancient doctor with my experiences of modern medicine. My concept of medical practice was also altered after reading Oliver Sacks' descriptions of extreme patient histories, highlighting the complex interaction between a doctor, a patient and a disease. I keep up to date with medical issues in the news and by reading BMJ and Eureka.

At my work experience at in Cambridge I met training doctors and the importance of and enthusiasm for continual self-education and for teaching colleagues was evident. Teaching ones patients of their own condition seems to me to be one of the cornerstones of good medical practice. Sailing has been a lifelong hobby and recently become more serious, sailing for the school 1st VI and teaching as a qualified RYA instructor. I also teach first aid to my peers resulting in a place on the Community Service Committee. I enjoy the solitary sport of running, and have put it to good use by completing a charity half marathon. However I prefer the rewards of working in a team. Whilst progressing through the stages to Gold Duke of Edinburgh it became clear that a good team must have a good leader and this is a role I took in my Gold Award and which I really enjoyed. In the same vein, I have been made a pastoral prefect which gives me the opportunity to help new pupils through their first year. I hope that this charge reflects the presence of the key skills required in the caring role of a doctor.

Elsewhere I am part of Uppingham Theatre technical crew and have achieved grade 4 bassoon, play guitar and sung in choirs at Bury St Edmunds Cathedral and at school. I firmly believe I have the drive, enthusiasm and intellectual rigor to succeed as a doctor. I intend to spend time in Vietnam with the Welcome Trust on a gap year in order to gain life experience which will ensure I am prepared to make the leap into medical school.

Universities applied to:
- ➤ University College: Offer
- ➤ Cambridge: Interview + Rejected
- ➤ Sheffield: Interview + Rejected
- ➤ Bristol: Offer

Good points:
The student presents themselves as a well-rounded and dedicated individual, interested and intrigued by the challenges and experiences associated with a career in medicine. They manages to provide a good representation of their varied impressions during their work experience placements. Their reflections on the value of these placements in the sense of providing an introduction to medical practice are reasonable and carry good weight in preparing them for the challenges of a medical degree and then a career. Understanding the importance of teamwork organisation, dedication, and communication is essential as all too often these central attributes and challenges are overlooked.

Bad points:
Some aspects of this statement carry little to no relevance in the form they are presented here. This applies in particular to the bibliography of books read by the student. Whilst it is interesting that the student chose to read literature dealing with medicine, it is highly likely that the majority of medical applicants will have read similar books. For this reason, the mere reading is no noteworthy achievement. The reading becomes relevant if it is reflected upon and put into context with particular interests or lessons the student was able to reach due to reading the books listed.

Overall:
Good statement. It gives good insight into some of the student's achievements and also describes their motivations for study in medicine. Furthermore the statement draws an interesting path of development of the student, highlighting particular experiences due to their worth and impact on the student's personal development.

NOTES

Statement 55

Robotic surgery, applications of nanotechnology in cancer treatment and research into synthetic life! In my opinion there has never been a more thrilling time to study medicine and I am ready for the challenge. Knowing that medicine was what I wanted to do, because of my desire to work hands-on with people and further my scientific learning; making sure I knew what it entailed was a priority. Aged 15 I gained my first hospital placement; this first look into the medical profession was invaluable as I learnt not only about the role of doctors but also about the team that supports them. At the end of my placement I had a better insight and my ambition to become a doctor was cemented.

My extensive involvement as an ambassador for the charity Kids Taskforce over the last 5 years has developed my communication skills through speeches and presentations at the UN in Geneva, Downing Street and New Scotland Yard. An ability to speak confidently in front of both influential people and my peers provided me with invaluable interpersonal skills that I have applied in my everyday life. For instance I have enjoyed volunteering at St. Catherine's Hospice over the past six months, where I have had to deal with difficult emotional situations. Being able to talk easily with both the patients and their families, even if just as a distraction for them, has made me feel that my volunteering there makes a difference. To ensure that I had a clear understanding of other aspects of the care profession, I arranged a short placement in a Home for adults with severe learning difficulties as well as, once a week during my free periods at college, volunteering at a day centre for the elderly. Although not medical, these taught me a lot about the challenges faced by professionals working in a care environment.

My time this summer with an Anesthetist in James Cook Hospital was one of the most insightful times I spent with medics. I learnt how each person on the team, from the Porter to the Surgeon, is dependent on one another and how detrimental a lack of communication at any point along the line can be. On reflection, I can see how effective teamwork is key to the whole process. My passion for rowing has taught me this importance through working together with my team to gain the best result. Similarly having had a job for 4 years, I have worked alongside a constantly changing team of people and my Silver Duke of Edinburgh award was where these teamwork skills came into their own. Leadership is a skill I have developed through prolonged association with the Rainbows Organization. Over my two and a half years with the children, I arranged activities and planned weekly meetings. As a Senior Prefect I had a team of 20 prefects to coordinate to ensure the smooth running of the school. In recognition of my work in this role I was presented with the schools leadership award.

I enjoy being involved in my community and since the age of 14 have regularly read and edited for Whitby's Talking Newspapers for the Blind. I am an active member of the local dance school. I have loved ballroom dancing since primary school and have worked my way up through many exams. I am proficient in conversational French having continued to learn independent of college. It serves as a welcome contrast to my more science based A Levels. My passion for playing the piano is my ultimate way of relaxing and relieving stress. It is a hobby I hope to continue.

Though all the placements I have undertaken have been incredible in teaching me about the responsibilities and challenges faced by Doctors, there was one particular day that cemented my desire to become a doctor. Whilst sitting in on consultations with my local GP I saw patients at their most vulnerable, people afraid to speak to anyone yet trusting in their GP. There is no way to describe the complexity of the Doctor Patient bond but I have seen how that trust can change people's lives. I want to have the opportunity to be that doctor.

Universities applied to:
- University College: Offer
- Manchester: Offer
- Newcastle: Offer
- Leeds: Rejected

Good points:

The student paints a clear picture of a long path of experiences dedicated to the pursuit of a medical degree. This long history of striving to get as much exposure to medicine as possible is very interesting and fundamentally highlights the student's determination and drive to achieve their goals. The large degree of exposure is bound to have influenced them in a variety of ways, supporting the acquisition of skills and impressions all supportive of a medical career. Community volunteering supports the notion of the student as a compassionate and responsible individual that takes a genuine interest in helping others. It will also invariably lead to a greater appreciation of the challenges faced by those battling illness, both chronic and acute.

Bad points:

Considering the large degree of effort this student has put into the accumulation of relevant experiences and qualifications, they fails to address their academic interests and how these have been influenced by their drive to becoming a doctor. This is not to say that they should list school awards and grades, but providing some insight into academic interests will give an idea of the student's ability to achieve the level of academic foundation necessary to practice medicine.

Overall:

A good statement that is dominated by the student's wide range of experience in medicine and their work in the community. It succeeds at providing good insight into the student's character and their work ethics. It is interesting to read about the long-term dedication to medicine this student displays. Whilst the statement is generally good, it does have some minor weaknesses, mainly related to the academic interests of the student.

NOTES

Statement 56

The basic science and the interaction with patients, combined with public health issues and the prospect of contributing to the healthcare of developing countries, makes medicine my career choice.

I have tried to understand the many facets of medicine, from laboratory research to its clinical application. A lecture in Cardiff University by Professor Neuberger revealed to me those discoveries in immunology which have allowed transplant patients to survive. I then spent time in a cystic fibrosis clinic as part of a hospital observation programme. It was shocking to hear how breathlessness had made one 17-year-old girl dependent on a wheelchair and oxygen cylinders. However she had recently had a double lung transplant and it was striking to see how her life had changed, and the satisfaction this gave her doctors. Her story also brought home to me how public awareness and involvement can change the practice of medicine but how complex the ethics can be. The basic research has been done, surgeons and physicians can transplant organs, but the public aren't always well enough engaged to make the transplant programme as successful as it could be. I witnessed similarly complex but different issues in the pulmonary rehabilitation clinic, where the majority of patients were suffering as a consequence mainly of their lifestyle rather than as a result of a genetic abnormality. These were very relevant experiences which introduced me to the ethics and politics of healthcare and made me more aware of the on-going debate about assisted suicide, and the relevance of Jeremy Hunt's views on abortion.

I learned about the financing of medical progress during a week at a cancer research laboratory during which I observed research into the mobility and growth of breast cancer cells. I was surprised to learn how dependent on non-government funding these laboratories were even though the research seemed so relevant. I learned more about medical research at Oxford University's UNIQ Biomedical Sciences course but it was the hands-on application of knowledge that particularly suited me. Reading books such as 'The Music of Life' and 'Why Do People Get Ill' has introduced me to the different perspectives within modern medicine.

Away from the hospital and research environment I spent a week at a school for children with severe disability, time in a nursing home for the elderly and, during an attachment to a GP surgery, I visited a children's hospice. This experience gave me an insight into the realities of custodial care for people for whom medicine has little more to offer. The hospice care required detailed medical knowledge but also catered for the patient's family, all of it in a homely environment. My weekly voluntary work in year 12 with children with learning disabilities helped me to realise the nature of long-term care and the commitment and dedication required. My school activities have enhanced my appreciation of good communication, particularly listening, when interacting with people. The school's debating society taught me the importance of other people's perspectives when forming my own opinions. I have helped establish a debating society for younger pupils, and have twice reached the UK final of the European Youth Parliament Competition. I have been a member of the school choir, which involved two European tours, and I have played county hockey for six years. I was a Gold Ambassador for the Olympics which allowed me to use my Sports Leadership skills (Level 1) and my Leadership and Management (Level 3). The Gold Duke of Edinburgh Award taught me the importance of team-work and about leading the tired and tearful! By my peers and teachers I was elected Head Girl, a position of considerable responsibility.

Having seen medicine from bench to bedside and the requirements of patients in the community I now fully appreciate what a broad subject medicine is. I am determined to make the most of the many opportunities that a medical career offers.

Universities applied to:

➢ Oxford: Interview + Rejected
➢ University College: Offer
➢ Bristol: Offer
➢ Birmingham: Interview + Rejected

Good points:

The student demonstrates a wide range of relevant and interesting experiences of primary care, secondary care and non-medical community care. It reflects a good dedication to gaining a varied impression of the challenges of medical care as well as the different levels of everyday life that are influenced by medicine, especially in people suffering from chronic diseases such as CF. The student demonstrates their hardworking and compassionate nature and reflects well on the experiences made in the hospital and at the GP by addressing how these experiences have influenced them in their perception of medicine. The different extra-curricular activities further support the representation of the student as a hardworking and dedicated individual.

Bad points:

Some of the points raised in the statement are factually a little off. For example, some of the challenges of transplant medicine are related to the difficulty of the procedure and the significant impact that life-long immune suppression has on the patient. It is important not to underestimate the huge impact and the magnitude of an intervention in transplant medicine. Other aspects of the statement suffer from being too superficial. The passage that is supposed to reflect the student's interest in current ethical events does not contribute much to the content at all as it stays very superficial and is not reflected upon.

Overall:

A good statement with many strong aspects and good at representing the student as an interested and dedicated individual. It is important to recognise the complexity of requirements for the individual when it comes to being a good doctor. The student demonstrates their awareness of this. This statement also demonstrates some of the limitations that medicine experiences that go beyond the mere medical side. This is particularly obvious in transplant medicine where many different aspects have to be considered, rather than exclusively medical feasibility.

NOTES

Statement 57

Volunteering at a summer camp for children with terminal illnesses in Romania this August highlighted two things to me: first, the injustice of this world and second, how I could work towards alleviating the pain of others. I am attracted to the medical profession because I care about people and wish to relieve human suffering. Furthermore, the fast pace at which scientific research is developing means that medics are at the forefront of an exciting discipline. Doctors are part of a team that will one day find a cure for the currently incurable. What once were 'terminal' illnesses may become only 'temporary'.

I am particularly interested in neuroscience, mainly because the brain is one part of the body we have great difficulty understanding, with the potential for considerable medical development. By studying medicine I aspire to expand my scientific knowledge, and then apply it in a clinical setting. Spending time with a neurologist in an out patients' clinic showed me the breadth of the specialty. However, my work experience also illustrated the more challenging aspects of the medical profession. One patient suffering from Parkinson's disease became violent to the consultant and a family member, demonstrating one of the many difficulties doctors face on a daily basis.

Whilst shadowing a consultant on a work experience placement at Frenchay Hospital, I learnt an important medical principle. He was confronted by an alcoholic whose drinking had spiralled to such a level that she was now suffering from liver cirrhosis. The consultant spoke with real conviction and I realised an essential skill of this profession: not to label people with their symptoms, but see every patient as an individual and to address the entire person, in order to improve their quality of life. I believe this would give me great job satisfaction.

From my time in Romania I learned that the emotional needs of the children were equally as great as their medical ones. I feel strongly about both these needs and realise that as a doctor I must try to meet both. Using a foreign language to communicate reminded me of the importance of using language to express information, a skill which I have developed through my studies in French A level.

Outside the classroom I am vice captain of my school's netball first team. I am a very determined individual, so I relish the opportunity to play in matches against tough opposition, and enjoy playing for a team. It was a privilege to be elected Head Almoner by my peers, which is a leadership role in my school. I am responsible for all the charity work that happens throughout the school community. I thoroughly enjoy the challenge of reaching targets and inspiring the entire school to participate in fundraising events and have developed my organisation, communication and time-management skills as a consequence. All of the extra-curricular activities and paid work I have done has encouraged me to be flexible and communicate effectively with other team members.

Weekly volunteering as a leader for my local youth group and helping on a children's summer camp in the UK have helped me gain my v100Hour Voluntary Award. However, what I have learned about myself is much more valuable than the certificate. All I have experienced has strengthened my desire to pursue a medical career: I am fully aware this will pose intellectual and emotional tests, but I feel I am equal to the challenge. It would be an enormous privilege to serve people in this country by practising medicine.

Universities applied to:

- ➤ Birmingham: Offer
- ➤ Sheffield: Offer
- ➤ Imperial College: Rejected
- ➤ Cardiff: Interview + Rejected

Good points:

Good connection between emotional motivations for studying medicine and specific academic and medical interests. The student demonstrates exposure to medically and emotionally challenging situations in the course of their work experience. The student also draws good conclusions from the reflection on their experiences, thereby putting them into context and giving them value for the statement. The student demonstrates that they has been exposed to the more challenging sides of medicine and has been able to acquire relevant soft skills such as professionalism, communication skills and organisation skills.

Bad points:

Some minor weaknesses mainly related to the choice of language. Whilst it is clear why the student chooses formulations such as 'the injustice of this world' they seem somewhat cliché. This weakens the statement somewhat as it distracts from the many strong and good points.

Overall:

A qualitatively good and well-structured statement. The student provides insight into an interesting development including academia, work experience and a wide range of volunteering work. This presents the student as dedicated, disciplined, and empathetic; all qualities very beneficial and sought after in doctors.

NOTES

Statement 58

When wounds are nursed, when pains are reported, when a baby is born, a doctor is needed. Numerous professions are found in every society which enrich our lives and provide a network of support for all. However, the one that everyone needs at some point in their lives is the Medical profession. Without health, life can rarely be enjoyed to the full. Therefore I believe being a doctor is the profession that will best allow me to change as many lives as possible and try to give, to the largest number of people, the quality of life every person deserves.

I have always been the 'problem-solver'. Whether an argument or an accident had taken place, I was the one calming and resolving any issue I was faced with. I have been Voluntary Service representative for several years in school, and since I was voted School Prefect, I have been able to take on greater responsibility organising charity events. My ongoing voluntary work at a local nursing home has allowed me to meet exceptional people, carers and residents alike. Since I began volunteering, my fascination with personalities and the human mind has grown. This has led me to secure a psychiatry work experience placement to gain insight into the day to day life of a psychiatrist. On meeting a thirty-year old, clinically depressed man and seeing his fear of himself and his own condition, I realised that depression is one of the most misunderstood diseases. It is not simply someone who is very unhappy with their life, but an imbalance in certain brain chemicals that are likely to cause them to act irrationally in a way that even they are afraid of. Hearing 'I'm scared of doing it again' from a patient made me eager to learn how to relieve this pain and to understand the patient's thought process.

The vast range of challenges and variety within Medicine greatly appeals to me; the array of work experience I have gained, such as shadowing a consultant Geriatrician and a Neuroradiologist, has made this clear to me. I initiated a work experience placement in Egypt where I enjoyed a few days in theatre, watching major operations such as a Mastectomy and a Thyroidectomy. Surgery requires a skilled hand and impressive patience which I witnessed and admired greatly in the doctors I shadowed. The contrast between operating on the chest and operating on the eye, which I attended during an Ophthalmology placement, throws into sharp relief the countless options available within the Medical profession and the range of health services people seek. The precision applied to every short operation in Ophthalmology determines the quality of a patient's sight and consequently, the quality of their life.

Being a doctor is extremely demanding and, whilst a love for and perseverance in work is vital, it is important to maintain a balanced lifestyle of work and relaxation. For me, acting is what allows me to take time off from daily pressures, whilst still helping me develop valuable skills. I am working on LAMDA Grade 8, having completed Grade 6 to distinction level. My love for acting has caused me to 'enter' the mind of various characters, helping me to identify with the people around me. This process, which I have used in many plays, such as 'Romeo and Juliet' has become part of my personality and every day life. This has allowed me to understand and empathise with the problems of others in ways other people without my experiences may not be able to do. I'm also a member of the Solving Science club for younger students.

Whilst relaxing on a beach this summer, there was a sudden disturbance a short distance away from where I was. I discovered that an eighteen year old boy had drowned. Had a doctor been at hand, this boy's life could have been saved. The shock of watching a life end so easily reinforced my wish to be part of the fight against untimely death. I believe that the Medical profession is the one that will best qualify me to change and improve the lives of people.

Universities applied to:
➢ King's: Offer
➢ Birmingham: Offer
➢ Leicester: Offer
➢ Nottingham: Interview + Rejected

Good points:

The student demonstrates a good range of clinical experience as well as a good academic basis for the pursuit of a medical degree. Having been confronted with different contexts of medical care is a definite strength of any statement. The greater the experience of medical care, the better. The student also gives good insight into their character and how this makes them suitable for a career in medicine.

Bad points:

Whilst the student is right in describing the challenges of depression, the attempt to describe the underlying biochemical cause backfires as it is somewhat imprecise and faulty. Even biochemically speaking, depression is more complex than a mere imbalance of chemicals in the brain. Simplifying statements like this one weaken the context of the statement. The conclusion of the statement is poorly written. Whilst it is generally good to include personal experiences in the statement, they have more value further to the front of the statement where they can be put into context and be analysed for their value to the student's motivation to study medicine.

Overall:

An acceptable statement with some weaknesses and a good degree of underlying medical experiences. The student gives a good account of their priorities in medicine and demonstrates a good degree of suitability for a career in medicine. The statement could be significantly improved by stylistic changes, making the statement more concise as a whole.

NOTES

Statement 59

Medicine is a subject that first caught my interest after participating in the National Pathology Week at school several years ago. I was intrigued to learn about the many different aspects of Science that could come together and be used to make a diagnosis. This practical application of scientific knowledge appeals to me not only because it is extremely interesting, but because it is relevant and can have a huge impact on people's lives.

As part of a week's Medical Work Observation Programme at a local hospital, I saw several clinics of which I thought cardiology was the most fascinating as I was able to see patients with a huge variety of both extremely rare and common diseases and conditions. The placement helped me to understand how vital a multidisciplinary approach to medicine is and how patients should be actively involved in decisions in order to make an informed choice about their care and treatment. I realise each patient must be treated as an individual, taking into account both their medical history and family background. I organised a visit to a GP's surgery in Northern Ireland where I observed the unique relationship between doctors and their patients: doctors must be friendly yet professional; they must be reassuring as well as being able to listen to and communicate effectively with a variety of people. I have attended several Science in Health lectures at Cardiff University which helped to broaden my knowledge on a variety of topics, for example, 'Medicinal Chemistry' and 'Diet, Drugs and Drink.' The Medlink course and a Hands-on Workshop at the Royal Glamorgan Hospital gave me an insight into different specialities and careers in medicine as well as giving me a chance to talk to doctors and different members of hospital staff about their jobs.

I have spent two weeks at a high school for children with moderate to severe learning difficulties. I helped the pupils with several activities including reading and writing which could be challenging yet ultimately very rewarding. I saw the importance of adapting to the needs of different students as well as the importance of clear communication and patience. Several months ago, after work experience at the school, I became a volunteer at a local Youth Community Project, where some of the pupils are members. At this weekly after school group, the children learn to cook, play sports and make music among other activities. My role involves encouraging and offering the children support which requires me to establish a trusting relationship with them.

I have been Irish dancing for 11 years and I regularly compete in national competitions. Not only has Irish dancing taught me the values of hard work, perseverance and commitment, but also how to pick myself up when things do not go as planned. I play the flute and I am currently working towards Grade 8. As a member of the school orchestra and participant of the Gold Duke of Edinburgh Award, I appreciate that organisation and communication are invaluable skills to be able to work successfully as a team. In school, my roles as Senior Prefect and Treasurer of the Rotary Interact Group allow me to work with both teachers and pupils across all year groups to organise events and to develop our school community. After taking on these roles, I noticed how they have helped me to organise and manage my time more efficiently. Having a part time job at a newsagents shop has enabled me to become more involved in the local community and work with the public on a regular basis. I enjoy going to the gym and I attend a weekly boxercise class which helps me to cope with stress.

I appreciate that medicine is constantly changing but for me this is what makes it an appealing science to study and practise. Medicine is a demanding career that requires determination and commitment but with the right guidance and education, I believe I have the skills and temperament to become one of tomorrow's doctors.

Universities applied to:

➢ Birmingham: Offer
➢ Oxford: Rejected
➢ Cardiff: Interview + Rejected
➢ Belfast: Offer

Good points:

The student provides a well-balanced account of their experiences and how they influenced them in the run-up to this application. Drawing from a background of clinical and non-clinical experiences, the student demonstrates a good understanding of the fundamental connection between scientific basis with non-scientific soft skills (communication etc.) in medicine. This is important as both sides need to be present and understood in order to provide adequate and appropriate medical care. Realizing the challenges of clear communication and the relevance of ensuring understanding are central to the medical profession. The student presents themselves as a well-balanced individual with a varied set of interests, including important attributes such as compassion, discipline, and organisational skills. In addition, having acquired practical hands-on experiences is another strong point, setting this student apart from other applicants.

Bad points:

At times, the student remains somewhat superficial with their argumentation, description and reflection. The statement could be improved by better exploration of the experiences drawn from confrontation with challenging and stimulating situations witnessed during work experience attachments.

Overall:

Good and well-balanced statement that reflects well on the student's achievements and interests and also presents the student as a motivated and disciplined character well-suited for the study of medicine. Some minor weaknesses reduce the overall strength of the statement somewhat, but overall the content is of appropriate relevance.

NOTES

Statement 60

Medicine is more than a subject; it offers a unique opportunity to combine science with practical and personal skills which I believe that I would be well suited to. Since childhood, I have been exposed to a medical perspective on life from my parents but, despite their discouragement, my interest in studying medicine has remained. I have the right mix of abilities, enthusiasm, practical and academic skills and personality to succeed in this demanding and competitive career. I am inquisitive and excited by studying medicine. I have experience of working in teams which I know is paramount to ensure that all medical activities are centred on the patient. In my opinion a doctor also needs to know the limits of their knowledge and ability.

During lower school I was a peer mentor to a socially isolated girl. This was when I first realised the responsibilities of a person in a position of trust and how small actions or words can have a significant impact on someone's experience or wellbeing. Similar care with communication is also needed by doctors who rarely give patients a miracle cure, but treat symptoms and reassure to make a difference to a patient's life.

I am an adult member of the St John Ambulance where as well as doing duties as a first aider, I volunteer as a simulated casualty. I find the first aid duties very rewarding as I am not only helping the charity but providing treatment and comfort to the general public at the events we attend. I remain a corporal in the St John cadets involved in supervising younger cadets, teaching and helping them deal with minor casualties. Volunteering with St John has enhanced my teamwork skills both through the leadership courses I have attended and the real situations I have encountered on duty, when it is essential to remain calm under pressure. The casualty simulation provides an insight into what it is like to be an injured patient and has given me a heightened sense of empathy for the casualties that I treat when I am on duty as a first aider.

I worked hard and had fun when volunteering for a week at a holiday centre for disabled people in 2009. I experienced the ethical dilemma of preserving all the guests' autonomy, including those with disruptive behaviour, while maintaining a relaxing and pleasant environment for everyone. My work experience in an orthopaedic hospital gave me a taste of the work and demands on a range of clinical professionals. The best session was observing an outpatient clinic with a professor of spinal surgery as he took the time to explain each patient's condition to me so I better understood each consultation.

I have been awarded school prizes throughout secondary school for my sustained effort and results in a range of subjects. My AS courses have extended my scientific knowledge which has excited me to pursue a career in medicine. I am committed to studying medicine and this has been reinforced by my work experience and a Pre Med Course in London. The Pre Med course involved lectures and practical sessions, participation in which increased my understanding of what it is like to be a doctor and reaffirmed my ambition to study medicine. I also attended the highly competitive Oxford University UNIQ Summer School, undertaking an academic programme like that of a medical student. This week's course gave me a greater insight into what it is like to study medicine; I particularly enjoyed learning a concept in a lecture and then seeing it in action in a practical session.

I enjoy playing the flute in groups, requiring teamwork and quick thinking to adjust to everyone around me whilst maintaining my own part. I also find it a relaxing and social pastime. Another passion of mine is the adrenaline fuelled hobby of downhill skiing. I ski in France which also gives me an opportunity to practice my French. Commitment to my hobbies coupled with my academic ability and varied experience show my motivation and suitability to study medicine.

Universities applied to:
- Oxford: Offer
- Birmingham: Offer
- Keele: Interview + Rejected
- Sheffield: Rejected

Good points:
The student demonstrates a wide range of clinical and non-clinical experiences. Particularly relevant is the actual hands-on experience with the St. John's ambulance. Being able to put learned medical concepts into practice and keeping a clear head under pressure is an essential skill for a doctor, and being able to demonstrate experiences having challenged these abilities is a strong bonus. Having conducted volunteer work with the disabled demonstrates the student's comfort with the application of efficient communication skills in challenging situations. Finally, the student also demonstrates good academic performance and interests stretching over a variety of subjects and over different levels of complexity and relevance for medicine.

Bad points:
Some parts of the statement do not actually have any value for the overall quality of the statement and could, therefore, be omitted, making more space for the discussion of relevant material such as experiences made on the student's different work experience attachments, which would be significantly more supportive of the overall progress and therefore quality of the statement.

Overall:
Good statement, well-structured and well-formulated. Some minor weaknesses, but the overall message is to present the student as hardworking, dedicated, well-rounded and disciplined. This makes them likely to succeed in the pursuit of a medical degree.

NOTES

Statement 61

My ambition is to be a doctor. I know care can become invasive because as a child I was a patient for years at Great Ormond Street hospital suffering with Immune Deficiency and Pancreatic Insufficiency. I was referred to the Royal Free where I became a part of Andrew Wakefield's discredited research into the MMR vaccine. Reading Tony Hope's, "A Very Short Introduction to Medical Ethics" I was introduced to the concept of capacity. From experience I now understand the doctor's duty to provide treatment, even when a person is not yet able or no longer capable of giving informed consent.

I gained work experience at the Bridge Lane Group Practice where I sat in on General Practice and Practice Nurse consultations and attended District Nurse home visits. I learnt the sensitivities of GP reception work and was inspired and challenged through observing an Alcohol Detoxification Clinic. I learnt the importance of honesty and communication between doctors and patients and the importance of building trusting relationships. Whilst at Bridge Lane I witnessed the rewarding nature of General Practice alongside the need for an enquiring mind, high professional standards and the ability to handle pressure.

Volunteering at The Beeches Nursing Home over the last year provided me with the opportunity to meet people suffering from Vascular Dementia and Alzheimer's Disease. I learnt to treat the residents with respect and dignity. Listening to their vivid life stories I now appreciate that long-term memory survives after short-term memory has diminished.
I participate in a Patient Awareness Course visiting Epsom Hospital for two hours a week and attend monthly sessions on Patient Welfare. This placement provides me with patient contact. I genuinely enjoy both reading to the elderly and helping to feed them. My visits were appreciated by those who live alone or have no relatives living nearby. Communication with patients is sometimes difficult but I have learnt patience and persistence through my time at The Beeches Nursing Home.

Attending the "So, you want to do medicine?" course at the Royal National Orthopedic Hospital strengthened my ambition to be a doctor. I watched surgeons perform a knee reconstruction to restore a patient's ability to walk again. This helped me appreciate the risks of infection carried with any surgery.

Taking part in The Medsim Course at Nottingham University I enjoyed practical sessions; we attempted phlebotomy and catheterization on medical manikins and simulated an ppendectomy by keyhole surgery. This course showed the need to preserve patient dignity and minimize risk whilst performing delicate yet embarrassing personal procedures.
Captaining the school 2nd team for hockey last year taught me to listen to the opinions of others and use them to inform my decision-making. Through the season I have learned to play to the gifting rather than the weakness of particular team members. In a hospital the varied specialist skills of doctors, surgeons and the care team are used to promote the quality of life, to save life and to prolong life. Medical teamwork is necessary to achieve the goals of medicine once defined by Socrates - to provide cure sometimes, to relieve often and to comfort always.

My interest in human biology increased through my reading about increasing rates of Sickle Cell Anaemia in James Watson's book "DNA: the secret of life." I continue to develop my interest in medicine through reading the student BMJ magazine and by attending a variety of talks at the University College of London on many issues.

I am also certain that my own medical experiences will ensure that when I complete medical training I will not forget the frailty and humanity of each and every patient. I believe I possess the necessary skills - a keen mind, an empathetic heart and a determined soul necessary to become a doctor.

Universities applied to:
➤ Nottingham: Rejected
➤ Birmingham: Offer
➤ Plymouth: Rejected
➤ Newcastle: Interview + Rejected

Good points:
Well-structured statement with a good degree of experience of the challenges of medical care in a clinical as well as a community-based environment. The student's personal experience of medical care is very relevant in the context of the statement as they reflect important lessons with regards to patient-centeredness in care and the challenges of treating particularly vulnerable patients such as children or patients with dementia. The student's volunteering work in dementia care further supports the appreciation of the challenges arising from this. The student demonstrates a broad range of medical interests and a well-balanced approach to the acquiring of pre-university skills relevant for medicine.

Bad points:
The statement has some minor weaknesses, mainly associated with the relevance of some points provided in the statement, The paragraph addressing books and journals for example does not contribute to the strength of the statement as a whole as it does not provide any information about the student.

Overall:
Good statement with some minor weaknesses. Could be improved by reducing the amount of less relevant facts in favour of more detail about experiences unique to this student. Ultimately, it is these experiences that will set the student apart from other students and through this will contribute to understanding and appreciating the student as an individual.

NOTES

Statement 62

Most people know little about the daily function of our bodies. Every minute the body performs countless miraculous feats in order to keep us standing and my aim is to understand how it works. I am fascinated by the body, particularly at a cellular level, for it seems surreal to me that a plethora of chemical reactions can lead to something as simple as lifting an arm or something as complex as fighting off infection. There is so much variety in medicine, and I am attracted by the prospect of constantly learning and adapting to new techniques. I believe a career in medicine combines perfectly the academic and the practical, providing opportunities to study scientific processes and then to apply that knowledge with patients. I have always enjoyed solving problems, and what better problem to solve than that of a diagnosis?

I have subscribed to the 'student BMJ', 'New Scientist' and 'Chemistry World' and I enjoy reading up on the latest medical advances such as a recent article on the Placebo Effect. I was intrigued by the ethical debate surrounding this topic and by the power of the placebo, and shocked to hear that there have even been operations conducted under a placebo anaesthetic! To this date my favourite book is 'Parasite Rex' by Carl Zimmer. I was fascinated by this study of the bizarre world of parasites, so perfectly adapted to living off others. I am following with interest the possibility that parasites may hold the key to relieving the plague of allergies in the western world. Studying immunology in A level biology has furthered my understanding of how the body reacts to foreign invaders.

Music means a lot to me and singing has given me the ability to perform under pressure and to communicate to different audiences. I find fly-fishing therapeutic, including the process of crafting my own flies. Gold DofE helped develop my time management skills and ability to cope in difficult situations. During CCF I learnt to combine leadership and the ability to work in a team. As prefect and Deputy School Captain I am developing my organisational and communication skills, particularly with younger pupils who come to me for help with problems.

When observing my first open surgery, 2 things became clear: I was capable of viewing a graphic situation with clarity of mind, and I would not faint at the sight of blood. Having seen surgeries in both Egypt and Britain I was struck by the similarities. It was interesting to see how the operating team cooperated, the anaesthetist starting the process followed by orthopaedic surgeons who seemed very grateful for the nurses' help throughout as they removed bones and various metal fixtures. Shadowing a radiologist was enlightening and I was surprised by the variety of activities undertaken, from imaging to interventional surgery. But it was in the operating theatres of Cairo's National hospital that I learnt the most. This was a stimulating experience and I coped well with being flung into major surgeries with little comprehension, at first, of what was going on.

When I first started voluntary work at my local care home I did not know what to expect but I soon found myself getting to know the residents and becoming involved in their activities. As a volunteer I was not legally able to help move residents, and when the carers were not around I helped those who were uncomfortable, not by moving them, but by calming them down by talking to them and reassuring them that help would be along soon. This was a rewarding experience and it felt good to know that I had made a difference, be it a smile when singing or reading to them, or a 'thank you' from someone who could not eat without assistance. It is moments like these that affirm my desire to become a doctor.

I hope to achieve fulfilment in life, and it is my belief that in pursuing a career in medicine I can achieve this.

Universities applied to:
- Cardiff: Offer
- Birmingham: Offer
- Oxford: Rejected
- Newcastle: Interview + Rejected

Good points:
The student gives an interesting account of their motivations for studying medicine as well as their interests in the field. The student also demonstrates good clinical exposure to the everyday business of medicine. Drawing on experiences from both the UK and Egypt adds a level of complexity which reflects positively on the student. A range of non-academic extra-curricular academics provided the student with the opportunity to fine-tune his communication and organisation skills, both very relevant for the pursuit of a degree in medicine. The student also provides some insight into personal interests in specific medical areas such as parasitology.

Bad points:
The introduction to the statement is too much prose and intrinsically contradictory. The student describes all processes in the body as miraculous and complex and then claims that the processes underlying the movement of a limb were simple. This contradiction distracts from the actual content and weakens the impression of the student's understanding and argumentative abilities. The writing style throughout the entirety of the statement is somewhat inaccurate and distracting. In addition, the statement is somewhat short of practical experiences, causing exposure to the challenges of patient care.

Overall:
Average statement that is reduced in strength due to the choice of language and writing style. The statement could be further improved by more in-depth discussions of the student's clinical experiences.

NOTES

Statement 63

There is remarkable brilliance in simple solutions. It appears that the use of checklists in surgery may prevent almost half of deaths according to a study by Dr Atul Gawande, a physician whose eloquence and insight into the field of medicine I find extremely stimulating. He wrote of how a surgical team overlooked a classic cause of asystole because too many other variables were at hand. Emphasising the often forgotten importance of teamwork and humility, this is a complication that checklists could have prevented. The challenge of combining ever-expanding academic knowledge with competence in an effort to heal the intriguing elegance that is the human
body inspires me to pursue a career in medicine.

Equipped with curiosity and an ambition to learn, I organised an internship at the Agaplesion Markus hospital Frankfurt's pathology unit to explore the laboratory aspect of medicine. I found examinations of biopsies under a microscope wonderful, yet it was the macroscopic analysis of an aborted foetus that rendered me speechless. This gripping experience triggered my interest in the ethical conflicts medicine involves, such as patient autonomy and super specialisation. I soon emailed the hospital to arrange another internship, where I spent time in different departments to learn how they interact. With the internists I realised how crucial the skill to quickly analyse and adapt to a situation is, because a station can go from calm to chaotic in minutes. Helping to clean a frightened patient with bowel and urinary incontinence required composure and highlighted the lack of stereotypical glamour in medicine. I enjoyed my time in the surgical departments the most; I learned how to take patients' blood, make surgical stitches and wash myself meticulously before a surgery - everyday activities that must be carried out to perfection. As I felt my enthusiasm and admiration for medicine grow I often stayed beyond the time planned to watch yet another appendectomy or PEG placement. My physical endurance was put to the test when I got to join physicians by the operating table to hold heavy muscle back with retractors. Besides such exhilarating experiences, I also witnessed the poignant moment of surgeons discovering a fairly large inoperable tumour. Only then did I truly appreciate how emotionally resilient doctors must be.

My four IB higher level (HL) classes have taught me to deal with stress and frustration, and that hard work reaps its own rewards. As my Biology and Chemistry studies brought to light how diseases such as HIV develop in the body and how they can be treated, I decided to take the two at HL. Missing physics from my IB studies, I gain basic understanding of the subject through private reading. Besides improving my ability to learn independently, an intriguing book about radiology led me to write my extended essay about radiation oncology. Via an internship at the Hospital Nordwest Frankfurt I compiled data of 308 mamma carcinoma patients. This not only improved my understanding of the bureaucratic constraints placed upon doctors, but also increased my abilities to work efficiently. Meeting frustrated patients with only palliative care left emphasised how indispensable compassion and interpersonal skills are.

Even pushing a patient's bed through the corridors of the Agaplesion Markus hospital helped confirm how much I would value a career in medicine. From being able to help individuals past the second level of Maslow's Pyramid of Needs, to constantly meeting new challenges, the prospect of becoming a part of the unpredictable world of medicine thrills me. The competitiveness of the field has only motivated me to work harder. I believe my devotion, analytical skills and appreciation of detail will help me further develop abilities to achieve my aspirations to become a good physician. I am certain the ten thousand hours that lie ahead will be worth every minute.

Universities applied to:

- ➢ University College: Offer
- ➢ Queen Mary: Offer
- ➢ King's: Offer
- ➢ Aberdeen: Offer

Good points:

The student demonstrates a well-rounded level of hands-on experience of medical care that will have provided them with a good exposure to the challenges as well as the complexities of medicine. Having some hands-on surgical experience will help set the student apart from other applicants and also supports the general impression of a well-rounded experience. Having had the opportunity to develop research skills and gaining insight into scientific methods is a valuable opportunity that again contributes to differentiating this student from other applicants that do not have this type of experience. It is all about standing out and leaving a positive impression.

Bad points:

The statement is written too informally, almost prose-like, at least in the beginning. This complicated form of expression distracts from the actual content and thereby reduces overall power of the individual aspects of the statement. In general, the complexity in which the content is presented makes it difficult to follow the flow of the statement.

Overall:

This statement demonstrates how important it is to keep the goal of the personal statement in mind. A concise representation of the individual and their experiences benefits greatly from a clear and simple presentation. Too complex a presentation only distracts. Other than that, the statement is relevant and provides good insight into the student's character, representing them as interested and hardworking.

NOTES

Statement 64

My attraction to medicine emerged through the valuable experiences I gained whilst working with patients suffering with Dementia. The satisfaction I attained from attempting to bring back their old memories combined with the happiness the residents felt while I was speaking to them was fundamental to my desire to study medicine. The holistic approach required to deal with patients, the caring attitude needed to persevere through medicine and my inherent personality to serve others have persuaded me to pursue this career.

During my work placement in the Urology department at Heartlands Hospital I gained an understanding of the medical problems faced by elderly patients and the emotional stress relating to their condition. I acknowledged the varying nature of illnesses that doctors are required to diagnose and treat in their clinical work, which makes the profession so rewarding. They were frequently called upon to respond to distressing and challenging new situations, which I found appealing. Shadowing a Paediatrician at Russells Hall Hospital, I understood the effectiveness of the different methods of communication used by the Consultant to deal with children and their parents. I was surprised by the level of detailed information given to the children about their surgery and their approval of it, contrary to my belief. These experiences gave me an insight into a secondary care environment in the NHS. In a contrasting country, I was able to appreciate how patients in India had to endure overcrowding and poor conditions compared to modern facilities in the UK, through a work experience I gained with a Gastroenterologist in Chennai. Having spent a week in Cardiovascular Research Labs I learned the process of testing new drugs through various phases of clinical testing when I observed surgery on a rat's brain. Electrodes were inserted into the visual cortex to test the efficiency of a cortical implant. I learned about the challenges in their daily tasks faced by patients with Dementia while volunteering at Limes Care Home once a week for the past eight months. Working with old people requires a lot of determination, patience and ability to converse enthusiastically, which are skills I am developing. Volunteering at a GP surgery every week for six months, gave me knowledge of a primary care setting. Whilst working in the reception I became aware of processes used for data protection and patient confidentiality.

As a senior mentor I have guided a Year Seven pupil throughout the year to help him with his homework, social interactions and to cope with the transition into secondary school. In this role I reflected on the communication skills that I had learnt while shadowing the Paediatrician to ensure I was approachable and supportive. I am currently undertaking an Extended Project Qualification on future uses of stem cells and their related ethical concerns. I have completed fifty hours of research and read books such as "Stem Cells and the Future of Regenerative Medicine" and "A Very Short Introduction to Medical Ethics". Through this, I have discovered that we are close to bridging gaps in organ transplant waiting lists as well as the ability to combat neurological disorders. Playing badminton regularly at a Performance Centre, funded by Badminton England, allows me to play competitively. I represent my school's Cricket and Hockey teams, which help me stay physically fit and focused. I was able to test my endurance when I completed expeditions for Duke of Edinburgh Bronze, Silver and Gold Awards. As the leader of my Envision group at school I organised a sponsored run to fundraise for The Children's Cancer Centre Appeal. Through teamwork, we raised GBP300.

The insights I have gained from my experiences have made me determined to face and overcome the challenges involved in medicine, to study in a field that will continually fascinate me and contribute to a career where I can be at the forefront of aiding others.

Universities applied to:
- Birmingham: Offer
- Cardiff: Interview + Rejected
- Hull York: Interview + Rejected
- Nottingham: Rejected

Good points:

A clear and well-structured statement that guides the reader from clinical work experience to non-clinical academics and social experiences, providing relevant lessons for a pursuit of a career in medicine. The student's ability to draw on experiences made both in this country as well as in India and the resulting reflections on the challenges resulting from differences in funding and general structure of healthcare provision provides a unique and interesting perspective. Experiencing the range of clinical exposure this student has is most certainly beneficial as it provides a well-differentiated impression of the challenges and complexities of medical care as well as the breadth of patient presentations. Non-medical engagement gives good insight into the relevance of soft skills such as communication and organisation as well as the adjustment of information to the need and the ability of the individual.

Bad points:

It would be interesting to read more about the student's experience of community-based care in contrast to hospital based care as both places offer different challenges for the healthcare professional in regards to patient interaction and treatment priorities. Being in the position of having experienced both, the student should probably be able to provide good insight into these differences.

Overall:

A good statement that presents the student as a well-rounded and disciplined student that has a great interest in the workings of the human body and the practice of medicine. Having been exposed to a variety of interesting stimuli, the student is in a good position to be able to comment on many of the challenges and exciting features of a career in medicine. The statement also offers ample information to discuss during an interview.

NOTES

Statement 65

A profession which strives to improve lives is one I would thrive in. Forming strong relationships with peers and working as part of a team to overcome health problems in the local community, is a patient orientated environment I want to be a part of. A doctor told me it is important to try and put oneself in the shoes of the patient. Reading a first-hand account of schizophrenia, I have recognised how difficult, yet effective this would prove to be. The effects diseases have on the physiology of the body fascinate me. I like to know what makes a disease unique; not just how it affects the body, but also how it affects the whole individual.

I read Student BMJ articles that grip me, from the inspiring work of doctors practising in rural India with minimum provisions but maximum risk, to the controversy concerning over-diagnosis in breast cancer screening. I have great interest in extending my knowledge, to gain full appreciation of the science behind life and the challenges confronting humanity. I designed my EPQ question 'is enough work being done to improve health in developing countries?' to allow me to research into some of the diseases crippling developing countries such as Rheumatic Fever and HIV. I discovered the causes, the behaviour, the treatment and then proposed ideas to prevent these diseases. The commitment to lifelong learning, in order to provide updated care, has been highlighted to me by my local GP. The fine line between safeguarding vulnerable patients and confidentiality was made explicit. I have witnessed the care of the elderly in both a care home situation and on an elderly ward. Elderly patients can be very confused therefore they need reassuring, they need company and they need to feel they are important. I have observed doctors do this by going through every step of a problem and solution with a patient, allowing them to feel much more settled and secure. On my work experience in a hospital I witnessed the significance of teamwork. Doctors and nurses form a vital team, all contributing consistent care and knowledge for the wellbeing of patients. The leadership of doctors is a great contributor to this and, as all team members are treated with equal respect, I saw how the expertise of a team can be harnessed. Initially when volunteering at The Stroke Association communication group I felt uncomfortable. Following training to learn about the consequences of the different types of strokes and strategies to aid conversation, I felt very confident speaking one-to-one with a stroke survivor and I realised the benefits of greater understanding. I met some very inspiring personalities too; one man made a particular impression on me with his determination to recover fully.

Through volunteering at my local youth centre and supporting more challenging students at my school, I have gained confidence interacting with an unfamiliar social group. I have played football since the age of four, captaining numerous teams. I am the leader of a sixth form site team, which entails managing my peers and meeting with senior staff. I have organised a charity event for CLIC Sargent and the Charlotte Blackman Memorial Fund at my school and I ensured decisions were made democratically. Part time jobs in retail and catering have furthered my communication and teamwork skills, as I have worked with varying age ranges from diverse backgrounds. I took part in a seven month long Engineering Education Scheme working as part of a team to solve a real life problem facing Rolls-Royce. After we finalised our project, we presented it to a panel of industry experts and responded to questions concerning our project - achieving the Gold Crest Award.

As a doctor and a medical student each day will present many challenges. I am not one to shy away from a challenge; I relish the opportunity to undertake something that will stretch and improve me as an individual and look forward to a rewarding career in which learning is endless.

Universities applied to:
- Birmingham: Offer
- Leeds: Interview + Rejected
- Newcastle: Rejected
- Sheffield: Rejected

Good points:
The student provides a well-reflected and diverse account of their experiences in medical as well as academic and non-academic fields. The student demonstrates a variety of skills acquired during their work experience attachment, spanning important areas of clinical medicine such as confidentiality, patient centred care as well as the challenges of appropriate communication with patients where communication might be challenging due to changes in mental capacity. The student also provides insight into non-medical volunteering works that allowed them to further hone their communication skills and also acquire teaching skills, both of which are very relevant in a medical career.

Bad points:
The main weakness of the statement lies in the inclusion of information that carries little weight in making the student stand out in competition with other applicants. One example of this is the inclusion of the student's interest in the BMJ. Whilst it is great that the student demonstrates an interest in medical literature, this is almost expected of future medical students and does not provide any differentiating features in comparison to others nor does it provide additional information about the student as an individual. Additionally, the passage addressing the engineering education scheme with Rolls-Royce could provide further significant and interesting information if it was developed to greater detail.

Overall:
Good statement with some minor weaknesses but many strong points. The student reflects well on their work experience and volunteering and manages to draw relevant and appropriate conclusions from their experiences and exposure. The statement could be further improved by accounts of practical hands-on experiences in medicine.

NOTES

Statement 66

My desire to study medicine has grown from a profound interest in Science that I have had for many years, and the responsibility I feel to employ this passion to work for people.

Whilst I know I have relatively little medical knowledge or experience, I have found myself fully engaged and enthusiastic with what I have explored. Medicine is an extremely wide ranging and incredible topic, and the area of genetics and genetic disease are especially interesting to me. The fast pace of development in this area is truly incredible; how through recent research potential risks to patients can be detected before they occur, or even before birth is fascinating. I am also interested in the moral debate surrounding genetics. I personally am in favour of genetic medicine. Advancement of medicine and the improvement of medical treatments are I believe two of the truly great things any person or organisation can achieve. Genetics opens wide new areas to explore, and this opportunity should be embraced. I would relish the opportunity to convince others that the curing and prevention of diseases, and so the prevention of death and the relief of suffering by modern methods must be a good thing.

Having spent a week in a GP's surgery and four months weekly volunteering at Didcot Hospital, it is clear to see how in all varied environments the doctor must be focused and respectful; I saw that although some people were tired, in pain or stressed, each patient values their time with their doctor and so it is important that the patient is at the heart of all medicine. The variety of medicine I witnessed during my work experience also astounded me. It showed that doctors must have a broad understanding of modern medicine, and this huge learning prospect excites me. Much of my volunteering work involved talking to patients and I found myself becoming ever more confident, realising that whilst all people are unique in some way, I could adapt to each situation. Outside of my academic life I participate in a wide range of extra-curricular activities: I play and referee football, where refereeing in particular puts me under pressure since I have to communicate with and control a large group of people. I actually enjoy dealing with high emotion situations, where conflict needs to be resolved. Highly emotional situations occur frequently in the medical environment; during my work experience I witnessed both ends of the spectrum: a mother crying with a mixed joy as her baby received vaccines, and a man in palliative care. Through dealing with emotion outside of a clinical environment I believe I am better prepared to deal with it in a medical situation. Being Head Boy of St. Birinus School, I have a wide range of responsibilities. In addition to representing the school and sixth form, I am part of an anti-bullying project led by Oxfordshire county council focusing on re-writing the county's current anti-bullying policy, and making it more targeted and accessible. I am also a high ranking Flight Sergeant in the ATC where I have a senior duty to teach and lead new cadets, as well as to provide help to Cadet Officers and staff. Also in the ATC I am the Mayor's Cadet meaning I spend time with the Town Mayor supporting him on civic duties. He uses me as a port of call for communication with the ATC, and relies on me to help him organise and run charity events. Having all these roles means I often have to work under pressure or with high workloads, but I thrive on being able to get actively involved in new areas, and am always eager. I find it incredibly difficult to remain idle.

My experiences in and out of school have increased my passion for Medicine, and given me transferrable skills that I will continue to utilise. I am really eager to study medicine at University, and to apply it later on in my career. I would be a dedicated and hard working student, and am looking forward to adding to the university community and showing a real enthusiasm for medicine.

Universities applied to:
- ➢ Oxford: Offer
- ➢ Nottingham: Offer
- ➢ Birmingham: Offer
- ➢ Bristol: Rejected

Good points:

Very honest and well-reflected statement. Being aware of the limitations of one's experiences is a definite strength demonstrating a reflective and evaluating nature, both very relevant traits for medicine. The student also gives good insight into personal interests and positions in regards to certain types of treatment. Being confident enough to take a position and argue it, though be it briefly, demonstrates confidence in one's reflective abilities. The student also provides evidence of good clinical exposure, allowing him to experience medical care in a different setting, appreciating the challenges that come with the different characteristics and priorities of medical care. Giving an account of his non-medical and non-academic experiences completes the picture of a well-rounded and interested individual.

Bad points:

Not per se a bad point, more a risk depending on the examiner reading the statement. Taking a stand in regards to the value of a certain type of treatment can usually go either way, good or bad. In this case, the student argues in favour of genetic treatments, followed by a brief explanation of his thought process. This carries some risk as there will never be enough space to fully argue issues such as the value of certain treatments, particularly when they are somewhat controversial.

Overall:

Good statement with no real weak points and many strong points. The only negative point to be aware of lies in the risk taken in regards to taking a specific position in the context of a controversial topic. This carries the risk of being misinterpreted by an examiner. It can also provide an excellent basis for discussion in an interview or be the point that sets the student apart from other applicants, so it is a bit of a gamble.

NOTES

Statement 67

A surgeon once posed me an intriguing question. He said he had once been compared to a knight in shining armour. He then asked me to work you out why in a battlefield if you had your stomach opened you would die whereas the equivalent in an operating theatre is safe. I realised that the safety of modern surgery lies with the design of the equipment and procedures. The most fascinating being the scalpel that utilises high voltage to sear the flesh and high frequency to prevent the cells discharging. This showed me that medicine is the matrimony of science and art; the blend of technology and physical skill. This revelation has fuelled my passion for medicine, and more specifically the complex science behind it.

I was privileged to witness this at two hospitals, a GP surgery and a hospital in Ghana. During this I witnessed multiple surgeries, the destructive effect of smoking and a variety of uncommon conditions in a tropical country.

I am also fascinated by the science behind medicine and human biology, especially research into future treatments. I find the complexity of the central nervous system and the immune response awe inspiring and believe they are vital in the production of new drugs. I have pursued this interest further than the syllabus, producing a research paper with friends entitled 'The Possible Uses of Nanotechnology in the Treatment of Brain Tumours', for which we were awarded a merit grade.

In my free time I volunteer at a care home and with St John Ambulance. In the care home I gained an insight into other aspects of the healthcare system and the effect of conditions such as dementia. With St John Ambulance I helped provide first aid at both local and national events, including the London Marathon.

I am also a keen athlete, completing in numerous triathlons and road races. I play guitar, drums, piano, sing and will soon be taking my Grade 5 in clarinet. I play in three different choirs and performed in my school's production of Bugsy Malone.

In addition to this I pursue other areas of science. I was Project Manager of my school's UKAY Roc Challenge team, reaching the national finals. This helped me refine my time management skills. I also represented the school's STEM club at The London Big Bang Festival and have volunteered at several of my school's family fun days.

Universities applied to:

➢ Cambridge: Offer
➢ Imperial College: Interview + Rejected
➢ Nottingham: Interview + Rejected
➢ Southampton: Rejected

Good points:

The student provides evidence of diverse clinical experience in a variety of environments and gives further information about experiences of non-medical and non-academic nature. The student also has gathered some hands-on experience volunteering for the St. John's Ambulance.

Bad points:

Poor writing style. The style of the statement is confusing and it is difficult to read as some sentences are very complex. This is unfortunate as it considerably reduces the amount of information transported by the statement. The experiences the student presents in the statement are generally underdeveloped in regards to their relevance for medical practice and the reflection of the student on their experiences. It is difficult to judge what impact the experiences had on the student and how they contributed to the student's development towards being a more suitable medical student. Generally, the statement remains very superficial and does not provide much information about the student at all. Combining poor writing style with little content makes for a sub-optimal statement.

Overall:

A bad statement. It is poorly written and delivers very little information about the student. The information that is delivered is superficial and serves little purpose to reflect positively on the student and on their experiences with medicine.

NOTES

Statement 68

Practising medicine requires not just an aptitude for science and a thirst for knowledge, but also the ability to communicate clearly with patients in order to deliver the best possible care. This has become evident as I have observed various aspects of the profession within different healthcare environments. For ten months now I have volunteered at the James Paget Hospital as a mealtime assistant, helping to feed patients incapacitated, for example, by strokes or falls. My role also involves recording how much of each meal the patient eats. I have learnt how essential good nutrition is to ensure a quick recovery, and the importance of rigorous monitoring and reviewing of patients to ensure the best outcome. While undertaking work experience at the Norfolk and Norwich Hospital, I was impressed by the empathy and compassion consultants showed toward patients, especially when all possible treatment had been exhausted and the priority was to allow comfort and dignity in the patient's final days. This notion was reiterated at Broadlands, a local residential home where I volunteer each Sunday for a few hours, as I witnessed the gentle, attentive manner with which the carers treated Stella, a resident suffering from Alzheimer's disease. Spending time conversing with, reading to and going for walks with Stella has given me a greater understanding of this debilitating illness and the effects it has on both the sufferer and those close to them. A news article linking good hygiene to higher dementia incidence rates inspired me to explore this "hygiene hypothesis" further and produce a research project on the matter.

At Westwood Surgery, a local general practice, I saw the importance of personal, one-to-one GP consultations and how therapeutic they can be, and observed the various approaches used to communicate with patients of different ages and from different backgrounds. During one consultation the doctor noticed that the patient's diabetic mother had become hypoglycaemic and promptly took steps to increase her blood sugar levels. I realised from this that a GP's role extends beyond the clinic and encompasses far more than I had imagined. Digitalising patient records and discussing the merit of summary care records with the locum provided an insight into the future of consultations as technology advances. Similarly, I found it fascinating to learn about the field of proteomics and its potential to revolutionise GP diagnoses in Dr David B Agus' book, 'The End of Illness'.

This summer I spent two weeks in Morogoro, Tanzania, shadowing doctors at a private health clinic and the larger regional hospital. After discussing the different human enterotypes with a surgeon following an ileocaecal resection to treat Crohn's disease, I was intrigued to discover more about them and how they may affect the body's reaction to drugs. The trip also highlighted some stark contrasts between healthcare there and in the UK, most notably the reduced reliance upon technology in Tanzania. The harsh realities I saw during ward rounds were a reminder of how fortunate we are to have the NHS, despite its shortcomings, as I saw how one man could not afford the cost of hip surgery so was given traction, an alternative treatment.

As Treasurer of the school's charity committee I help to organise fundraising events and manage finances, while my role as School Prefect involves acting as an ambassador for the school and maintaining discipline. I am a keen swimmer and have competed at national level for four years, also helping to teach five year olds how to swim in my spare time.

I am under no illusion that practising medicine will be an easy task - speaking with both junior and senior doctors I have realised that the journey will be long and fraught with difficult decisions, demanding hours and testing circumstances. Nevertheless I believe that I possess the tenacity and motivation to overcome these challenges, and it is a journey upon which I cannot wait to embark.

Universities applied to:
➤ Oxford: Offer
➤ Birmingham: Offer
➤ Bart's: Offer
➤ Newcastle: Interview + Rejected

Good points:

The student demonstrates good reflections on the subject of studying medicine and also seems to be well aware of the challenges that come with such a demanding course. They demonstrates a variety of medical work experience placements, all of which have given them the opportunity to experience healthcare from a first-hand perspective and in different environments. Being able to contrast medical practice in the UK with that in other countries is a benefit, allowing for an appreciation of the challenges that arise in medical care when resources are limited. Experiencing both primary and secondary care will give good insight into the importance of clear communication and patient-centred care. The student has also had the opportunity to hone organisational skills in additional roles, adding to further qualities to the impression of a well-balanced, hardworking and disciplined student.

Bad points:

The statement is somewhat short of information about the student's academic interests. It would be interesting to know if the student has any particular medical interests as this offers itself very well for interview conversations.

Overall:

A strong and well-structured statement that gives good insight into the student's character, providing an image of a well-balanced and outstanding student. The experiences listed in the statement are largely well-reflected and all serve a specific purpose in the context of the statement.

NOTES

Statement 69

It is impossible to consider the human body without being moved by its intricate components and complexities. My love of science developed during my secondary education, and I was led towards the field of medicine because I have a passionate desire to aid and interact with people. As I applied myself to some serious research into what a career in medicine would entail, I became more convinced that this would be the correct option for me. I enjoy challenges, particularly when working towards a rewarding objective, and although medicine is a tough career choice I am sure that it will be an enormously gratifying one.

To gain further insight into my potential career, I shadowed a Medical school student at an Oxford hospital in April 2008. This gave me the opportunity to attend lectures and clinical teaching sessions on the Neurology Ward. It was satisfying to see some aspects of the basic foundations of my AS Biology course applied to more complex specialties. In addition, I participated in a work shadowing week at James Cook University Hospital, Middlesbrough in August 2008. I spent the most time with the Orthopaedic and Paediatric teams and was privileged to observe various clinics as well as Physiotherapy. I came to appreciate the importance of other Medical staff such as nurses; without good teamwork and communication skills, there would have been ineffective patient care. The highlight of the week was the opportunity to shadow an A&E doctor which was unpredictable and very exciting. I witnessed the management of a seizure in an alcoholic patient, and the repair of a traumatic amputation of the thumb in another. I also gained a greater understanding of the pressures that doctors face and the need to be empathic towards patients. I have since spent a week in my local GP surgery, which exposed me to another facet of the Medical profession. These experiences have been enjoyable but more importantly have confirmed that medicine is my chosen career.

My A Level choices reflect my aspiration for a Medical career. I am studying Biology, Chemistry, Mathematics and History because I believe there are aspects of each that will furnish me with the basic knowledge required to embark on a Medical career. I especially enjoyed studying the Health and Disease module in Biology because I have a genuine interest in finding out about the pathogenesis of disease. The logic of Mathematics, with the requirement for problem-solving has also been invaluable in helping me to develop a scientific mind. The three sciences are brought to balance with the study of History, where analysis and evaluation skills form the substance of the discipline.

Outside the academic environment, I have several other interests and commitments. I am a School Prefect, which involves organising groups of students to carry out activities. This has helped me develop time management and leadership skills, which entail motivation and providing good examples for others. I also enjoy participating in sports such as badminton, athletics and netball for which I have been on school teams. I have undertaken a few paid jobs at the weekends including babysitting and retail work in a shop. I also briefly worked in a local home for the elderly which gave me an opportunity to learn more about the issues that are important to them, which is imperative for the practice of Medicine in our ever-ageing society. In addition, I volunteer as a Shop Assistant at a charity shop for a few hours every fortnight. I have had a part in organising fundraising activities at school for various important causes such as cancer research. Finally, I am an avid reader and entertainment enthusiast and I indulge myself in many genres, eras and cultures of film, music and literature.

I look forward to the academic and social challenge of studying medicine at university with great enthusiasm, positive that the rewards will be worth the challenge.

Universities applied to:
➢ Birmingham: Offer
➢ Newcastle: Interview + Rejected
➢ University College: Rejected
➢ Imperial College: Offer

Good points:
The student provides a well-balanced insight into their motivations for pursuing a career in medicine. This is important as the clearer the reasoning, the more understandable it is for the examiner. The student also provides evidence of various clinical experiences, all of which contribute to his representation as a well-rounded and well-suited candidate for pursuing a degree in medicine. The student reflects well on his work experience drawing conclusions related to the importance of communication, academic ability as well as organisational skills and approachability. All of these are relevant and important skills as a doctor.

Bad points:
The paragraph related to the student's choice of their A-levels is unnecessary since the student already explained earlier in the statement that they has an interest in the scientific side of medical practice, sparked by the science subjects at school. Additionally, the choice of A-levels presented here is basically going to be the same for all medical students due to the university requirements of 3 science topics.

Overall:
Good statement with a wealth of different work experiences and a good reflection on the experiences during the attachments. This is probably one of the most pivotal points as this is the area where individual talents and preferences are the most likely to reflect and make a difference between individual students.

NOTES

Statement 70

Despite the glamorous portrayals of the medical career in numerous television dramas, it was a rather less flattering depiction of life as a doctor which first sparked my interest in studying medicine. The world portrayed by Max Pemberton in "Trust me I'm a Junior Doctor" was appealing due to the challenges it presented. I found myself drawn to the complexities of this career and my academic curiosity was roused by the chance to learn about the intricacies of the human body.

I have undertaken two hospital placements and spent a day at a GP surgery. Both hospital placements provided me with contrasting but equally valuable insights into life as a doctor. My week at Epsom Hospital was made particularly interesting due to the unexpected absence of the consultant endocrinologist I had been allocated. Rather than spending time in the library as suggested, I went and found alternative clinics that were happy to let me observe. By the end of the week I had spent time in obstetrics, haemato-oncology, paediatrics and on a care of the elderly ward amongst others. At Great Ormond Street, I shadowed a world leading specialist in paediatric electromyography. I look forward to studying the brain in more detail during my A2 biology course this year which will enable me to better understand the procedures I witnessed. The most valuable aspect of the experience was learning to appreciate the importance of the triangular relationship between doctor, parent and child. The case of Ashya King is a current illustration of the problems that can arise when parents' opinions clash with those of doctors. Along with 3 science subjects, I chose to continue studying French at A level as I believe it has taught me invaluable communication skills. Whilst at GOSH I was impressed by the consultant's ability to talk to his patients in both French and Arabic, and noted how this helped to put them at ease. These placements, along with a five day Medlink course, cemented my desire to study medicine. For the past year, I have been a weekly volunteer at Riding for the Disabled (RDA). This commitment has enabled me to interact with people with disabilities including Chronic Fatigue and Cerebral Palsy with right-sided Hemiplegia. I feel lucky to be a part of the team helping them to achieve something they had not previously thought possible, and am fascinated by how the movement of the horse's body relaxes the muscles of the more physically disabled clients.

I have always enjoyed the sciences and have received gold awards in Chemistry and Maths challenges, and been nominated for the SCI Young Chemist 2014. I read "Bad Pharma" by Ben Goldacre with fascination; the intrinsic flaws within the clinical trials that Goldacre describes struck me as having potentially disastrous impacts on our healthcare system, and I was interested to see this listed as one of the five key issues facing the NHS in the latest edition of the student BMJ. Working with sufferers of Chronic Fatigue syndrome at RDA and an article I read investigating the biological causes of Gulf War syndrome prompted me to give a talk to the school's Medical Ethics Discussion Society exploring the social stigma surrounding these diseases. Through this I learnt the importance of using language appropriate to the audience in order to ensure the message is well understood.

I am aiming to complete my Duke of Edinburgh's gold award, alongside my roles as a School Prefect and Deputy Head Girl. Through this I have learnt the importance of teamwork, managing my time and prioritising. I enjoy horse-riding and I continue to take part in British Eventing competitions throughout the school year. I am a member of the school equestrian team, and Captain of the 1stVII netball team.

To me, medicine presents the perfect opportunity for a challenging but immensely rewarding career and I am excited by the prospect of joining a profession in which the capacity for learning and applying knowledge is constantly expanding.

Universities applied to:
- Liverpool: Rejected
- Birmingham: Offer
- Nottingham: Offer
- Oxford: Offer

Good points:
Realistic approach to the medical profession. This is a strong point as being aware of the challenges and the very nature of the profession makes it less likely for the student to become disillusioned and lose motivation. The student also demonstrates good clinical work experience stretching over primary and secondary care, taking into account the subtle differences in care provision between the two. Being able to work in Great Ormond Street is a great experience, as working with children is always a challenging yet rewarding experience allowing for good reflections on communication challenges and traits that make for good doctors. Appreciating the role of parents in the environment of paediatrics further underlines the impression of the student as a well-rounded and alert individual.

Bad points:
The only minor weakness of the statement is the somewhat limited discussion of pharmacological research in response to having read 'bad pharma'. It is important to realise that this only represents one perspective of many and taking sides can back fire.

Overall:
Excellent statement with many strong points and a minor weakness that in this case has little impact on the overall quality of the statement. There is a very fine line between taking a specific position and reflecting on an issue of significant relevance. It is important to be aware of the challenges that come with taking a side, especially in controversial matters.

NOTES

Statement 71

Witnessing a patient on the verge of death wake up depicted how effective healthcare brings joy and empowers people. Life is precious, and I want to raise people's quality of life. Continual learning in science, and constant exposure to new methods and technologies make me want to commit to medicine, as it will be satisfying to apply my knowledge to help society.

I believe studying A-levels has provided me with many skills useful for medicine. Multi-tasking and being organised was essential for success. Participating in an online course on vaccine trials made me realise how fulfilling research is, as it can profoundly affect many lives. Working on a novel idea in a research project at Rutherford Appleton laboratory enabled me to use maths and physics to solve problems creatively. Health was a key topic in biology, and to learn more I enrolled in a 'Nutrition for Health Promotion and Disease Prevention' course. It was fascinating to learn genetics plays a part in many ailments. Wanting to discover more, I read: 'The Language of the Genes' by Jones, and 'Mutants' by Leroi, where I learnt that people have misconstrued how great a role genetics or genetic technologies have on our lives. So, when partaking in an online course on Epigenetics for an independent Crest Gold Award, I was more able to critically appraise the information.

To better understand life as a doctor, I arranged to shadow clinicians in various departments in a teaching hospital. Being inquisitive, 'What is wrong?' and 'What is the remedy?' were the two questions I frequently asked. I gained insight into the importance of a concise and honest approach in building a rapport with patients. To improve my communication skills, I participated and trained other students in public speaking and debating. Here, I was awarded a prize for my bubbly spirit and gracious nature. At a community hospital, I worked with occupational therapists, physiotherapists and nurses in treating sufferers of Parkinson's disease, highlighting that a doctor plays a role within a multidisciplinary team. At another hospital, I learnt about infection control measures when I helped to wash and dress patients. There, I began to understand how important it was to treat the individual, and not just the symptoms of the disease. So, I cared for dementia sufferers, and engaged elderly patients in conversation. Being approachable, confident, and compassionate made it enjoyable for them and me. It was humbling to see the wider social impacts that these simple acts had. These experiences made me aware of how central teamwork and empathy are in providing the optimal outcome for patients. Working in a GP surgery illustrated how vital administrative aspects are for the best result. Observing the medical system in India gave me a global awareness of the advantages and disadvantages of service delivery in various settings.

As a St. John ambulance cadet, I have remained calm under pressure to make clear and timely decisions for the last 4 years. I am a prefect and was a member of the student council for 3 years, which established my leadership and teamwork skills. In my free time, I participated in community programmes and volunteered at Oxfam and various libraries. This developed my time management skills. Acting has given me the aptitude to interact with people from all walks of life, and improved my ability to teach inspiringly but assertively. Drama also reveals how fascinating the human mind is, which reading New Scientist has enforced.

I realise that a medical career is demanding, but I consider delivering quality care to supersede the hardships of pursuing it. I believe I have the drive, resilience, dedication, and conscientiousness to be a useful member of the medical community, and I am looking forward to contributing to university life.

Universities applied to:

➤ Oxford: Offer
➤ Imperial College: Offer
➤ King's: Offer
➤ Leicester: Offer

Good points:

A well-written and well-structured statement. The student provides a well differentiated and well-reflected insight into their work experience and the particularly interesting lessons regarding medicine. Recognising the particular importance of communication skills and addressing them specifically reflects very positively on the student and their awareness of the challenges of medical practice. The practical hands-on experience of working with the St. John's Ambulance and acquiring the skills relevant for working well under pressure further demonstrate the student's proactive nature.

Bad points:

The introduction is somewhat too cliché positive. Whilst it is amazing when treatments are successful and patients that were already on the verge of death recover, more often than not, this is not the case. Recognising the essential limitations of medicine is just as important as being passionate about the success and the many things medicine can treat now.

Overall:

A very strong statement with only very minor weaknesses. The statement is dominated by the student's excellent insight into the challenges of clinical medicine and their varied experiences, both clinically as well as non-clinically. The student manages to present themselves as a well-balanced individual, driven to succeed but also aware of the inter-human skills required for being a good and successful doctor.

NOTES

Statement 72

My childhood notions of medicine were the hallmarks of TV dramas. TV doctors have it easy. They are heroes barking orders who, in the end, save the patient's life. When a friend of mine passed away from muscular dystrophy, his demise began my journey of exploring what it really means to be a physician – and I discovered a vastly different world of medicine.

Last year I undertook a 12-week voluntary placement as a ward clerk at a local hospital, which gave me the opportunity to gain a deeper understanding of the medical and social needs of patients as well as helping me to hone my communication skills and to develop a high degree of empathy. To gain more patient contact, I volunteered in a nursing home, feeding patients and assisting in moving and handling. It was here that I discerned the lesser-known aspects of healthcare: paperwork, understaffing and even violence to healthcare staff. Seeing patients in palliative care, I found that not everyone's lives are saved and that if I were to become an effective clinician, I must be resistant to great emotional demands, but not immune to all emotion so as to breed apathy. My experiences in palliative care inspired me to base my EPQ on Traditional Chinese Medicine as adjunctive therapy for pain relief, in which I systematically reviewed journal articles on how the quality of life of palliative care patients can be improved.

I have been fortunate to shadow many doctors on the wards and in theatre, observing mastectomy, coronary artery bypass surgery and seton placement. I saw how the multidisciplinary team-work together in a demanding hospital environment. The doctors' focus on patient-centred care hugely impressed me; the duty of a doctor to respect patients' decisions (providing the patient has capacity and has made an informed decision) reminds me that doctors, aside from being highly competent, must also recognise patients' moral values. To learn about other aspects of healthcare, I spent two weeks at a pharmacy where I learnt about confidentiality. I also volunteered at a dental clinic, practising manual dexterity in aspiration.

Being an MD (Medical Devotee!), I run a weekly Medical Club at school, a forum to explore medical research and ethical debates. I also lead a team of students in running and editing a blog (TheMedSchoolProject.com), where I write reflections on my work experience and reviews of medical books; I also write articles on recent medical advances such as gene therapy and the nerve allograft. Since our website's conception, it has received over 60,000 views. This year, our film exploring the ethics of saviour siblings won a competition run by the Nuffield Council on Bioethics. I have also organised medicine-related trips for my team, including trips to genetics lectures and a biomedical research open day.

The challenges of my last years at school have highlighted my strengths. Leading the school council allowed me to take on a position of responsibility. Taking part in a three-day 'Skills for Management' conference and in a 'Health Sciences Masterclass' has given me a greater appreciation of the allied health professions in the NHS and has provided me with valuable skills such as teamworking, managing conflict and time management. Time management plays a huge role in my somewhat hectic life as aside from my love of blogging, I also enjoy playing classical guitar and I practise kickboxing to help me unwind.

Gone now are my childhood notions of doctors in TV dramas. I have come to realise that being a doctor involves commitment to the welfare of humanity. This commitment is deeply imbedded within the core of heroes the likes of Edward Jenner and John Snow, their modern counterparts Atul Gawande and Oliver Sacks and the thousands of unsung heroes who dedicate themselves to the NHS each day. Being determined to follow in the footsteps of these pioneers and to stand on the shoulders of giants, I hope to make significant contributions to medicine someday.

Universities applied to:
- Oxford: Offer
- Imperial College: Offer
- University College: Offer
- Birmingham: Offer

Good points:
A very well-written and structured statement that provides a balanced view between academic and work experience related ideas and reflections. The student succeeds in giving a very detailed in-depth analysis of their perspective on medicine and how they improved their understanding of the subject. The student manages to make most described experiences relevant to the statement and to the course of medicine as a whole by tying their reflections to specific requirements of a career in medicine. The general impression resulting from this is that of a hardworking and dedicated student that is well aware of the challenges of the medical profession and the requirements this career poses on the individual. The student demonstrates that they has acquired a wider range of skills relevant for medicine such as communication, organisation, commitment and discipline.

Bad points:
Whilst the statement is already very strong, there are some points that could be improved and elaborated on. In particular, this includes the ethical issue of saviour siblings. The student describes having taken part in the production of a film addressing the topic. It would be interesting to learn more about this.

Overall:
An excellent statement with many very strong aspects. The student manages to present themselves as a well-rounded individual that is well suited for the pursuit of a career in medicine. The choice of work experience placements and the reflection on associated experiences demonstrates the student's strong understanding of the challenges and requirements of a career in medicine.

NOTES

Statement 73

Medicine is a fascinating combination of different subjects, ranging from biology and chemistry to philosophy. Studying the human body in all its complexity, it provides endless challenges and an opportunity for lifelong learning - two essential parts of a stimulating scientific career I want to pursue. However, healthcare is much more than a science. Medicine is the art of healing and helping people - an aim I feel very passionate about.

This summer I spent two weeks with nurses in a cardiac ward. Assisting them, even just making sure a patient got to the procedure unit safely, was very rewarding. Meanwhile, I learnt a lot about working in healthcare. While observing the blood-taking and injections, I noticed how flexible and quick-witted one has to be to keep every patient calm, no matter what their mood and attitude are. I have also come across some upsetting situations there. I met a patient waiting for a heart transplant, and seeing him having to put his life on hold whilst waiting for a suitable donor was heart-breaking. Nonetheless, I think the difficulty of coping with negative emotions is worthwhile, because, once you have acknowledged these feelings, you can set them aside and concentrate on helping the person. The experience furthered my determination to study medicine to eventually be able to play an active role in aiding people's recovery.

To gain more insight, I went to a pre-medical summer school in Britain. I enjoyed working with pupils from all over the world to explore the human body and various aspects of medical ethics. Discussing the moral issues in healthcare and the NHS prompted me to read around the subject, and I found McCartney's 'The Patient Paradox' especially thought-provoking. At the same time, meeting current medical students, who shared their experiences and showed us some basic procedures like cannulation, was exciting and motivational.

Medicine is a diverse field with many career options. For me, there is one thing that makes doctors stand out: they make final decisions in patient care. Such a level of responsibility can be intimidating, but it allows you to make a real difference - something I want to do in my life. Being a doctor also requires problem-solving. Careful observation and logic necessary for working out the right diagnosis and treatment are appealing to me. Having studied at a highly competitive mathematical school for the last three years, I know problem-solving is my strong side and an activity I never want to give up, if I can use it to help people.

Although my high school curriculum is considerably challenging, my time-management skills have allowed me to pursue my other interests. I take a deep interest in literature and languages. Reading widely has helped me develop empathy and open-mindedness, qualities essential for a good doctor. Moreover, I love sharing my passions with others, so I have been organizing literary activities with my classmates during our school trips. What is more, I am lucky to live in Moscow, where museums have allowed me to take my knowledge beyond what I have learnt in classes. Eager to give something back to the community, I started volunteering at the Museum of The Theory of Evolution. There I help children to explore interactive displays in an exhibition. Working to enhance visitors' experiences was very satisfying and presented a communicative challenge I was happy to accept.

I am aware that there are many difficulties when studying and practicing medicine. However, having taken steps to explore a medical career, I believe I can meet these challenges. I am highly motivated, enthusiastic about science and committed to providing good care.

Universities applied to:

➤ Oxford: Offer

➤ Imperial College: Interview + Rejected

➤ King's: Interview + Rejected

➤ Nottingham: Rejected

Good points:

Well differentiated and well thought through statement. The statement gives good insight into the student's endeavours to get as much exposure to clinical medicine as possible. The student's description of his experiences with a heart transplant patient and the impact the waiting for a suitable donor had on the patient is particularly interesting as it provides and represents an emotionally challenging situation. The sum of the student's experiences as provided in this statement paints them as a hardworking, interested, and well-dedicated student that is aware of the different facets of medical care.

Bad points:

The student's conception of the role of a doctor seems to stand in some contrast to the role doctors fulfil in the UK. Whilst it is true that they are the ultimate decision-makers when it comes to the deciding on treatment and management, the journey to this point is very much influenced and shaped by the input of other healthcare professionals. The multidisciplinary team is essential in effective management and treatment plans. The recognition of this needs to be adequately reflected in the statement.

Overall:

A well-written and well-structured statement that gives good insight into the character of the applying student. It is interesting to read about the student's experiences and their interests in medicine. The student succeeds in providing a balanced review of academic as well as clinical experiences that all contribute to a well-rounded reflection of the student as an individual.

NOTES

Statement 74

Combining my commitment to helping people with my thirst to understand the intricacies of human anatomy, physiology and biochemistry I believe that medicine offers the perfect vocation for me. Extended periods of work experience have helped confirm my direction. Attending the Medical Work Observation Week in Llandough Hospital, I shadowed consultants in Gastroenterology and Cardiology outpatient clinics; I saw the importance of communication skills and a compassionate yet professional relationship. When asked to take patient histories I realised the need to respect patients and to be sensitive to their situations; sympathy and empathy are clearly essential. After following a ward round I attended a multi-disciplinary meeting, seeing the many healthcare professions working together closely as a team. I undertook a five month placement as an NHS Ward Volunteer in Barry hospital. There I spent four hours a week talking with patients, gaining a clearer picture of patient needs and also the day to day running of a hospital. From conversing with F1 doctors I appreciate the constant work, long hours and dedication required throughout a career in medicine and am eager to make that commitment.

I am naturally inquisitive and as such eagerly embraced the challenges of school work, an attitude which won me numerous awards throughout my school life; finally culminating with The Headteacher's Cup - given for outstanding effort and a positive attitude. In the upper 6th I was pleased to be elected Head Boy and took on a leading role in the school community. The experiences that followed tested and developed many skills from public speaking and organisation to people management and delegation. In completing the Welsh Baccalaureate I was given the opportunity to participate in large amounts of charity work, I found this a pleasant contrast with the strict academia of my A-Level studies whilst being highly rewarding. Leading on from this I also spent 2 weeks in Sri Lanka teaching English and running sports activities for underprivileged children in orphanages. This was a particularly moving experience giving me an understanding of a very different culture, but also helping me to develop a broader perspective on life.

Rugby has always been a passion of mine and I continue to play for Barry RFC; in school my commitment was rewarded with a place in the senior starting line-up. In my spare time I am a keen member of the Llancarfan change ringing band; I also led and taught a band of youth bell ringers for 13 months. I enjoy playing the cello and found it an invaluable method of relaxing during exam periods. I believe my ability to balance these interests with my school life is a key skill to bring to a medical profession. Whilst re-applying I plan to use the time constructively and take a gap year; I hope to gain important new skills and experiences that will be invaluable for a career in medicine. I have worked in Techniquest as a Science Communicator for two years. When giving public lectures I have become aware of the need to tailor the talk to different audiences, a skill that will be needed to deliver personalised patient dialogue. Alongside employment I am preparing for a unique experience with VSO. I intend to travel to China in April where I will work with a developing community for three months building schools, delivering healthcare and teaching English.

My experiences of life so far have helped me to work hard and keep calm in high pressure situations. I feel that I am sympathetic to others and have a willingness to listen - qualities and skills which I hope will help me become a skilled medical professional. I believe that I am now sufficiently mature and able to meet the challenges and rewards of modern medicine with excitement and enthusiasm.

Universities applied to:

➢ Oxford: Offer

➢ Liverpool: Interview + Rejected

➢ Edinburgh: Rejected

➢ Southampton: Interview + Rejected

Good points:

Well-written statement highlighting the student's achievements, both clinically as well as non-clinically. The statement paints an interesting picture of a well-rounded and curious individual, motivated to work hard to achieve his goals. The student reflects well on lessons learned during his work experience placements and comes to valuable conclusions regarding the challenges and realities of medical care in the NHS. Having the opportunity for further voluntary engagement in Sri Lanka, the student demonstrates his awareness of the relevance of good communication skills and highlights his curiosity in regards to new experiences.

Bad points:

The statement lacks insight into academic interests and performance. Whilst this is not necessarily an area of high relevance, it would be helpful to understand the student's perspective on academia and learn about any particular interests that might guide the student's studies of medicine into a particular field or specialty. This is particularly relevant as the student describes the amalgamation of science and helping others as one of the core motivators for his choice of pursuing a career in medicine.

Overall:

A well-written statement that focuses on clinical as well as inter-human experiences in order to demonstrate the student's character as a well-rounded and hardworking individual. The statement loses some strength as the student ignores the relevance of academic pathways.

NOTES

Statement 75

The allure of medicine is that it combines a wide range of sciences into one field with fantastic results. I have always been intrigued by how different scientific disciplines can be applied to detecting and treating illnesses. There is great appeal to me in using my scientific knowledge in my future career and each science is a source of great enjoyment to me. Although I have some ideas of where I want my career in medicine to lead, I recognise that I have very little experience in many of the aspects of medicine and I anticipate that the path I take may be very different from the one I plan.

Studying Biology, Chemistry, Physics and Maths taught me to use logic; consequently I shine in problem solving exercises. This key skill will provide excellent preparation for developing my diagnostic skills in the future. My subjects complement each other well and taught me to draw on my knowledge of each subject to resolve challenging questions. Medicine is a diverse and challenging field with complex cases requiring specialised problem solving skills. I have taken an EPQ entitled 'How feasible is cloning and how ethical is the process' which furthered my independent learning skills, and gave me an insight into an area of medicine that is advancing quickly with massive lifesaving potential.

I have undertaken work experience in three separate areas that would confirm to me that I had chosen the right career and was well prepared for it. Not only did they confirm this to me, but they inspired me to work even harder to reach my goal. I have been a St. John Ambulance first aider since June 2011. This was a very rewarding experience, and it gave me confidence with the experience of treating patients. A placement at the Oncology department of the Leeds Institute for Molecular Medicine highlighted to me that medicine is a combination of advance scientific techniques along with highly specialised interpretation techniques, which I saw used in a research setting to treat, screen and monitor oncology patients. Many procedures required a high level of understanding of each science and that reiterated to me that a broad knowledge base was vital. I also volunteered as a care assistant at a local nursing home which was the most valuable work experience I did. Speaking to the residents shocked me initially, because many spoke of being ready to die. To overcome this I had to understand the situation from their point of view. They had lived long, happy lives and simply wished to live the rest of their lives in a safe and caring environment without further suffering. Nurses prioritised a resident's happiness over medical treatment which emphasised to me that there are some patients for whom a painful treatment is inappropriate and instead need care and love far more than any drug.

Music and sport were both introduced to me at a very early age. I have played the violin for over 10 years and I am now working towards my grade 7. Last year I also took up the viola and achieved a merit at grade 6. I now play in the Leeds Youth Orchestra, one of the most prestigious youth orchestras in the country. Sport has also played a significant part in my life and much of my academic success can be attributed to the competitive attitude I gained from it. My participation in a wide range of sports has meant I am a focussed individual who also flourishes in a team environment. Over the years I have devoted more and more time to athletics and now I train for more than eleven hours a week. This dedication has seen a return of two Yorkshire Steeplechase titles and a top 25 placing at the English Schools Championships. My involvement in athletics doesn't just lie as a competitor; I have also helped in coaching the local primary school athletics team. Both athletics and music will continue to play a considerable role in my life at university and beyond. A medical degree is merely the beginning of my passion, becoming a doctor will be a lifelong challenge that I relish.

Universities applied to:
➤ Oxford: Offer
➤ Imperial College: Offer
➤ University College: Offer
➤ Birmingham: Offer

Good points:

Very well-written and structured. The student approaches the statement very sensibly, acknowledging their limitations with regards to making a judgement on clinical experiences. In general, the student provides a good overview of a well-balanced range of relevant work experience, all geared to providing them with the best possible introduction to clinical medicine. The student recognises the importance of a good scientific basis for medicine. Being confronted with end of life questions in a residential home is a very relevant experience.

Bad points:

The student very much focuses on the relevance of science for medical care and only acknowledges the necessity of soft skills such as empathy in a side note. Unfortunately, this ignores a very relevant side of medical care. Whilst a sound scientific basis of knowledge is vital for a safe and efficient practice of medicine, a good grasp of the relevance of inter-personal skills is equally as important.

Overall:

A very strong statement with regards to work experience and scientific relevance. The student succeeds in presenting themselves as hardworking and dedicated as well as aware of the challenges that come with the pursuit of a career in medicine. The statement also provides a good range of topics that could be addressed during an interview.

NOTES

Statement 76

Success in medicine relies upon a combination of excellence and enthusiasm for science, supported by personal diligence ensuring good patient care. The modern-day doctor requires knowledge and understanding, detachment and personal connection. The life of a doctor is rigorous, demanding and yet rewarding, and this is the life I aspire to.

Work experience has reinforced my decision to read medicine. Volunteering in a care home educated me in patient care, this involved performing observations on the residents and drug rounds, requiring both patience and precision, and in return giving me an insight into the holistic nature of geriatric care. Working with sufferers of Alzheimer's and Parkinson's disease was challenging, yet gratifying, as it was obvious that the residents appreciated I was taking an interest in them and time to build a close rapport. The pharmacy also proved to be a stimulating environment. Working behind the counter dispensing drugs alongside pharmacists led me to appreciate the importance of the close link between GPs and the local pharmacy to ensure that the patient receives the correct medication, and that the drugs do not interact to cause an antagonistic effect. During two weeks spent at University Hospital Coventry I joined handover meetings, shadowed consultants on ward rounds, and observed clinic so I was able to follow the progress of patients. From observing bronchoscopies and ERCPs in the operating theatre, I came to appreciate the importance of teamwork in hospitals, for it is not just the doctors who are vital to improve the condition of patients. For the successful ERCP, five people (surgeon, radiographer, nurses), each with a different role, worked together to guide an endoscope into a patient's bile duct to remove a gall stone.

Scientific excellence is the foundation of effective medicine. New scientific developments are constantly being made that shape the medical environment, which enhance our understanding of the human body and allow us to treat conditions more successfully e.g. The discovery of the antibiotic streptomycin revolutionized treatment of tuberculosis. Having learnt about the composition of cell surface membranes, the differentiation of stem cells and the intricacies of DNA, I am intrigued by the way in which these microscopic elements are essential in the correct functioning of the human body at the macroscopic level. Preparing for the British Biology Olympiad and reading Chemistry Review help me learn more about science beyond the A-level syllabus.

Preparing for undergraduate study, I attended extra-curricular science lectures, the most memorable being by Prof. D. Nutt, exposing the politics influencing medicine, such as in classing drugs. Developing my interest in medicine, I frequently read BBC Health, and my extended project is on how cosmetic surgery is affecting society, questioning whether cosmetic surgery is really medicine and engaging with the ethics that surround all medicine. Representing my school in the European Youth Parliament, I chose to research how mental disorders affect European youth. I was shocked to find that so many young Europeans experience mental disorders such as anorexia, anxiety and depression, due to a range of social issues. As well as the sharp thinking and intuition required for debating, I am completing my Gold Duke of Edinburgh Award, and shouldering the responsibilities of being Deputy Head of House and School Monitor, including supporting and mentoring younger students. I also enjoy sport, representing the school 2nd XI rugby team, and studying French and Spanish has given me the flexibility to adapt to new situations and allowed me to teach Spanish to children.

I am looking forward to reading medicine, and a career in it will be both challenging and rewarding. The combination of interpersonal skills, academic discipline, ambition and commitment that I possess make me an ideal candidate for the study of medicine.

Universities applied to:
- Oxford: Offer
- Manchester: Offer
- Birmingham: Interview + Rejected
- Cardiff: Interview + Rejected

Good points:

A well-written and well-structured statement that succeeds to give good insight into the student's motivations and interests in medicine as well as providing a good overview of the student's activities aimed at gaining as much clinical experience as possible. Having good exposure to medical practice in a variety of contexts is very relevant. The student reflects well on his/her experiences, recognising the importance of sound scientific knowledge as well as other factors affecting good medical care such as team-work between all professionals involved in the care. The student succeeds in presenting himself/herself as a disciplined, hardworking, and well-rounded individual with a wider range of interests; all attributes well sought after in medical professionals.

Bad points:

There are two basic weaknesses in this statement. Firstly, the student overestimates the speed at which medical practice changes. Whilst it is true that our understanding of some aspects of the human body is changing, this has little impact on medical practice, or at least, impacts it on a significantly slower pace. Furthermore, the student pretty much ignores, with the exception of team-working skills, the relevance of non-academic, inter-personal skills for medicine until the conclusion of their statement. The involvement of the patient in their own care is essential for the delivery of good medical care.

Overall:

A strong statement delivering a picture of strong academic performance and a well-rounded clinical experience. The statement is weakened somewhat by the lack of recognition of soft skills and an associated over-valuation of scientific knowledge. Remember, medicine is an art, not just a science.

NOTES

Statement 77

Attending the Medical Society lectures at my school and hearing the doctors speak with such enthusiasm about their careers first made me consider a medical vocation. I was particularly moved by a talk on reconstructive work performed on burn victims, which showed me that medicine provides the opportunity to really make a difference in people's lives. Whilst I appreciate that a medical career can be very demanding, I believe that the opportunity to improve the quality of life of others will far outweigh the challenges I will have to overcome.

To inform myself further about a career in medicine, I arranged to shadow consultants from various departments at Hillingdon Hospital for three weeks. I saw medical students taking patient histories, as well as an MDT meeting, highlighting the importance of good communication skills with colleagues and patients as a medical professional. I also saw a thyroid removal operation, which I found immensely interesting. The second thyroid removal I was due to attend was cancelled mid-operation as the patient was at risk, a stark reminder that the patient's wellbeing must always be the priority. I also arranged to sit in on a GP's clinic in Putney, where I was struck by the doctor's level of empathy, and how comfortable the patients were discussing matters with him, showing me the importance of being approachable and compassionate.

For a number of months I have been volunteering for three to four hours every week at a local residential home, where I organise activities involving arts and crafts, as well as helping to serve and clean up lunch and talk to the residents. This has given me an opportunity to make lasting relationships with people, and speaking to the patients who suffer from dementia has given me an insight into how emotionally stressful a career in medicine can be, and the patience it requires.

I am now on the committee of my school's Medical Society. I help to organise meetings and entertain speakers before their talk, and after hearing Dr. Alexander Young speak on his career in orthopaedic surgery, I read "Bones" by Caroline Shreeve, a very accessible book on the assortment of diseases that affect our skeletal system. I was interested by the cause and treatment of rheumatoid arthritis, and subsequently wrote an eight page dissertation on arthritis for the school medical essay prize, for which I have been shortlisted.

After reading an article on influenza vaccinations in the Biological Sciences Review, I was interested in the science behind pandemics. I read "The Viral Storm" by Nathan Wolfe, which was a thought-provoking and highly alarming read, and attended a lecture given at my school's Medical Society on the spread of HIV. This led me to write an 8000 word essay on viral pandemics and why we are so susceptible to them, using HIV as a case study.

Working as part of a four-person team, I won a national 'Voices of Conservation' competition aimed at rhino conservation. Our innovative idea to monitor rhino heart rates won us a trip to South Africa, where we worked with experts in the field in an attempt to find a solution to rhino poaching. I have since given talks to my school and written articles in the school magazine on the topic of environmental conservation.

I am a keen sportsman, competing for my school in a range of sports including rowing, athletics and football. I am a black belt in kickboxing and the head of martial arts at my school, which involves helping to organise competitions and assist in coaching the younger students. I completed a 33 mile bicycle course across London to raise money for The Stroke Association, and have completed a half marathon for SCOPE. Competing in sports at a high level has helped me to maintain composure under pressure. This has proved useful in my role as House Captain, where I advise and support younger pupils. I am currently working towards my Grade 7 on the piano, and I find music an excellent way to complement my academic work.

Universities applied to:

- ➤ Oxford: Offer
- ➤ Southampton: Rejected
- ➤ Newcastle: Rejected
- ➤ Birmingham: Rejected

Good points:

A very diverse statement demonstrating a wide range of academic interests, clinical experiences and non-academic extra-curricular activities. The student succeeds in presenting themselves as a well-rounded individual with many strengths that provide a good basis for the successful study of medicine. Recognising the basic skills required in medicine (scientific knowledge, communication skills, empathy as well as a good patient rapport), the student demonstrates a good degree of reflection on their experiences in the hospital, the GP, and the care home.

Bad points:

The statement could be strengthened further by giving more insight into the student's work on pandemics as infections still represent one of the major challenges of medical care. Not only viral, but also bacterial. In the latter, antibiotic resistance is a particularly relevant topic. Being aware of these challenges would be a further representation quality of the student and also aid setting him/her apart from other applicants.

Overall:

Good statement that succeeds in providing good insight into the student's character, motivation and interests. There is some room for improvement that would further increase the student's chance in competing with other applicants. Since the point of the personal statement is to set yourself apart from the masses, being on the lookout for opportunities to be different is always relevant.

NOTES

Statement 78

I would love to study medicine because it is a scientific profession with a human twist. Science intrigues me because it attempts to explain almost everything in our lives while constantly evolving to fit new evidence. This excites me and I aspire to use my knowledge for the benefit of others through Medicine. My desire to become a doctor was cemented after careful reflection on my work experience which gave me a deeper insight into the field of medicine.

At one of my hospital placements I shadowed a cardiologist and was impressed by the professional and compassionate way in which he interacted with the patients and gained their trust. Rotating through various specialities in the hospital taught me how specific a doctor's skillset can be. I was fortunate to watch a knee-cap replacement in theatre and was amazed by the efficient teamwork involved in the procedure. Further work experience at a GP practice made me appreciate the role of a primary care doctor in holistic treatment of patients. Through observing the practice nurse and helping at reception I understood how the different professions work together for the benefit of patients. I saw how being a doctor can be stressful such as when attempting a lumbar puncture for the first time or when consoling a family of a patient whose condition was bleak.

I have seen that doctors need to communicate complex ideas clearly to patients, a skill which I have developed while volunteering in the care home and on the till at Oxfam over the past year. At Oxfam I found working in a team more efficient than working alone on a task which reflects the teamwork I saw on my work experience. I have become more empathetic and a good listener through my voluntary work at the care home by chatting with the residents. Now I better appreciate some of the problems doctors will face in the future due to our ageing population such as dementia.

Last summer I did work experience in a private hospital in India where I saw a team of doctors work calmly to save an unconscious patient with cardiac arrhythmia. I feel my responsibilities at school as Prefect and member of the Sixth Form Committee have helped prepare me for working under such pressure. I have learned how to skilfully negotiate with students which will help me as a doctor when dealing with difficult patients. On the same trip I helped organise a medical camp in a remote village and was struck by the disparity between the healthcare service in the village and the city.

I have represented the school in various science and linguistics Olympiads and challenges and I'm proud to hold an academic scholarship. Being an editor for the school magazine has improved my time management and organisation skills. My interest in my science A levels have enthused me to read interesting articles in scientific magazines. I was inspired to do my EPQ project on developments in cardiology after my work experience which will help me prepare for the independent style of learning at university.

I like to use my IT skills by heading up the school's six student technicians where we run the IT component for school assemblies and events. I was the IT director of my Young Enterprise team where I designed a website and social pages for our company and led negotiations with a Chinese manufacturer for our product.

My hobbies include playing the violin and cricket. I have achieved grade 5 on the violin which I have played in various orchestras and I have also taught myself guitar where I have improved despite initially finding it hard. My hobbies have taught me patience and perseverance which would be useful in a medical career.

I am a hardworking, enthusiastic and self-motivated individual and I look forward to the independence of university. I am aware that medicine is a demanding though rewarding career and I believe I have the aptitude to become a good doctor.

Universities applied to:
- ➤ Oxford: Offer
- ➤ Newcastle: Offer
- ➤ Nottingham: Interview + Rejected
- ➤ King's: Interview + Rejected

Good points:

A well-written and well-structured statement. The student provides insight into a wide range of clinical experience spanning primary and secondary care in the UK as well as private secondary care in India. This broad experience of medicine will be helpful by providing a good degree of insight into the realities of medical practice and the personal challenges coming with the profession. Recognising some of the skills necessary for efficient medical practice further reflects positively on the student.

Bad points:

In the introduction, the student misjudges the significance of the 'human twist' in medicine. Medicine amalgamates scientific excellence with inter-personal excellence, at least in a clinical setting. Good doctors will possess equal parts of scientific excellence and human excellence. Other weaknesses include a choice to provide information that adds little depth to the statement. Whilst this is a minor weakness, it highlights the importance of relevance, in particular, in a document such as this where the main goal is to set yourself apart from other applicants.

Overall:

Good statement representing a well-rounded, hardworking and disciplined individual that has a good basic awareness of the challenges of medicine and the skills necessary for a successful pursuit of a medical career. There are some gaps and minor weaknesses in the statement preventing it from reaching its full potential.

NOTES

Statement 79

I didn't always want to be a doctor. For most of my life the bureaucracy, the emotionally draining nature of comforting the ill, and the sheer amount of stress seemed too overwhelming. Yet through my experiences the harshness of these factors dwindled and I was drawn to medicine.

My interest in the life sciences led to an online course about drug compounds and their development. Although fascinating, it made me realise that research alone wouldn't be satisfying enough as it was too distant from the people it helped; thus my search for a career that fused both research and care steered me towards medicine. "Bad Science" by B. Goldacre gave me insight into evidence-based medicine, whilst "How We Die" by S. Nuland taught me about the clinical reality of death and helped me appreciate the emotional tension involved. To discover another dimension of the career, I read "Medical Ethics: A Very Short Introduction" by T. Hope which highlighted the hard decisions that often need to be taken by doctors. By this stage I wasn't deterred, but enthused by seeing that medicine offers varied challenges, a responsibility for care and a solid basis in science.

Two weeks of work experience in the past year confirmed this. During a week in a medical laboratory in Cairo I came to understand the 'multidisciplinary team' as I observed doctors working with nurses, secretaries and lab technicians; emphasising the importance of teamwork and sound leadership in doctors. I arranged the second week in a hospital in the UK for a more patient-oriented experience and was particularly surprised by the importance of humility in doctors as they dealt with difficult patients with admirable courtesy and respected patient autonomy even when the decision was against their professional judgement. My observation of orthopaedic surgery led to taking an online course in musculoskeletal anatomy to understand what I had seen; as well as reading A. O'Donnell's "Anaesthesia: A Very Short Introduction" to learn about how that remarkable process is performed.

These experiences showed me that the relevant skills for medicine are the ones I have most enjoyed developing throughout my life. Two international MUN conferences enhanced my communication and collaboration skills with people from a range of backgrounds and cultures, preparing me for handling patient diversity. Tutoring struggling students developed my talent in explaining complex concepts to others in a friendly manner; while mentoring teaches me how to empathise with each student as an individual in order to advise them, skills which doctors need to explain a patient's diagnosis. Out of compassion, I visit elderly couples which has taught me to be a respectful listener, as well as how to quickly build rapport.

Seeking new challenges, I became the youngest camp director in our church, leading a group of thirty in planning and delivering a three-day camp. My leadership, teamwork and organisational skills grew as I delegated tasks and encouraged my team throughout the intense preparation process and during the camp. Involvement in the sound design of my school's musical taught me how to remain calm and adapt when problems arise, as well as how to endure the long and arduous days that are all too common in medicine. I was also elected Secretary of our student council last year, a position I sought because it would empower me to help my peers and school. This role further refined my ability to handle responsibility and listen to others' views. Due to my extensive involvement in school and community life, I realise the importance of relieving stress hence I have been playing the piano for ten years, participating in choirs and receiving two Trinity Exhibition Awards.

My systematic approach has made me confident in my decision to study medicine, and I am sure I can maintain the same commitment, energy and enthusiasm that I have put into both my academic and extra-curricular endeavours on the lifelong path of medicine.

Universities applied to:

➤ Oxford: Offer
➤ Leeds: Offer
➤ Nottingham: Interview + Rejected
➤ Sheffield: Rejected

Good points:

Very honest statement. Providing insight into how the student has come from not wanting to study medicine to deciding on a career in the subject is very interesting. Especially since this change is catalysed by experiences made in hospitals and laboratories, during exposure to real-life medicine. This supports the perception of the student as a well-rounded and reflective individual that likes to look at all the evidence before making a decision; a very important characteristic of doctors. The student demonstrates good reflection on experiences in hospitals and outside of medical attachments. Stressing the most relevant lessons for him/her in relation to the medical profession further underlines the reflective nature of the student.

Bad points:

Whilst this statement contains a lot of very valuable and relevant information, some information provided is less relevant and distracts from the strong parts. In a piece of work as short as the personal statement, being concise and goal-oriented is key. The mere listing of books read, for example, is of little relevance. The reading needs to serve a purpose in improving the student's grasp and understanding of medicine.

Overall:

A well-written and well-structured statement that delivers a very clear picture of a hardworking and motivated student that approaches problems with reason and ensures that they has sufficient information for an appropriate judgement of the impact and consequences of their decisions. Being of a reflective nature, avoiding rash decisions is a definite strength in doctors.

NOTES

Statement 80

My passion for medicine stems from attending a lecture on infant malnutrition in developing countries and how this negatively impacts on development. The complex workings of the body fascinated me and made me driven to study medicine and become a doctor.

For the last two years I have obtained as much clinical work experience as possible. The week I spent on an Endocrinology ward was my first time seeing the complex workings of a hospital beyond A&E, and provided me with an insight into the world of medical professionals. During this time, I witnessed what a mentally and emotionally draining job being a doctor can be. I was present when a lung cancer patient's results of a biopsy came through, indicating that the cancer had metastasised to her brain. This made me realise that a career in medicine will have distressing moments, but as a doctor you can improve the lives of people through your knowledge and compassion.

I have gained direct patient care experience through volunteering for a care home and a local children's charity called WECAN, which enables children with additional needs to access community leisure facilities. My work as a voluntary playworker has made me aware of the range of conditions grouped under the term 'disabilities', as I work with children with a variety of infirmities, who therefore require different levels of support. Working closely with the children has humbled me, making me aware that medicine is often about management rather than cure, and as a doctor you are in the privileged position of being able to positively influence the lives of patients in ways beyond just prescribing medication.

Many of the topics I have studied in A Level Chemistry and Biology have interested me throughout my school years; primarily the human elements of the Biology course. Work on the human brain fascinates me; an interest I have pursued through reading Suzanne Corkin's "Permanent Present Tense", which examines the case of a Henry Molaison who developed severe amnesia resulting from a neurological operation. This compelling book recounts the testing and treatment that was done to determine how and why a supposedly safe operation left him with no capacity for memory lasting beyond a few seconds.

Throughout year 12, I undertook an EPQ. My final presentation explored the causes and treatments of obesity, with the aim of answering the question "Should obese patients be treated for free by the NHS?" I learnt a great deal throughout researching and producing my presentation, and my attitude towards obesity changed as I became more informed about the topic. Furthermore, I developed the good organisation and time management abilities that were required in order to be successful in the self-directed course.

In recent months I have organised and participated in several bike rides, raising many hundreds of pounds for charity. In my role as expedition leader, I was responsible for the safety of the other cyclists through the decisions I made; a role I felt comfortable taking. Also, when completing my Duke of Edinburgh award earlier this year, good leadership and teamwork was necessary in order to be successful on the expedition, for example when we had to change our planned route in order to stay safe walking on what was the hottest day of the year.

Outside of school, I teach guitar locally. Tutoring children as young as 7 has improved my ability to communicate in a way that is suitable for my audience, which is very important in order to have successful consultations with patients. In my role as a tutor, making myself understood is vital to maximise my students' enjoyment and development in music.

The responsibility I hold as both a role model and tutor has required me to behave in a professional manner; imperative for those who work in healthcare.

I am determined to continue my studies and become a doctor. A medical career demands a continuous updating of knowledge in order to be able to positively influence the lives of people limited by illness; therefore I believe that medicine is the perfect career for me.

Universities applied to:
➤ Oxford: Offer
➤ Sheffield: Offer
➤ Leeds: Interview + Rejected
➤ Nottingham: Offer

Good points:
The student recognises the emotional challenges of medicine. This is important as it is an aspect that tends to be overlooked and that also tends to be ignored in common depictions of medical practice in TV shows and in books. Describing a wider range of clinical experiences aimed at understanding the delivery of medical care and being exposed to as much clinical medicine as possible is a very relevant strong point of the statement. Addressing the ethical issues of diseases that in part are dominated by the individuals choices (obesity in this case) helps demonstrate the student's awareness of these challenges. The student also provides good evidence of a range of soft skills such as organisational skills and communication skills.

Bad points:
It would be interesting to learn more about the student's reflections on the patient receiving news about his metastatic lung cancer. This is a very significant event and likely a scenario the student has not experienced previously, therefore, reflection will provide good insight into the student's character.

Overall:
Good and well-presented statement suffering from some minor weaknesses that mainly keep the statement from reaching its full potential. The student presents themselves as a self–motivated and disciplined individual with a good awareness of current ethical issues as well as many of the challenges of healthcare. The student demonstrates an ability to reflect on their experiences and draw relevant conclusions from them.

NOTES

Statement 81

The respect I felt watching my mother practise as a Recovery Nurse reinforced my motivation for a career in Medicine. I believe the challenge of patient diagnosis would suit my love of problem solving. I recognise that although not all medical issues can be resolved, the opportunity to improve someone's quality of life or to support them to a dignified and comfortable end would be fulfilling.

Each week last year, I volunteered at a school for disabled children, supporting Noah, an eight year old boy with severe autism and cerebral palsy. The continual encouragement by the staff when following routine activities such as feeding him through a tube emphasised the need for developing a strong rapport with those in your care. A week shadowing several doctors at GWH, Swindon, highlighted the variety of career directions available. Whilst observing a victim of a road traffic accident in A&E, I saw the medical team's collective efficiency in protecting a man's spine using braces and log rolls as he vomited due to trauma; this taught me the relevance of good communication and teamwork. Watching a registrar in the Special Care Baby Unit attempt to insert an IV line into a premature neonate highlighted the importance of manual dexterity and perseverance for a doctor. I was fortunate to spend two weeks in a hospital in Tanzania where the priority of patient confidentiality was emphasised: AIDS patients were referred to as ICD positive to prevent discrimination from others. The poverty underlying the Tanzanian healthcare system, such as lack of facilities which necessitated risky, invasive surgery, made me realise how valuable the NHS is. During my visit, I learnt the importance of leadership when an obstetrics consultant made sure his staff all knew their roles as a distressed baby was safely delivered by an emergency C-section. Observing the mother's swing in emotion from preoperational apprehension to the thrill of its success was particularly moving.
I was proud to gain the school prize for my Extended Project Qualification, "Is the prevalence of anterior cruciate ligament tears in women explicable?" which developed my ability to analyse data logically and critically. I thoroughly enjoyed researching the impact of hormones on the strength of our ligaments and gained a detailed understanding of the anatomy of the knee, appreciating the role scientific knowledge plays in making clinical decisions. I have always been a committed student with an enquiring mind. I engage in regular debate in my school's Scholars' Society and was instrumental in setting up a society for potential Medics who meet weekly to discuss various topics. I also relish studying Mandarin GCSE in addition to my four A-levels.

As Head of a boarding house for 60 boys I liaise frequently between staff and pupils, lead groups to carry out responsibilities and ensure the welfare of the boys. I enjoy such interaction with people of all ages and have also worked as a volunteer at a home for the elderly, at a summer school caring for 3-5 year olds and have provided maths support at two primary schools. I am a good team player and have represented my school at football and golf at first team level. I enjoy developing my own ideas and seeing these through as demonstrated by the charitable initiative I undertook in the summer; I gave a presentation to 350 Sixth Formers, spread awareness using posters and managed to collect 104 donated football shirts which I persuaded an airline to transport to Tanzania free of charge. Having already organised fixtures at local orphanages and schools, I was able to distribute every shirt to an underprivileged child; their reactions made it an extremely rewarding experience.

Observing my mother and others involved in healthcare has made me realise the commitment required in pursuing a career in medicine; I strongly believe that I am up to the challenge and look forward to both the dilemmas and the opportunities that lie ahead.

Universities applied to:

➤ Oxford: Offer
➤ University College: Offer
➤ Manchester: Interview + Rejected
➤ Bristol: Rejected

Good points:

A well-structured statement that demonstrates a wide range of extra-curricular activities and a high degree of social awareness and social engagement. The student demonstrates a powerful sense of charity and desire to help others. It is interesting to read about the student's endeavours to alleviate suffering already at this stage. This compassion and empathy is a great strength when it comes to being a doctor. Exposure to different systems of medical care will have provided valuable insight into the differences of healthcare that come with lack of funding and lack of medical infrastructure.

Bad points:

At times, the writing style of the statement is somewhat clumsy. When addressing their experience in Tanzania, the student seems to claim that risky invasive surgery is a hallmark of a poor healthcare system. This is not true. There are plenty of risky and invasive procedures being undertaken in the NHS every day. It would also be interesting to learn more about the type of charitable initiative the student undertook. Was this in the framework of a specific organisation or cause, was it self-driven, what outside help did the student receive?

Overall:

A well-rounded statement with some weaknesses. The student succeeds in presenting themselves in an excellent light, underlining their charity activities and their dedication to the wellbeing of others less fortunate. This provides a strong motivational basis for a career in medicine. The statement makes for an interesting read and provides a good basis for further discussion in an interview.

NOTES

Statement 82

The ability to change and save lives is a unique skill, which comes with great challenges and even greater responsibility. This is why I aim to pursue and excel in a career in medicine.

I am involved in several groups and activities that have helped me to develop numerous skills in anticipation for life after college. These include voluntary work as teaching assistant for Key Stage three students studying science. Attempting to explain particular scientific theories to younger students was very challenging and highlighted the necessity to convey and explain ideas in a concise and effective manner in a pressurised situation. From this I developed an appreciation of the demanding circumstances which medical professionals face daily. I am currently participating in a Peer Mentoring programme in association with the Voluntary Service Unit. This involves working with and supporting young people with social and personal issues such as bullying. This experience greatly enhanced my ability to work positively in a team in response to real community needs. Additionally, I am a member of my college's sixth form committee; the main role of which is to review and discuss improvements for the sixth form. These are subsequently presented to the school board. This has helped me develop teamwork skills and effective communication, both of which are vital in the world of medicine.

As an individual I take great satisfaction in helping others. I have undertaken voluntary work in order to make a positive impact on both my school and local community. This has brought me into contact with people from many different backgrounds. I volunteered to take part in my college's Summer School Programme, which helps incoming year seven students become accustomed to life at secondary school. I also take part in a paired reading programme at college, helping younger students to gain confidence in their reading ability. I am also a volunteer at Age Concern where I take part in a befriending programme. This involves regular visits, providing company to elderly individuals suffering from illnesses that keep them housebound.

Working with the young and elderly has taught me the diverse ways in which socialising through effective communication and a good attitude can encourage and help people of all ages. Furthermore, good communication skills are a vital component of patient-centred care.

I am an avid sportsman, participating in a variety of sports, particularly football where I play for my school and a men's team. I also enjoy athletics for which I represented my school for five years at district level. Taking part in these sports has helped promote a strong sense of team ethic, leadership, commitment and a competitive edge. I am driven to doing and being the best, a quality that is reflected in my education. In my GCSE's, I achieved the best results in my school for which I was awarded the Governor's Award for Excellence and recognised in the local newspaper.

To gain further understanding about what a career in medicine entails, I organised two weeks of work experience at Gravesend Medical Centre. I observed minor surgery including the excision of a cyst lodged near an eye. I also observed a practice nurse during a NHS quit smoking programme. In addition I also did some work experience in a pharmacy unit where I learnt about different medicinal drugs and their effects on the body. In addition I learnt about the stringent security procedures to prevent misplacement or patient abuse of drugs. This placement gave me valuable insight into how much dedication, endurance and perseverance is required to succeed in such a fast paced and challenging job.

The world of medicine is ever evolving, providing a daily mountain to climb. I am totally committed to my decision to pursue a career in medicine and would truly appreciate the opportunity so I too can join those with that unique opportunity to change and save lives.

Universities applied to:
- King's: Offer
- East Anglia: Interview + Rejected
- Southampton: Rejected
- St George's: Offer

Good points.

The student provides a good account of some of the reasons why he believes a career in medicine would be suitable and fulfilling for him. He provides some insight into experiences that helped him acquire necessary skills such as communication and organisation skills as well as responsibility and discipline. The student also demonstrates a dedication and discipline to academic work, by underlining his desire to perform to the best of his abilities. Including information on community based care experiences is relevant, as this supports the development of soft skills such as empathy and underlines a desire to improve the life of others.

Bad points:

The statement is somewhat thin on clinical work experience. The student provides very brief and superficial insight into his work experience, but the passage generally lacks reflection and purpose in the context of the statement as a whole. Also, whilst the award for the student's GCSE performance is impressive, it carries limited weight in this statement as it lies too far in the past to be overly relevant.

Overall:

Good statement somewhat let down by the limited amount of reflection on clinical work experience. Whilst the student provides evidence of different types of work experience, he fails to make the most of the lessons learned during these placements. This is a pity as there is ample opportunity to provide very valuable insight into the challenges experienced during clinical work.

NOTES

_____

Statement 83

My longstanding ambition to become a doctor stems from my enthusiasm for the sciences and a caring, respectful interest in people and their cultures.

To confirm medicine is the career for me, I have spent over two weeks in many healthcare settings, including health visiting, respiratory medicine, obstetrics and gynaecology, and microbiology. Working with an Infection Control Team, it struck me how often staff are required to wash or gel their hands, and brought home to me the need for good general hygiene; I was able to realise the impact of simple measures on patient safety, while seeing three wards closed with viral gastroenteritis showed me what can happen if standards slip. When shadowing ward rounds at Leeds General Infirmary I was surprised how patients with similar symptoms can have countless different conditions, and how mental and physical responses to illness and treatment can vary just as widely. A two-day Liverpool Medical Institution Taster Course introduced to me the many career pathways open to a doctor, which was reinforced by subsequent discussions with health professionals.

The varied, challenging nature of a medical career also attracts me, a theme reflected in my A-level choices. The human aspects of Biology particularly interest me, not least the study of proteins. It fascinates me how a single altered amino acid can have such implications on the body, as in sickle cell anaemia. German is also a subject I enjoy, so much so that I participate in an advanced evening class to improve my conversation. A second language, along with my Geography and Equality and Diversity qualification, has enabled me to appreciate the complex issues in our world from different perspectives, preparing me for a people-centred working life in the increasingly global world of healthcare.

For three years I have worked as a waiter, which has developed my interpersonal skills. I must remain calm in stressful situations, particularly when managing the restaurant, and have to make considered decisions quickly and prioritise my workload. Spending an afternoon a week in a primary school and, latterly, a care home since September 2010, along with my work during the holidays at a day nursery, has enabled me to further this experience working with people, and opened my eyes to the issues facing all ages. I've seen at first hand the value of tailoring communication, support, and care to suit different social groups.

At school, I find mentoring of younger pupils requires similar patience and empathy. Leading Year 7 Science Club last year, which involved creating engaging practicals and writing risk assessments, developed my confidence at teaching groups, while helping to coordinate Fairtrade Fortnight strengthened my time management and organisational skills. As a House Captain, I am proud to be a role model, and must work in a team and communicate effectively with both staff and fellow pupils. I also happily go the extra mile, often helping out at weekends and evenings.

I enjoy rugby, football and mountain biking, which allow me to relax and enjoy the great outdoors, and am the Equipment Officer at a local cycling club, which I joined at the age of eight. I recently completed a St John Ambulance first aid course, and am now Deputy First Aider on the rides that I lead; I love being able to safely introduce youngsters to the thrills of the outdoors. To give something back, I helped with the restoration of a local cycling track and have been involved with the St John Ambulance for six years, where I help to maintain the medical kits and raise funds.

In conclusion, I am someone who always relishes a new challenge. Medicine is such a diverse, demanding and lifelong science, and the potential this creates to continue developing understanding and skills beyond graduation excites me. By becoming a doctor I realise I will not be able to cure everyone, but am still inspired by the opportunity to help people to the best of my ability.

Universities applied to:
➢ Birmingham: Offer
➢ Queen's Belfast: Interview + Rejected
➢ Edinburgh: Offer
➢ King's: Interview + Rejected

Good points:
The student demonstrates a wider range of characteristics as well as medical experiences stretching over many different areas of clinical and non-clinical areas. Gathering good experiences in a hospital setting is very important as it provides good insight into the everyday life on a hospital ward and also highlights the challenges of the medical profession. Working as a waiter will have taught the student discipline and responsibility as well as valuable communication skills which will positively influence their ability to perform well as a doctor. Hands-on experience at the St. John's Ambulance serves to provide the student with some practical experience whilst also challenging them in their confidence.

Bad points:
The student's understanding of infection control is limited and in the way it is presented in this statement suffers from some shortcomings. Whilst hand hygiene and personal cleanliness are important, they play a partial role in the overall complex of infection control and it is somewhat difficult to attribute outbreaks of infections solely to lapses in this area. This type of superficial sweeping statement distracts from the content and reflects poorly on the student's ability to draw reasonable conclusions from their experiences.

Overall:
A well-balanced statement that provides good insight into the different experiences that helped shape the student and influence them in their decision to follow a career in medicine. The student presents themselves as a well-disciplined, driven, and well-rounded individual, generally well-suited for becoming a doctor.

NOTES

GRADUATE PERSONAL STATEMENTS

Statement 84

I have recently graduated with a degree in Psychology, during which time I immersed myself within the topic of the human mind, achieving high academic success as well as gaining valuable presentation, research and study skills that I will carry for the rest of my life. However, studying mental health and illness fuelled my desire to understand the human body and I often found myself studying beyond the syllabus to learn more of the chemistry behind the diseases. Whilst I have a firm understanding of mental health and the brain, I now desire to take this further and develop my knowledge of other facets of human biology in a clinical setting. I believe that my sound understanding of biology combined with an in-depth knowledge of the human mind and behaviours will give me a valuable and unique foundation on which to base my medical education and provide the best possible care to patients.

A two week placement within general medicine and anaesthetics provided me with great insight into the wide variety of specialities the field of medicine offers. I had the opportunity to spend time with patients before, during and after a number of surgeries, offering them comfort when they were nervous or in pain. Following the satisfaction I gained from this, I am currently beginning employment as a Healthcare Assistant where I will work during my gap year and gain hands-on experience with patients and an in-depth understanding of the healthcare profession.

A week I spent in an orthopaedics department was invaluable in understanding the importance of teamwork and communication within the field of medicine. The efficient correspondence of information between a team of nurses and doctors at the morning meeting meant that a patient narrowly avoided amputation of a finger. A day shadowing an F1 on ward rounds revealed a different side of medicine, emphasising instead patient contact and long-term care. The compassion with which the doctor cared for a patient recovering from a suicide attempt was inspiring and I have subsequently begun training as a telephone volunteer for Samaritans. Here I will provide a first point of contact for individuals contemplating ending their lives, gaining skills that will be invaluable to me as a doctor.

An empathetic nature is crucial in the field of medicine and is a quality I have developed through a number of voluntary projects I partake in. While at school, I utilised my musical training to teach music classes to pupils from a nearby special needs school. Through this, I improved my skills of communicating with children, especially learning how to articulate tangible explanations from more complex ideas. I also learned how to adapt my approach from one individual to the next, since each child possessed a different level of disability. Regular voluntary work with individuals suffering from dementia at my local hospital has taught me the importance of palliative as well as curative care. I have learned that it is often small gestures such as a kind conversation that can make the biggest difference to a patient's happiness and wellbeing.

I enjoy feeling part of a team and the independence of self-sufficiency, and have therefore held a job alongside my studies since I was 16. I am often praised for remaining upbeat and helpful at all times and I believe that my unfaltering positive attitude is one of my strongest assets that will guide me successfully through a career in medicine. In order to relax I am an avid runner, both individually and as part of a team, representing my school on many occasions.

Medicine is a demanding profession, however I relish the challenges ahead and believe I have the personality and motivation to excel as a doctor, becoming a valuable asset to both my university and the field of medicine. My eagerness to learn and adapt makes me perfectly suited to the ever-changing world of medicine and each of my relevant experiences have only confirmed my drive to become a doctor.

Universities applied to:
➢ Birmingham: Offer
➢ Southampton: Rejected
➢ Warwick: Rejected
➢ Newcastle: Rejected

Good points:
The student provides good evidence of their motivation to pursue a career in medicine. Having studied psychology gives the unique perspective of having unique insight into the non-physical side of medical practice, therefore being able to appreciate the role of soft-skills in medical care. The student demonstrates a good range of clinical experience and also demonstrates the ability to reflect well on their particular experiences, drawing reasonable conclusions and motivation for personal development. The student also demonstrates a good exposure to the chronic aspects of medical care by volunteering with patients suffering from dementia, highlighting the burden of chronic disease as well as the specific challenges of a neuro-degenerative disease.

Bad points:
Due to the student already having undergone a degree, it would be interesting to learn how this experience has influenced them and has put them in the position of being a better doctor, even beyond the mere syllabus of their degree.

Overall:
A good statement written by a student with a unique set of experiences and skills that will come in handy in the good and successful practice of medicine. The student demonstrates to be welldisciplined in the pursuit of their career as well as aware of the challenges a career in medicine holds. Having already successfully completed a degree demonstrates the student's self-motivation and their ability to work well in an academic environment.

NOTES

Statement 85

As I have contemplated what I wish to do with my life I have been increasingly drawn to medicine, a profession that is intellectually and mentally challenging, varied and constantly evolving. I am attracted to its practical nature and the emotional reward that comes from working for and with other people.

In order to gain a realistic understanding of the life of a doctor I undertook a number of varied work experiences. At the Radiology Departments of the Royal Free and QMC I observed a stent dilatation, fibroid embolisation, the coiling of a cerebral aneurysm and an MRI enteroclysis. I was struck by the intricacy of the procedures as well as the dexterity, physical stamina and mental focus of the radiologists. I also attended sessions in CT and MRI scanning. I was captivated by the anatomical displays and their exquisite detail compared with the 'primitive' X-rays I watched my father read as a child! In particular I remember seeing a patient with TB granulomas of the lung, liver and brain. When attending various GP surgeries and the Chest and Allergy Clinic at St Mary's the holistic way that the doctors engaged with their patients impressed me. Their awareness of non-verbal signals and their ability to extract pertinent clinical information was vital to arriving at an accurate diagnosis.

This summer, after ten days of intensive training in emergency medicine, I spent two months as a volunteer EMT for the Israeli Ambulance Service working one or two eight-hour shifts daily. I learnt to work as part of a team, to assess situations quickly, follow protocol precisely and communicate effectively in highly pressurized situations. I felt a deep satisfaction when implementing basic medical skills and calming and comforting patients in distress.

During my work experiences and through my preparation for A-level Chemistry and Biology I have re-discovered a deep appreciation and enthusiasm for the biological sciences. In particular I have been intrigued by Neurology, having read 'The Man Who Mistook His Wife for a Hat' and 'Phantoms in the Brain'. I was enthralled by the creative approaches taken by the authors and how understanding of the abnormal provides insights into the normal.

I have had two internships at HM Treasury. In 2008 I compiled a report on corporate governance creating and applying my own methodology and liaising directly with civil servants from across Whitehall. In 2009 as a member of the RBS team I developed communications products for the public. Whilst at school I volunteered at a local primary school and during my gap year I spent three months teaching ESL to students from disadvantaged backgrounds, initially under supervision but later organising and running classes on my own. The experience of building trusting relationships with my pupils taught me valuable lessons in patience, attentive listening and sensitivity to others. I also learnt to express myself simply and clearly. At University I took an active interest in student politics. Prior to the recent European elections I initiated the 'BEAT THE BNP' campaign, working with individuals and groups from all political and religious sectors. I am an independent, outgoing and intellectually curious person, open to new experiences. I therefore seized the chance to spend a semester at the University of Maryland. I enjoyed immersing myself in a new culture and adapting to a new academic environment. As a keen sportsman I play team football regularly, although not the most skilful I compensate with guts and determination!

I know that medicine is an extremely demanding profession. I feel I have a good understanding of the pressures doctors face but also of the rewards. All of my experiences have not only confirmed my desire to practice medicine but also shown me that I possess the necessary stamina, drive and emotional maturity. I believe that my varied background, empathetic nature and determination will help me to become a well-rounded doctor.

Universities applied to:
- University College: Offer
- King's: Rejected
- King's Graduate: Rejected
- Bart's: Offer

Good points:
Well-written and good style. Very varied experience in the past which is good as it gives insight into the students as a well-rounded individual. The student also demonstrates a wide range of previous experiences that will help set him apart from other applicants that will not necessarily have the same level of experience. Having a degree is also an interesting component, but it should maybe be elaborated on a little further.

Bad points:
Because the student has such a wealth of previous experiences, it is easy to get lost in details that have only limited relevance to the study of medicine. It would be more useful to focus on fewer experiences and use them to convey specific messages about lessons learned that will make the student a better doctor. Some of the past experiences offer themselves particularly for this such as the EMT experience as well as the teaching experience. Teaching is a particularly good point to provide details on. The student's motivation for studying medicine is somewhat unclear as well. It almost seems like the student chose to study medicine after being bored with their current choice of career.

Overall:
A decent statement. It gives a good overview of the student's past and previous experiences. Unfortunately, because of the wealth of experiences, the statement stays too superficial. It would have been a lot stronger if the student could have tied his experiences better to the medicine.

NOTES

Statement 86

Working at Great Ormond Street Hospital as a pre-registration pharmacist has been the most challenging and fascinating experience of my life so far. Every day I have the opportunity to be a working part of a diverse team of professionals, caring for patients with an incredible range of conditions.

Working alongside doctors on a daily basis has highlighted how much I would like to study medicine. I am always captivated with how doctors can take a wealth of clinical information, histories and observational data, then appraise and apply it to reach an effective decision. I feel that I would be very well suited to this. I love to question, investigate and collaborate with others to solve problems. I am fascinated by the disease states I see when working with patients on the wards. I always spend time researching and trying to understand their condition, talking to them about it wherever possible.

As well as my job, I have had the opportunity to shadow a wide range of doctors in orthopaedics, endocrinology and general practice. I have learned a lot about communication with patients through this, and have seen how medics are able to balance their agenda with that of their patient. Although my current role does feature some patient contact, I would love a role where I could spend more time communicating with them, as it is the most rewarding aspect of my work. Recently I have been volunteering with the London Ambulance Service, caring for patients in a wide variety of acute situations. This has been an important and challenging experience and it has shown me the significance of adaptability when communicating.

I studied pharmacy at the University of East Anglia, where I was thrilled to be awarded a first class degree and received merit as one of the top students in the cohort for two consecutive years. I particularly enjoyed pharmacology and applying it to real patient scenarios. During my final year I took part in a research project investigating novel anticancer agents, the results of which went on to form part of a published research paper. I was also a national semi-finalist of the annual 'Responding to Symptoms' competition, which I attribute to my passion for clinical skills during my degree.

As well as a strong and relevant knowledge base, I believe my degree has given me a high standard of skills in patient communication, applying evidence, team working and leadership. I was delighted to be elected as LGBT welfare officer at my university, where I set up my own support group for those struggling with their sexuality whilst studying. I feel that I was able to assist them by discussing these issues, whilst they taught me a lot about trust and compassion. I also represented the student body on my school council and worked regularly as a student guide. At the end of my degree the head of school awarded me with the Alumni Prize for outstanding school contribution.

My principle interests are design and photography. I enjoy visiting galleries, exhibitions and taking my own photographs. Creativity consistently plays a part in my life and I believe it has an important role both in my leisure time and my work. I am a keen cyclist and enjoy combining it with exploring new places. I have always been passionate about politics, and a few years ago I was invited to speak at the House of Lords, which was an honour and something I will never forget. I have continued this passion through participation in my university debating society and I also participated in an intercollegiate medical debating competition.

It has been quite a journey for me to get to this point. I have worked hard to try and demonstrate that I have the work ethic, ability and attributes necessary to study medicine. I am keen to develop myself further and feel prepared for this challenge.

Universities applied to:
- Birmingham: Offer
- King's: Rejected
- Queen Mary: Rejected
- Warwick: Offer

Good points:

A well-structured statement that demonstrates a well-balanced and diverse background as well as a wealth of non-academic experiences contributing to the individual development. The experiences as a pharmacist provide a unique perspective as they guarantee a wide range of clinical exposure, both to patients and disease as well as more managerial aspects of medicine. Depending on the course type applied for (graduate v undergraduate) this provides an important advantage compared to the average applicant just leaving school. The student also demonstrates a varied non-academic history of commitment and activity. This further underlines characteristics such as compassion, empathy, communication skills, and dedication.

Bad points:

The writing style of the statement is somewhat sub-standard. This takes some of the strength of the experiences away as it almost seems trivialising. Furthermore it would improve the statement more if the student applied his unique standpoint of previous experience further. Having already successfully completed a degree the student will be aware of the challenges of university, expanding on this, for example, will set him apart further from other students.

Overall:

A good statement with the potential to be great. This student clearly has a very varied background and has a lot of interesting experiences to draw from for their statement. It is let down in strength by a lack of in-depth development of ideas and reflection of previous experiences.

NOTES

Statement 87

At some point in our lives we will become ill; when that happens, the people that we will have to rely on are doctors. Almost by definition the professional life of a doctor equates to easing the suffering and improving the health of the general population. I have a strong desire to be part of this as I am inspired by the idea of a profession where there is a need to be constantly up to date with the latest developments: a lifetime of learning and moving the boundaries forward.

Recently I read the book 'The discovery of the Germ': it provides an interesting insight into modern medical history. What shook me was the rapid pace of development between 1880 and 1900: in just twenty years, medicine was transformed. The role of germs in producing ill health was for the first time fully understood, resulting in doctors abandoning ideas that had persisted for thousands of years.

I am a frequent listener of "Inside Health", which discusses current medical issues. In one broadcast, a doctor working in a HIV clinic noticed that almost all of the patients he had treated did not have Multiple Sclerosis; this led him to link the possibility of using antiretroviral drugs to treat people affected with MS. To understand more about how people are affected by this disease, I researched MS and developed some knowledge of this life-long condition. I have taken a particular interest in motor-neuron diseases to better understand the impact of this condition on residents of the disability home where I volunteer.

I have come to understand some of the essential qualities a good doctor needs through my personal achievements and interests; I was able to explore the primary care of medicine during a three day work placement at a Birmingham surgery, where I shadowed several General Practitioners. I found the experience very insightful; it allowed me to value the importance of communication between a doctor and patient and the need to always remain empathetic and patient. I observed that not only did the GP change her approach to different patients, but the patients themselves saw the GP as a trustworthy figure to whom they confided their problems. The approach that I observed from this experience has greatly aided me during my voluntary work at a local Leonard Cheshire disability home, where I have built one to one relationships with residents; it has given me the confidence to be more friendly and engaging. I have also extended my understanding of long term care and the issues arising from genetic conditions through joining the Local Aid Buddies Scheme where I participate in a variety of activities such as art and crafts with young people with learning disabilities.

A work placement at Glangwili Hospital gave me the opportunity to participate in ward rounds. This experience allowed me to appreciate the importance of team work: it not only relieves pressure but also leads to a more accurate decision because opinions are expressed from people with different skill sets and knowledge of patients. Last August I took part in a First Aid Course, qualifying with a Level 2 in Pediatric First Aid: I believe this has made me a more responsible person, as I will now be able to act confidently in an emergency situation.

As a positive consequence of moving around during my childhood (I spent 7 years in China), I am fluent in Mandarin and find it easy to adapt quickly in a new environment. Outside of school I enjoy music whilst working towards Grade 7 in piano and 6 in flute; I have found it particularly enjoyable playing in the school wind band, participating in concerts both in and out of school.

Medicine presents to me an opportunity to further my interest in science; to become a part of the profession which is at the center of society. It is a career which requires extensive knowledge, compassionate commitment and excellent inter-personal skills. I believe that I possess the qualities needed to become the devoted and dependable doctor which I aspire to be.

Universities applied to:

➤ Birmingham: Offer
➤ Cardiff: Interview + Rejected
➤ Bristol: Rejected
➤ Warwick: Offer

Good points:

Well-written and well-structured statement that contains a lot of useful information about the applicant and the reasons for their choice of medicine as a career. The student demonstrates good and well-reflected experiences from hospital and general practice attachments, all of which will contribute to making the student a well-rounded individual, exposed to the challenges of medicine and familiar with some of the skills required for a successful career in medicine. The student recognises the ever-changing nature of medicine and acknowledges the challenges for doctors that come with this characteristic.

Bad points:

Some of the statements the student makes are factually oversimplified. In particular, this applies to the paragraph addressing the progress in microbiology between 1880 and 1900. Medical development is significantly more complicated than the student makes it out to be and recognising this complexity is an important quality doctors should be able to demonstrate. Furthermore, that introduction to the statement is generally good in regards to the underlying principle but is very poorly formulated, weakening it significantly.

Overall:

A principally good statement that works along some generally good ideas. Unfortunately, it is somewhat let down by inaccuracies and stylistic weaknesses. The concise and well-written passages related to the student's work experience make a big difference in the overall quality of the statement.

NOTES

Statement 88

I have always aimed for a profession where I can meet and engage with people from all sorts of backgrounds. While medicine satisfies this, it also combines my love of learning and compassion, and I am convinced it is the right vocation for me. Living with doctors in my family and university has given me a realistic view of life as a doctor, as has medical work experience, and my involvements through school and university have shown me that I am capable to handle the challenges of in a career in medicine.

Medical work experience has given me further insight into clinical practice and the importance of communication with patients and carers. In 2011 I shadowed a paediatric endocrinologist at Great Ormond Street Hospital. It was fascinating to see congenital diseases I had learnt about in my degree, and to see how a deeper understanding of medical science facilitates more articulate patient counselling, which is essential in guiding treatment. I have always enjoyed studying the pathogenesis of human disease. I look forward to the academic aspect of medicine and putting what I learn into practice.

I consider social care and awareness to be significant factors in effective medical treatment. Through work experience in my GP surgery I met a spectrum of patients visiting the GP, nurse, health trainer and drugs clinic. This not only increased my understanding of the NHS and appreciation of public health campaigns, but also reinforced the importance of gaining patients' trust and addressing psychosocial issues. This year I am volunteering full time with XLP, a youth charity in East London, working in council estates and schools to help young people escape gang culture and achieve their potential. I am eager to see the difference this will make to individuals, and I expect to gain valuable insight into more challenging aspects of society and social factors affecting health. I know this year will be most worthwhile preparation for work in the NHS.

My Natural Sciences degree encompassed biology, mathematics and chemistry, gradually focussing on human biology and statistics. Cancer genetics became my particular interest, and I was able to further this during my Masters year. I devised a method of statistical analysis of DNA methylation and gene expression in germ cell tumours, resulting in a publication next spring. I gained experience in the scientific basis of medical research, while eight-week summer placements in 2010 and 2012 at Birmingham's Cancer Research Clinical Trials Unit gave me an appreciation of the administration of clinical trials. I hope to follow this research as I progress through medicine.

At university I have led and been part of numerous societies. As leader of Christians in Sport and president of the Natural Sciences Society I learned the value of cooperation, communication, motivation and delegation. As welfare representative in halls I looked after the needs of three hundred people, representing their concerns to the university. This meant gaining the trust of students and staff and communicating appropriately with all. My role on the Athletics Club committee involved organising races on campus. This required detailed planning and time management, which I excel at, having balanced studies with sport, orchestras and youth groups since primary school.

I am proactive in seeking opportunities to develop and stretch myself. I find particular appeal in physical challenges; having completed two half marathons, sprint and olympic triathlons, three treks in the Himalayas and a long distance kayak trip on the Yukon River, I have learnt the reward of training and perseverance. I believe this has given me the physical and mental capacity to deal with more demanding aspects of medicine.

I am eager to throw myself into the many and varied situations that medicine will offer. While I know it will be challenging at times, I feel confident and ready to take on the responsibilities and embrace the rewards.

Universities applied to:
- Birmingham: Offer
- Nottingham: Offer
- Southampton: Offer
- Warwick: Rejected

Good points:
A well-written and well-structured statement that provides very good insight into the personal development of the student as well as their academic interests. Coming from a natural science background is of obvious benefit in the study of medicine, and the students previous research experience clearly demonstrates an interest in the academic side of medicine. In regards to the non-academic, soft skills of medicine, the student provides several examples of experiences they feel taught him valuable lessons in communication and problem solving. This complements well with the academic achievements.

Bad points:
Whilst the student has a natural science background, it would be interesting to read more about this and get some deep insight into how the student intends to apply some of the knowledge acquired for their study of medicine. They briefly touches on the subject, but a more concise passage would increase the value for the statement. In regards to the beginning of the statement, there are some minor weaknesses in the content. The beginning almost seems to contradict the rest of the statement. The student claims that they is convinced that medicine is the right choice of vocation, this is somewhat difficult to believe considering the student has already completed a different degree prior to applying for medicine. Also, the statement is somewhat short of actual clinical experience.

Overall:
Good statement, with obvious trying points, but somewhat short of hands-on clinical expense and exposure to the intrinsic workings of the NHS. Due to the background of the student, this statement has the potential to be excellent but sells itself short by a lack of attention to detail in regards to context.

NOTES

Statement 89

The elderly lady collapsed to the floor, emptied her bladder and started foaming at the mouth. I rushed for the doctor. The speed at which the physician stabilised the patient whilst remaining calm was inspiring. Within minutes he had administered a diazepam injection, fitted both a glucose drip and catheter and put her swollen arm in plaster. I felt helpless, a feeling I no longer want to experience. I want to have the knowledge, the skills and the appropriate manner to put someone at ease when they are sick and vulnerable. What's more, I think I have the potential required.

This woman was a patient at the medical clinic funded and run by myself and other students in rural Nepal. Although lack of clinical expertise restricted my medical contribution, I took basic observations in order to triage patients and dispensed drugs following consultations. This experience not only allowed me to interact with patients with a variety of conditions, including some rarely seen in developed countries, but it also gave me insight into the necessities for providing efficient healthcare services.

I have also done work experience in two NHS hospitals. Ward rounds demonstrated how the multidisciplinary team works together to determine the most suitable treatment and patient care. During a neurology consultation a patient presented with reduced sensation of his 4th and 5th fingers which I identified as ulnar nerve entrapment. Applying my anatomical knowledge to problem solve in this way was hugely satisfying. As well as being knowledgeable, the consultant showed a genuine interest in all his patients and his light-hearted yet professional approach reassured even the most apprehensive. In my final placement I adopted a similar bedside manner when taking a patient's history and performing a basic cognitive assessment.

These skills were also useful whist volunteering as a St John's Ambulance first aider and a dementia befriender. As a befriender my role was to encourage engagement and communication. For some patients visual cues would stimulate old memories which they would happily entertain me with. For others, in the later stages of the disease, my presence comforted them when they were distressed or confused. This role was extremely gratifying and it has taught me the importance of emotional care alongside physical care. I will continue to reap the rewards of patient interaction in my new position as a bank HCA.

During my neuroscience degree I developed the ability to critically analyse and think independently. These skills will be useful throughout any medical career enabling me to interpret clinical research so my patients receive the best treatments. My fascination with the brain has grown throughout my studies and neurology is a speciality I would certainly consider. Alternatively, the opportunity to build long-term relationships with patients makes general practice equally appealing. I am aware that, in all specialities, medicine is a demanding profession requiring a breadth of knowledge and long hours which can be physically, mentally and emotionally exhausting. However the prospect of having a stimulating and rewarding job in which I would be continually learning is exciting and would motivate me throughout medical school. I know it would be tough but I enjoy a challenge. I have recently completed my Gold Duke of Edinburgh Award and taken part in the 3 Peaks Challenge. Both experiences required effective teamwork and taught me that achievement comes from determination. As well as working well in a team my leadership qualities led to my selection for the roles of Head Girl at secondary school and social secretary for my university tennis club. Whilst at medical school I would continue play tennis for both enjoyment and to alleviate stress.

Through a combination of work experience and volunteer work I believe I have developed a realistic desire to study medicine and I look forward to both the challenges and rewards ahead.

Universities applied to:

- Leicester: Rejected
- Bristol: Rejected
- Cambridge: Interview + Rejected
- Birmingham: Offer

Good points:

Very diverse background and interesting experiences. The experience in Nepal and volunteering in the UK allow for a good comparison of the differences of care delivery in environments of different wealth and economic standards. Having run a clinic is interesting as it provides good insight into effective resource management and organisation skills- a quality very desirable in doctors. Volunteering as a dementia befriender is an excellent opportunity to improve communication and inter-personal skills as well as getting exposure to the reality of chronic and debilitating diseases.

Bad points:

The beginning of the statement is too melodramatic. This is supposed to be interesting, yes, but it is not prose. Drama is not a quality sought in doctors. Also, the feeling of helplessness will not fully leave, even as a doctor. There will always be challenges and situations of uncertainty. The structure of the statement could also be improved. Achieving a previous degree is interesting and relevant and should come closer to the front. Especially since it has relevance for medicine. It is also relevant to learn what lessons the student took away from their degree with regards to academic work and self-motivation. In regards to the student's description of their work experience, the student could be more efficient in providing a framework of their experience and detailing their conclusions and reflections in more depth.

Overall:

Statement with good potential. In the form presented here, a lot of this potential is wasted on poor style. The melodramatic entry reduces the strength of the statement significantly, being very distracting. It would be significantly more appropriate to describe the patient as experiencing a seizure. This would allow for the same feeling of helplessness motivating the student whilst sounding less dramatic.

NOTES

Statement 90

The NHS saved my cousin's life.

The NHS cared for my Grandparents through a range of illnesses.

The NHS has provided my Mum with a fulfilling career.

I am not alone in feeling gratitude towards the NHS and those who work for it, I place great value on their role and see worth in the positive impact they have upon others lives. This, together with my great interest in science has urged me to study medicine. I am not naive to the dedication that this requires; indeed I have endeavoured to ensure that I am aware of what a medical degree and career will entail. This understanding has not deterred me. It has enhanced my ambition to pursue a career that I believe is truly valuable to society.

My education has given me a firm foundation of scientific understanding. Consistently, I have been drawn to health related fields of study, an interest that persuaded me to pursue a year-long internship at the pharmaceutical company Janssen. I was able to apply my scientific knowledge and research skills to successfully complete projects that enhanced my understanding of the link between R&D and patients. Ultimately, this work experience highlighted my attraction to the clinical application of medicine, motivating my current application.

This appreciation encouraged me to seek placements to shadow a number of clinicians. I gained an awareness of the high pressure clinicians' face and the breadth of variation between different medical specialities. My ambition also led me to volunteer at a local hospice, and since leaving university I have volunteered on the Dawson Ward at Kings College Hospital. This weekly commitment gives me the chance to support healthcare professionals and gain satisfaction from interacting with patients and their families.

Currently, alongside this I work as a Healthcare Researcher at a communications agency. In this role, I have become adept at multi-tasking and used to working as part of changing teams, for which my ability to communicate effectively has proven invaluable. It is essential that I have an up to date awareness of the healthcare policy landscape, this has given me a realistic understanding of the environment the NHS functions in. One of my proudest achievements has been completing a literature review for a company who produce robotic exoskeletons, which allowed the company to reach out to more patients with a stronger evidence base.

Additionally in my role, I have supported development of the communications launch plan for a genomics company. Genomics was the focus of my final year dissertation, a project which required commitment and perseverance to achieve a first class mark. I am excited and curious to understand how innovations in this technology and the future of personalised medicine will impact patients and I look forward to being able to exploit their potential.

Studying medicine is academically challenging, I believe I have proven my capability though my university grades and by being awarded the Robert Eisenthal prize. A medical degree will also require me to balance a demanding workload, something I have become accustomed to. Whilst at university, I studied extracurricular French, volunteered, held a peer mentor role and was selected to be a university Ambassador. As an Ambassador, I developed my leadership skills by giving tours and presentations to large groups of prospective students and parents from a range of different backgrounds.

I have proven my ability to work both in teams and on my own and I have also demonstrated flexibility, having adapted to new geographic locations, working styles and colleagues. I am a passionate, motivated and caring individual with a desire to make a positive impact in people's lives. I believe my academic history together with the invaluable work experience I have gained has established that a career in medicine is the best path for me.

Universities applied to:
➢ Birmingham: Offer
➢ Imperial College: Interview + Rejected
➢ University College: Interview + Rejected
➢ Brighton & Sussex: Interview + Rejected

Good points:
Well-written statement providing a good demonstration of the student's background and their abilities and skills. It gives a wide range of medicine-related work experiences, which provided the student with the opportunity to gain insight into the workings of medicine and relevant skills such as communication and team work. Having experience from a paid full-time job is also a strong point supporting the student's ability to focus their productivity as well as being goal-oriented. The student's interest in individualised treatments provides an interesting starting point for conversation in the review and also gives a good insight into the student's individual interests.

Bad points:
It would be interesting to know more about the student's previous degree. This would provide more information on the student's interests as well as potentially being relevant for medicine providing a scientific basis. The previous degree will also help greatly distinguishing this student from other applicants.

Overall:
A good statement that is well-written and provides good information about the student. There are some minor weaknesses, but these are well offset by the strengths of the statement. It could, however, be improved by having additional information about the student's previous degree as this would provide an additional academic source of information about the student.

NOTES

Statement 91

Feeling frustrated and helpless at my grandmother's three-month stay in hospital cemented my decision to become a doctor. Though I have had an interest in health and disease since studying 'medicine through time' at school, being affected by my relative's illness and the trust put in medicine drove me to begin placements, giving me firsthand experience of the challenges faced by modern doctors.

Speaking to pre-operative patients during hospital work experience about their anxieties allowed me to understand the expectations patients have from their healthcare; the anaethetist I was shadowing used his enthusiasm and interpersonal skills to relax patients of all ages. Observing the doctor respond calmly using his experience when a patient reacted badly to an anaesthetic relayed the importance of how clinicians must be adaptable in pressured situations. In the community I attended multi-disciplinary meetings, showing me the value of teamwork as allied health professionals shared expertise to discuss new strategies when a treatment was ineffective. This taught me the importance of patient-centred care. Observing mental health assessments allowed me to appreciate doctor-patient relationships, it was important that respect was gained in order to reassure the sensitive patient. I began to understand the role of education in treatment, as clinicians taught patients how some massage techniques may improve their lymphoedema using demonstrations and anatomical diagrams.

The past year of weekly volunteering as a Hospice Ward Helper has taught me to be realistic and I am reminded that doctors have natural limits. I continually learn that palliative care involves supporting individual needs when a cure is not available; while it is distressing when patients die, I find comfort in knowing I have had a positive impact on their lives. I was pleased to use my strong interpersonal skills to calm a delirious patient.

Being asked to train as a lymphoedema assistant with the hospice is a testimony to my reliability and work ethic. I continue to practice my bedside manner and gain hands-on experience of chronic illness and its affect on patients as well as those around them. Assisting with personal care has helped patients gain trust in me. As a social activities volunteer in the NHS I aid the independence of patients that have had brain injuries which has helped me understand the importance of empathy and compassion. I learnt that flexible approaches alongside a personal and patient nature are vital as it can be challenging when individuals have dysarthria.

During my degree I researched an association between cognitive function and incontinence in the elderly, which helped me value patient confidentiality. Through studying Biomedical Sciences I have become a motivated and independent learner, and whilst my degree has strengthened my interest in human disease, the lack of patient interaction has reinforced my desire to pursue medicine.

Working in retail has helped me develop initiative and strong teamwork skills; as a member of the social committee I organise events using my supportive leadership and decision-making skills, which are essential in solving medical dilemmas. I have transferred these skills as a high school mentor, utilising my impartiality and patience working with a student with a stammer. Running regular 10K events, baking and participating in choir help me achieve a work-life balance, vital for facing the demands of a medical career. Enjoying travel, I helped improve a women's refuge in Chile. Currently, I am taking the opportunity to gain further insight into the workings of the NHS as a trainee clinical coder.

Varied experiences over five years have shown me that medicine encompasses teaching, research and the clinical application of science, progressing my desire to study and practice medicine. I possess the commitment and drive to succeed in this rewarding, ever developing profession that requires lifelong learning.

Universities applied to:

➢ Birmingham: Offer
➢ Keele: Rejected
➢ East Anglia: Rejected
➢ Lancaster: Rejected

Good points:

A well-written and well-structured statement that provides good insight into the experiences of the student. The student provides an interesting account of their work experience and also reflects well on the lessons learned in the wards. The reflections on the hospice experiences are particularly strong. Recognising the limitations of doctors and medicine and also being aware of the role of palliative care further adds to the strength of the statement. Applying lessons learned during their previous degree that goes beyond the purely academic experience is a further strength of this statement.

Bad points:

Whilst the statement is generally very strong, it has some minor weaknesses, mainly related to the degree of detail provided for the individual points. The wealth of experiences make it difficult to address them all with sufficient detail, but further reflection would improve the strength in support of the statement.

Overall:

A very good statement that provides good insight into the student, their motivation to study medicine as well their personal background. The student demonstrates a wide range of interesting experiences, characteristics, and also provides much basis for discussion during the interview.

NOTES

Statement 92

Medicine is a field that is constantly advancing and this challenges doctors to continually adapt and learn. My desire to be a part of this dynamic profession stems from my experience as an impressionable 10 year old when I watched with great concern the expert care and treatment my father received following a diagnosis of grade 2 chondrosarcoma of the proximal left femur. This initial childhood interest continued to develop and as a 16 year old I was invited to spend a week shadowing the consultant who successfully treated my father, thus my passion for medicine as a career was confirmed.

A love of science and interest in the human body led me to explore the field of medicine beyond my academic studies. Over the past five years I have learnt much from three weeks of intensive shadowing of surgical consultants and two years of volunteering at a local hospice.

Studying Biomedical Science has prepared me for Graduate Medicine both academically and psychologically. Completing modules in pharmacology, immunology and biochemistry has given me a core scientific knowledge that I am ready to develop and apply in clinical settings. Studying B-cell immunology inspired my research project at Southampton General hospital on chronic lymphocytic leukaemia. By using a novel cytotoxic drug, currently undergoing stage 2 clinical trials, my research aimed to increase apoptosis of leukaemia cell lines. This haematological research led to me achieving the Society of Physiology award for physiological excellence and has given me an insight into a specific area of medicine that I am keen to explore in the future.

As a weekly volunteer at the Countess Mountbatten Hospice I was a member of the multi-disciplinary palliative care team where I continually learnt from their expert care of terminally ill patients. I particularly enjoyed completing the hospice's Meal Time Assistance training. Meal times are a special time of day and this work has allowed me to grasp the sensitivity and care that doctors give their patients. I have also learnt that medicine doesn't always cure but high quality care at the end of life is very important.

Shadowing surgical consultants on three separate occasions, at two local hospitals, helped me to understand the work of, and demands on, a doctor. Spending time in radiology, outpatient clinics and theatre reminded me that medicine is a multi-disciplinary field where every member of the hospital team has a key role in providing care. The two weeks I spent shadowing a Breast Consultant highlighted the difficult decisions and challenges that doctors face every day. Observing numerous surgical procedures widened my understanding of clinical practice. Viewing a sentinel lymph node biopsy was particularly fascinating and enabled me to couple my prior knowledge of metastatic cancers with the practicality of surgery.

Aside from my academic studies I enjoy captaining a football team in a local league. In 2009 I travelled to Uganda for three weeks on a school exchange. The trip opened my eyes to a different cultural way of life and the daily struggle of living in a third world country. Although my exchange partner's English was limited, I learnt how listening carefully bridged the communication gap and I believe this valuable lesson will help me in my medical career. On leaving school I travelled to Australia, New Zealand and South East Asia. This experience developed my independence and confidence, and helped prepare me for university.

Broad work experience and academic study has fuelled my ambition to study medicine. My focus on clinical practice for the past 5 years has taught me that medicine is a profession where I can continually engage, develop and learn. All I have discovered so far about medicine confirms to me that this is the profession I wish to pursue and believe that I can make a contribution to.

Universities applied to:
- ➤ Birmingham: Offer
- ➤ Warwick: Rejected
- ➤ Bart's: Rejected
- ➤ King's: Rejected

Good points:

Well-written and well-structured statement providing a good balance of clinical and non-clinical work experience, providing good insight into the student's interest and characteristics. They reflect well on their experiences and give a good account of how these experiences are relevant to medicine. The student's research history and exposure to clinical medicine are a further strength of the statement as they are clinically relevant providing insight in to the clinical practice of medicine and the human side of treatment. Additionally, this experience demonstrates valuable insight into scientific methods and work as a part of a team. The biomedical science background further contributes to setting the student apart from other applicants.

Bad points:

In the beginning, the student chooses formulations that weaken the statement by reducing the value of the content. The student reduces the emotional aspect of the introduction by de-valuing himself in the situation which weakens the value of the argument as a whole. In relation to the rest of the statement, at times the student could be more concise with his statements, making them more valuable and clearer with regards to their impact on them.

Overall:

Good statement that benefits greatly from the student's wealth of experiences, both academically and non-academically. The experiences made in the environment of their previous degrees are definite strong points and help to set the student apart from other applicants.

NOTES

Statement 93

I cannot lie and say I have wanted to become a doctor all my life, but I have always known that I want to work by helping people, and that I have a huge love of science. However, as a teenager I was diagnosed with rapid onset scoliosis and kyphosis, resulting in 2 major surgeries and a lot of time as an inpatient, the latest only last year after my original Harrington rod implants snapped in multiple places. Ever since, my life has been changed. I suffer from chronic neuropathic pain in my spine, and as a 21 year old graduate, it is very hard to contemplate that this will probably be the case for the rest of my life. Nonetheless, I believe it has made me a much better person today. I have had a huge insight into many levels of hospitals, and during my last surgery I could not speak higher of how I was treated. Every single person that worked there helped me get through every day. Whether it was the surgeon, anaesthetist, or simply the person bringing me my food, every one of them aided my recovery by just being kind, caring and supportive, showing me just the sort of doctor I know I am going to be. There is just no other career for me now.

However, I did love my time reading pharmacology, and there is so much that I have learnt from my time at university. I have found a particularly strong passion for the neurological side of medicine and disease, for example depression and analgesia, along with my favourite topic, anaesthesia. Because of this keen interest I still find myself reading papers that stand out to me in this field. I also believe that my social skill set has really developed during my time at Bristol, something that will only aid me in a career in medicine.

I am currently working full time as a healthcare assistant in a private hospital outpatients department, with some work also in both theatre and on a ward. This is so valuable to me, as it involves helping people when they are at their most vulnerable, which is where my passions lie. The hospital OPD where I work covers a broad range of specialities from orthopaedics to cosmetic surgery; I see a huge range of clinics. There is a great range of things I do in this job, giving me experience in removing a few sutures to chaperoning patients in clinic. There are many things that this job has taught me – mainly how tiring shift work is! I have learnt that many medical techniques take a long time and a lot of hard work to master. However the main thing I feel I have learnt from this is how quickly and easily something can go wrong, putting the lives of vulnerable patients at risk, and this has taught me how careful and particular everything must be, even if it will take much longer.

As well as this, I do a weekly placement on a NHS dementia ward, reassuring patients who are often confused and lonely, to help them through their stay. This is really important to me, as it exposes me to one of the many difficult faces of medicine; that not all your patients are going to return to full health. This is a very harrowing experience, and I believe that it is very important that I am learning to cope with it before I even start my career. I really enjoy my work on the ward, as the reward of helping the patients cope is one I value so highly. Furthermore, this past summer and the one before I have done work experience in a GP surgery in one of the poorest areas of my home city, shadowing the GPs and nurses in clinic. This was an invaluable piece of work experience, as the high majority of patients had emigrated from other countries and therefore struggled with communicating in English. It was amazing to see how well all the doctors dealt with this and managed to make the patients who were often anxious or confused feel at ease in the surgery. This has demonstrated to me how important it is for a doctor to do everything in their power to help patients feel relaxed and comforted, in what can be a very intimidating environment.

I know that medicine isn't the glamorous or lucrative career that people may perceive it to be. I want to become a doctor, because to me, the most rewarding part of life is being able to help other people. I find it an alluring career because I can't think of anything better than being able to feel that every day at work, meeting people from every walk of life, who just need someone to care for them in ways they simply can't themselves.

Universities applied to:
➢ Birmingham: Offer
➢ King's: Offer
➢ Bart's: Offer
➢ University College: Rejected

Good points:
Well-written and well-structured statement. The student chooses a very honest and personal approach to the reason of why medicine. This is definitely a very strong point as it provides good insight into what motivates the student on their path to becoming a doctor. The student furthermore demonstrates a varied range of previous work experience that allowed them to further their experience of clinical medicine behind the patient-based experience. The student's previous degree is relevant to the field of medicine and, therefore, a strong point to include in the statement. The student also demonstrates a good awareness of the reality of the medical profession, supporting the impression of a well-rounded and well-balanced personality.

Bad points:
The statement suffers somewhat from the wide range of the student's experiences, predisposing it to lack in detail in some passages. This is unfortunate as an appropriate development of ideas and reflections is essential for the quality of the statement.

Overall:
A very strong statement suffering from some minor weaknesses mainly related to the range of experiences available to the student to draw from. The personal approach to the statement as a whole is one of the most obvious strengths as it provides valuable insight into the personal development of the student.

NOTES

Statement 94

Medicine is a career that is both challenging and demanding, however, it is a highly rewarding field where I can combine my scientific interests with my compassionate nature in an environment where the wellbeing of the community is the doctor's first priority. Through personal experience I developed an understanding about the many years of continual training required for a doctor to provide effective patient care. When my father was diagnosed with diabetes, I became intrigued into how the doctors were able to interpret data and graphs to provide the best management possible. After observing their professionalism and continued support, I hope to strive to provide a very high level of care in reflection of what my family has received.

The challenging nature of the theoretical and practical aspects of my biochemistry degree has provided insight into the work and effort a medicine degree requires. Pressured work surroundings have refined my study and organisational skills required to succeed as a physician.

For two weeks, I shadowed a GP and learnt about the day to day running of the surgery. Observing consultations, I became aware of patient confidentiality and the attention to detail required to determine the correct course of action. Working with doctors and nurses at a BUPA clinic, I was taught how to interpret blood sample results and the importance of the relationship between different health professionals. Volunteering at a hospice enabled me to appreciate patient centred care beyond their illnesses and the importance of palliative care. I was able to empathise with and comfort not just the patient, but also their families in a holistic manner offering them conversation away from their daily routine.

Volunteering on community projects has proven to be rewarding and instilled empathy within me. Working alongside GP's on a community project, the teams aim was to aid patients in their everyday problems and make them aware of how to alleviate and manage stress. Patients have so far garnered this project with the highest of accolades leading to its improvement and growth. I was able to hone my listening and communication skills as English was not the first language of many of the patients. I organised a summer working at two hospitals in Gujarat, India. From this experience, I gained a great appreciation for the NHS where the population has access to a modern organised healthcare system in stark contrast to the sheer poverty in India. Being bilingual, I was able to talk to patients in a sensitive manner. This taught me how to deal with the emotional side of medicine by stepping into the shoes of the patient. It was intriguing to see and learn how to assess patients given the limited resources available. Observing a haematologist, I learnt that sickle cell anaemia provides some protection against malaria which is prevalent in India and whether this can be classified as an advantage. In a multi-cultural society, doctors should be able to remain respectful of a patient's beliefs and customs when treating him or her. Working with people from various backgrounds has helped improve my understanding of the differing needs of the patients.

Teamwork is imperative to work efficiently and effectively within a multidisciplinary team. This requires understanding, patience and mutual respect which I have gained from playing netball and as Head Girl at my school. Acting responsibly and communicating with my peers and juniors developed my interpersonal and leadership skills.

Whilst the role of a doctor is demanding and emotionally challenging, the ability to positively influence numerous lives is truly inspiring. I possess a strong work ethic which I believe is essential to succeed in a rapidly advancing medical field. My journey thus far has given me a firm foundation of knowledge, experience and drive that I can bring to medical school and build upon. I am enthused and excited for the opportunity to prove my potential and succeed.

Universities applied to:

> Birmingham: Offer
> East Anglia: Interview + Rejected
> Aberdeen: Rejected
> Lancaster: Rejected

Good points:

Well-structured statement demonstrating a wide range of experiences, both nationally and internationally, demonstrating the student's ability to comfortably act in new environments and leaving their comfort zone. The student demonstrates relevant clinical experience that provided them with valuable insight into the workings of medicine. Having experienced medicine in both a developed and a less developed environment is relevant for being able to recognise challenges in medical practice.

Bad points:

The role of the doctor is only partly the maintenance of the community's well-being. The primary focus of a doctor lies with the individual which in a sum leads to the wellbeing of the community. This is an important differentiation to make as medicine today revolves around the individual patient. Unfortunately, the personal statement contains some factual errors - the protective attributes of the heterozygous sickle cell trait in malaria is well established and demonstrated on the example of some regions in Africa.

Overall:

Well-written statement of good quality that demonstrates a good range of experiences and skills as well as good insight into the individual interests of the student. The statement addresses some relevant challenges of modern medical practice, especially in relation to the contrasts that come with increased economic status of a country.

NOTES

Statement 95

My passion and deep interest in human biology led me to study Cellular and Molecular Medicine, specialising in Microbiology, with the intention of pursuing a career in research. However, the deaths of two close family members whilst I was at University caused me to reassess my aspirations and to seriously consider a career in medicine for the first time. Witnessing the high standard of world class, one-to-one care given to my Grandfather whilst he was in ICU, despite being 87 and having lung and heart failure, had a profound effect on me. The emotional support and empathy my family received from the medical team highlighted another, often undervalued, part of their role.

It is this commitment to patient wellbeing, and a desire to work directly with patients on a daily basis, which has inspired me to pursue a career in medicine. Work experience I have undertaken to better inform me about the career has only served to reinforce my ambitions.

I volunteered once a week for several months as a ward visitor on a dementia ward at a local hospital. I was able to spend long periods of time talking with patients and building a rapport with them, something I found immensely enjoyable and which would be crucial as a doctor. I was also able to shadow doctors and other healthcare professionals, such as nurses, healthcare assistants and occupational therapists, on this ward. I attended multi-disciplinary team meetings which impressed on me the role of teamwork in order to plan and implement individualised treatment programmes for each patient. This work showed me some of the challenges of working with dementia patients and just how devastating this disease can be for both the patients and their families. I was, however, inspired by how the doctors and other healthcare workers responded to the stresses of their job, working calmly under pressure to consistently maintain high levels of patient care. During work experience at a local GP surgery, I was able to shadow not only doctors but also nurse practitioners as well as district nurses, which gave me a much better understanding of medicine in the community. Witnessing GP consultations left me with a greater respect for the role that GPs have as the first point of contact for many patients, having to distinguish between relatively mild and life threatening diseases, as well as having to manage and "fine-tune" chronic conditions.

I volunteered, and was later employed, as a play worker for Routeways, a local charity running play schemes and activities for children with a range of learning difficulties and mental disabilities. This developed my skills in interacting with vulnerable children with a very wide range of abilities and needs, and taught me how important it is to treat every child as an individual and not as a case. This was particularly important in disorders as varied as Autism Spectrum Disorder. Being able to improve the quality of life for these children, by just a small amount on a daily basis, was hugely rewarding and has reinforced my desire to become a doctor.

Outside of academia, I regularly exercise and play sports. I played football for my school team and for my University Halls of Residence team, which required dedication and helped improve teamwork and discipline. I am a keen road cyclist and a member of a cycling club, something I believe is very beneficial in order to keep fit and help with relaxation. I was a full school prefect and pupil mentor whilst in secondary school which required maturity and leadership skills.

I have all the attributes to become a successful doctor. I am an extremely empathic individual and have achieved highly in academia, resulting in a sound knowledge of the science underpinning modern medicine. My opportunities to undertake work experience have shown me the varied and, at times, harsh realities of being a doctor. Ultimately, however, a career in medicine is an extremely rewarding endeavour and one which I would relish and excel in.

Universities applied to:
➤ Birmingham: Offer
➤ Warwick: Rejected
➤ Southampton: Rejected
➤ Bristol: Rejected

Good points:

The student provides a very intimate and personal account of his motivations to pursue a career in medicine. Drawing on this emotional connection to the field adds an additional degree of depth to the statement, making it more relevant. It also provides good insight into the student's motivation for studying medicine. The student also demonstrates a good range of medically related work experience that will have provided them with a good insight into the challenges of medical care. The student's non-medical work is also interesting and relevant as the student identifies the beneficial characteristics of this work by having improved their communication and organisation skills and allowed them to become a more responsible individual. Furthermore, recognising the impact that disease has on the patient as well as on the patient's relatives is very relevant.

Bad points:

The conclusion of the statement could be improved to maintain the high quality of the statement. Whilst it is important to be aware of one's strengths, it might not be the best idea to claim that one possesses all attributes to become a successful doctor. This seems exaggerated as the student's experience of medical care to this point is very limited.

Overall:

Averagely well-written statement that provides good insight into the student's motivation and character. The student demonstrates a good range of clinical experience, but the overall strength of the statement is somewhat reduced by a misjudgement of experiences towards the end.

NOTES

Statement 96

Our health is something we so often take for granted. Yet during illness, both the wonders and the fragility of the human body become apparent. Its resilience in the face of trauma and disease is remarkable, something that I have witnessed in even the youngest of patients during my work at the Birmingham Children's Hospital. Although this may be so, both our physical and mental wellbeing are still so fragile. Medicine offers substantial relief from suffering and provides many individuals with the opportunity to live in a way that may otherwise not be possible. To deliver this opportunity is what principally draws me to the profession of a doctor.

As part of my undergraduate research I volunteered at a hospital cardiac rehabilitation centre. Over a period of 4 months I became one of the team, building a close rapport with patients who allowed me to monitor them during therapy. I thoroughly enjoyed learning about their conditions and found great pleasure in witnessing their recovery back to health. I felt confident in my ability to communicate and empathise with a variety of patients as well as interacting and communicating with health professionals. Additionally, I conducted my own research regarding mortality and hospital readmission. It was a topic for which I became passionate about and I was overjoyed to become a co-author in what I hope will be the first of many research publications.

In addition to my research experiences, I have strived to increase my understanding of the role of a doctor. Firstly, I undertook a one week placement with an anaesthetist at the Queen Elizabeth Hospital. I found the operating theatre to be an inspiring environment: a demonstration of the great advancements within medicine which now allow for the treatment of the previously untreatable. I also spent an insightful 4 weeks in India shadowing a surgeon, witnessing conditions unlike those I have seen in the UK, along with alternative methods for treating them. I learnt of a healthcare system vastly different to our own in an ongoing struggle against overpopulation and financial difficulty. It broadened my understanding of the many challenges present in healthcare provision.

Throughout my time at university I took on various roles of responsibility. I was the vice president for the Barnardo's charity society, an anatomy study leader, and a mentor to six prospective medical students whom I assisted with university applications. These roles required me to delegate jobs, chair meetings and organise events. Consequently, I proved myself to be a confident and capable team leader. Additionally, as a member of 'Sexpression', I was given the task of independently providing sexual health lessons to classrooms of school children. It was a unique role, and one which tested my initiative during pressurised situations.

Currently, I am employed as an operational assistant in a management team at Birmingham Children's Hospital. The role will allow me to increase my understanding of the NHS and to observe the job of a doctor from an alternative perspective. I am working with senior consultants on several exciting projects; one to improve the care of medically complex children and another to improve patient experiences in outpatient clinics. I am hopeful this will provide me co-authorship in a further research publication and I am sure the experiences will be of benefit to me not only as a medical student, but as a practicing doctor.

Despite the challenges facing our health service in an ever growing, ageing, diversifying and demanding population, I am excited by the challenge that a medical career presents. At the core of my character I am someone who values others above myself, is filled with compassion for those around me and is always eager to utilise my abilities for the benefit of others whether it be friends, family, patients, or co-workers. I endeavour to be an honest, respectful and competent doctor, whose values are centred on the patient.

Universities applied to:
- ➤ Warwick: Rejected
- ➤ King's: Rejected
- ➤ Birmingham: Offer
- ➤ Newcastle: Rejected

Good points:

The student demonstrates an interesting background of research and clinical work experience as well as professional exposure to clinical medicine. Having already undertaken research in the context of a degree, the student demonstrates the ability to perform well in an academic environment and also demonstrates an understanding of good scientific methods. Having been exposed to medical issues in this context is a further strength, setting this application apart from others. Having been able to experience healthcare in different financial settings is also interesting as it provides insight into the relevance of cost-efficiency and resource limitation. Furthermore, recognising the challenges facing the healthcare system in the UK demonstrates the student to be well-versed in identifying issues and problems.

Bad points:

It would be interesting to learn more about the student's previous degree and the student's motivation for studying medicine. The passage addressing the experiences related to the degree could also be more concise allowing for more information. The structure of the statement could also be clearer, making it easier for the reader to proceed through the statement.

Overall:

Good statement with interesting and relevant content. It has some minor weaknesses, omission of which would further improve strength. The statement provides sufficient information about the student's experiences but lacks information about motivation and individual interests.

NOTES

Statement 97

As the youngest of a big family I have always enjoyed the company of others. Volunteering at a dance school as a teenager allowed me to communicate with a huge variety of people which has given me confidence in myself, instigated my interest in the body and made it clear that I was destined for a career working with people.

I am self-motivated, always striving to get the best out of myself, not just in academia. At school I was Head Girl and set up schemes which are still in place today. My favourite subject was Maths; the satisfaction of solving problems to reach a final outcome I'm sure draws parallels with the diagnosis of patients. However, the content of biology and chemistry led me to read Biomedical Science. My interest for the body developed as I focused on physiologically related subjects. Being awarded the Prize for achieving the highest mark on my course was great recognition for the passion I had for the subject. An internship at the Genome Centre gave me the opportunity to explore the field of research. It was a fantastic experience, however I learnt that I'd like to use my knowledge to help people more directly.

In 2011 I backpacked around India. An operation while away has been instrumental in my desire to study medicine. When septic shock became a possibility, the Doctor's compassionate attitude made such a difference. I have endeavoured to learn from this experience and use it in my current employment. The dedication of the medical staff in the financially challenged circumstances was inspiring, highlighting the variety of situations in which medical care is delivered across the world. If given the opportunity to pursue medicine, travelling and learning about different cultures is something I hope to do. I have considered becoming a medic in the forces. Being at the forefront of advances in protocol, tackling complex cases and with a brother in the military, protecting people like him makes frontline medicine very attractive to me.

To discover whether medicine is for me I decided to work with vulnerable people. I care for the elderly in their homes aiding with various tasks. Initially the responsibility was scary, but now I enjoy it. I aim to maintain individuality, get to know and create a good rapport with the people I visit. Maintaining dignity and respect is vital in doing this, protecting them from neglect and abuse which the elderly are too often subjected to. The exposure I have had working with dementia sufferers and my interest in pathology and neuroscience has led me to support the Alzheimer's Society. I was inspired to raise over £250 at a 'Memory Walk' when volunteering at dementia cafes, which provide amazing support for those directly and indirectly affected by dementia. As a healthcare support worker I care for a 3 year old with Tracheobronchomalacia in the home on 12 hour night shifts, requiring me to troubleshoot and be calm under pressure. Empathy and good communication have led to a respectful, professional relationship with the parents which is important in an unusual working environment. These long hours will be good preparation for medical training. Both jobs require confidence to work alone and cooperate in large care teams.

Shadowing at the Royal Sussex has been a valuable experience. A ward round with a Respiratory Consultant emphasised to me how important professionalism and the people skills I have learnt in my employment are in the reassurance of patients. I saw a huge variety of cases while with a Radiologist, as imaging is often part of a patient's care pathway. It was fascinating to see the variety of experts working towards a common goal, opening my eyes to the network of communication in the NHS. I strive to be part of this network of professionals, one day using my expertise to help to provide the best care for people.

A culmination of my love for science, desire to make a difference and work with people have lead me the decision to pursue a career in medicine.

Universities applied to:
- ➤ Birmingham: Offer
- ➤ Cambridge: Rejected
- ➤ Southampton: Rejected
- ➤ Warwick: Rejected

Good points:
The student provides a well-reflected and well-structured insight into her motivations for studying medicine. This is very helpful in ensuring appropriate communication of this very relevant aspect of the statement. The student also provides good insight into clinical experiences and how they influenced her in the decision of becoming a doctor. Having a clear goal, in this case serving as a military doctor, is an additional strength of this statement. It supports the impression of a student that reflects appropriately on experiences and uses them to draw conclusions about the future. The student also provides evidence of her experience of soft skills such as professionalism and communication.

Bad points:
The student is somewhat unclear in regards to the time running up to the application. It would be interesting to learn more about how the time since leaving school was spent and how experiences made during this time have contributed to shaping the individual into a suitable candidate for a medical degree.

Overall:
Good statement that has some minor weaknesses and could be improved by further details regarding the student's preparation for their degree as well as the student's interests in disease and medicine as a whole. This statement demonstrates the relevance of both, having a plan for the future as well as being able to demonstrate reflection on the subject.

NOTES

Statement 98

Observing a doctor lead an A&E multidisciplinary team during work experience reinforced to me exactly why I want to study medicine; the opportunity to make a real difference to people's lives by combining the theoretical aspect of science with hands-on care. The lifelong learning involved further draws me to medicine, having the opportunity to overcome challenges such as our changing population and provide successful healthcare to patients. Whilst in A&E I saw how each patient is a new case to be solved and from talking to doctors I have learnt just how rewarding making a diagnosis is. One doctor particularly inspired me with her ability to see the person behind the patient. I learnt from her that good communication is essential to gather information, that ever expanding knowledge is vital to make a correct diagnosis and excellent team-work is needed to implement a treatment plan. I have demonstrated I have these skills through various experiences.

Working as a healthcare assistant on an ENT ward gave me hands-on experience. I enjoyed working as part of the health team, assisting patients with personal hygiene, feeding, and taking their observations. Through talking to patients I learnt how daunting hospital can be for them and that doctors need to show compassion alongside clinical excellence.

For three years at university I was a member of the 'Buddy a Granny Society'. I made regular visits to a care home to work with the residents, many of whom had Alzheimer's disease; here I was able to establish both empathy and trust with the residents. I was elected president of the society, and lead a team of volunteers in a way which ensured all felt valued as well as dealing with any problems that arose within the society. When one of the residents expressed some concerns I liaised with social services in a mature and confidential manner to ensure the problems were resolved. Whilst I was president, the society was nominated for the 'Best Student Volunteer Group'.
I also volunteered at a play scheme for disabled children. On one occasion a child with autism ran off and I was able to use my abilities to quickly gain trust and form relationships to bring him back safely. Such qualities are vital in a career in medicine.

To gain research experience and an appreciation of evidence based medicine I spent a week at the Centre of Evidence Based Dermatology at the University of Nottingham. I assisted with a systematic review of treatments for atopic eczema by extracting data and screening published trials to determine whether they were suitable for inclusion in the review. I was also able to observe some aspects of clinical trials, from grant proposals to data analysis.
Through reading human biology at university I gained a broad yet detailed understanding of biological principles. I learnt how to collect, analyse and interpret information to enable conclusions to be reached, an essential skill in medicine. Gaining a 1st in my dissertation demonstrates my ability to learn and work independently. My degree has given me the confidence and independence to enter medical school academically focused and mentally prepared.

I strive to keep a good work life balance and at university played korfball to relax. Always keen to learn, I am now studying Spanish part time whilst applying for a full time job as an HCA. I enjoy independent travel and during my time in Mexico I volunteered in a school where I learnt to control my emotions when dealing with people who had so little. Controlling emotions is vital as a doctor for although you need to be approachable and empathetic, the patients' medical needs must remain the priority. Next year I am volunteering with a medical team in India, getting basic hands-on experience in a very different environment.

Together these experiences have given me a realistic view of what a career in medicine involves and they have made me even more determined and committed to become one of tomorrow's doctors.

Universities applied to:
➤ Birmingham: Offer
➤ Hull York: Offer
➤ Warwick: Rejected
➤ Bart's: Rejected

Good points:
Interesting statement providing evidence of a wide range of clinical and non-clinical experiences of caring for others. The student demonstrates actual hands-on experience through their time as a healthcare assistant which is an excellent distinguishing point from other applicants. Having worked in a healthcare environment ensures that the student had appropriate time to reflect on the challenges of medicine. The student's previous degree provides a good scientific basis to build on during the study of medicine and also provides evidence of exposure to medical research giving insight into scientific methods and the workings of medical research.

Bad points:
The statement is somewhat poorly structured. It could be improved by providing it with a more logical structure addressing topics in logical order. It would make more sense to start the passage addressing the experiences at university with the academic side of things as this will guide the reader through the experience better.

Overall:
Good statement with some structural weaknesses. These affect the quality of the statement mainly because it disrupts the overall flow. In general, the statement is built on a wealth of experiences and appropriate reflections from the side of the student.

NOTES